Not Quite the Way You Heard It in School...or, Everything Is Relative:

Lighter Side Memories of Vietnam

Charles (Chick) Freund, III, Lt Col, USAFR (Ret)

DORRANCE
PUBLISHING CO
EST. 1920
PITTSBURGH, PENNSYLVANIA 15238

Dorrance Publishing Co
585 Alpha Drive
Pittsburgh, PA 15238
Visit our website at *www.dorrancebookstore.com*

ISBN: 978-1-6470-2245-7
eISBN: 978-1-6470-2872-5

IN MEMORIAM:

CHARLES ALBERT MAUPIN
4 November 1919—19 October 2019

He was on Normandy Beach at D-Day Plus One, 7 June 1944. Among his other awards, he was presented with a Bronze Star and a Purple Heart. On 4 November 1919 he would have been one hundred years old; he died sixteen days short of becoming one hundred. He had been asked to be the grand marshall of the Veterans Day Parade on 9 November 1919 in Columbus, Georgia, where he lived. Charlie had been my stepfather since 1957.

CONTENTS

PART 2

PART 3

BRIEF COMMENTS FROM THE AUTHOR

As I was reading the introduction to The Complete Calvin and Hobbes, Book One by Bill Watterson, I came across a cartoon that fitted me perfectly when I contemplated writing this book. Since the cartoon was not from one of his published comic strips, it was not available to reprint. However, I recently thought to ask if I could have permission to use just the verbiage from the cartoon, and permission was granted.

Imagine a drawing (by Bill Watterson) of a harried guy (himself) at his desk, paper in hand, trying to write something for his college yearbook:

"Two pages. Great. How am I ever going to stretch an explanation of the Viet Nam war to five pages?!?"

My sentiments exactly!

FOREWORD

Although this book is mostly military oriented, I have written it so that a civilian Reader can follow all the military acronyms and abbreviations that would not require explanation for a Reader with a military background. For example, a military person would know that Q or VOQ refers to housing, whereas spelling out Visiting Officers' Quarters clarifies it for the civilian. I am also an advocate of the Oxford comma, in case you were wondering.

(Here comes the "disclaimer" . . .)

I have taken the time to do research on many topics and details in an effort to maintain accuracy wherever I can. However, often I have had to rely on my memory of events and details from nearly five decades ago which, I readily admit, is sometimes easier than remembering which shirt I wore to church last Sunday. Speaking of which, I have a system I use now to actually remember just which shirt I did wear.

Throughout this book I have attempted to maintain a sense of humor, keeping my writing on the lighter side, with the intent of entertainment. That orientation extends to some otherwise dry topics which I have attempted to make more readable, including all of the appendices. My personality is reflected from the cover page to the last page, with just a few exceptions where humor would be inappropriate.

So, pour yourself a glass of Chateau Margaux or other preferred beverage and read on . . .

ACKNOWLEDGMENTS

Of course, my loving, tolerant, proofreading, and patient wife of (all these) years who shared nearly all of these experiences—or at least heard about them first-hand at least once—Andrea Freund (née Daskivich), who always warrants first, both on paper (or screen) and in my heart. (Okay, so I got a little schmaltzy. Our 50th wedding anniversary will have passed by the time you read this, so I think I am justified. If you disagree, feel free to skip over the schmaltzy parts.) In a sort of crisscross of roles, she taught English and reading in high schools (mostly) while I was an Air Force pilot and, for an all too brief period, a pilot for Eastern Airlines (R.I.P.). Years later she retired from teaching, and a few months later she was hired as a flight attendant (stewardess to you old folk), and I became a writer.

Andrea is a first soprano in our church's Chancel Choir. She is also responsible for having applied quasi-irrefutable logic to get me to join the choir years ago, something I admittedly and unexpectedly learned to enjoy immediately. Andrea is the singer in the family; she was a soloist on the record album her college choir made. As part of the bass section, I am in my element with fellow smart mouths. In my defense, however, I have never been accused of being a singer; I participate. (One must wonder why "bass," when referring to music, rhymes with base, as in baseball, but when referring to a kind of fish, it rhymes with gas, as in gasoline, except that "bass" has an extra "s"—or perhaps gas is short an "s." No wonder English is such a difficult language.)

First Presbyterian Church, Marietta, GA Writers Support Group (WSG)—When I first read about the creation of a writers group at our church, I thought I would go to the first meeting and see what it was about. When I mentioned that I had thought of writing a book but had no idea of a topic, the others attending suggested I write about what I am familiar with—advice very similar to what a management professor in business school suggested years ago. Thus began the fun with writing my military memoirs. I just so happen to really like writing with multiple parenthetical expressions. It is almost like a game to me, making sure that the number of closed parentheses equals the number of opened parentheses. However, those writers in the WSG who are more experienced than I am have vehemently discouraged my use of such a plethora of distracting (their opinions (not mine)) sidebars. Alas, finally conceding (somewhat (I still find many places where the (and the) are necessary (in my (not so) humble opinion))) to majority opinion, I have eliminated many dozens, actually, and you, the Reader, will never miss them. I thank the WSG members past and present as a group and as individuals:

David Blake—young professional-author-to-be of a trilogy of fiction/fantasy books —apparently somewhat influenced by J.R.R. Tolkien; he set up the WSG Google Drive site; alas, he is no longer among the living; I never had the opportunity to read his third book.

Buck Buchanan—professional author, working on his next novel; a tenor in our Chancel Choir; fellow wine apprecianado; plays golf left-handed for some strange reason, but it does not seem to affect his card playing. Bennett (mentioned below) once said to Buck after he (Buck) had made a particularly bad shot, "Buck, that's how bad I would hit the ball if I played left-handed."

Jody Fidler—former Wall Street Journal reporter and contributor to Barron's.

Bennett Frye—one of the original members of WSG; co-owner with his wife Karen of Aquarama Pools & Spas; jack of many trades, amateur author, former Chancel Choir bass but now a tenor (he must have changed to wearing tight underwear; I am only guessing here), fellow smart mouth, the king of making combination shots in pool, my chief rival in our card group (but my partner when we are playing cards with our wives). He is a fellow wine apprecianado, my chief rival at shooting pool, and a very good friend and buddy; it is sometimes scary how much we think alike, frequently at the same moment. My wife says we must have been brothers separated at birth—good trick, as he is a year and a half older than me, making him really old.

Dr. Joan Gray—pastor and professional author of several books.

Howard Kramer—professional author and blogger on the subject of religious sites around the world.

Bill Lewis—one of the original members of WSG; professional author, longtime freelance writer, former fellow bass in our Chancel Choir (unlike me, he can actually sing); he probably has what must be the most colorful and exotic sock drawer in Marietta.

Sally Moreland—retired teacher, amateur author.

Jeff Plowman—one of the original members of WSG; retired attorney and amateur author.

Bob Sloop—had the good sense to marry Lynne and is a fellow wine apprecianado, golfer, pool shooter, and card player.

Dr. Lynne Sloop—directly related to Bob by marriage; alto in our Chancel Choir; hand bell choir ringer, pianist, organist, wine apprecianado, and card player; although she is a doctor, she knows nothing about rocket surgery.

Patricia Sprinkle—one of the original members of WSG; professional author of twenty mysteries and various other books, and she is still writing.

Carolyn Tiede—amateur author, soprano in our Chancel Choir.

Bruce H. Vansickle, LCDR. USN (ret)—amateur author.

David E. Brown—retired USAF major and navigator extraordinaire (PRI) and longtime friend; he spent a number of hours proofreading for me and finding numerous items that required my attention; I have known his wife Sheila since high school (although she was not his wife at the time).

Roger Elstun—retired USAF colonel and pilot, friend since AFROTC in college. He dated Carol, a sorority sister and roommate in college of my (now) wife, who fixed them up together, and they got married before we did.

Mark L. Spencer—retired USAF major who started in avionics before going into pilot training and subsequently flying B-52Gs; he and his wife Sue have been good friends since college days in the late 1960's; fellow bridge players.

Rick Hanson—English major, USAF UPT classmate, former crop duster, now a glider instructor and (snow) skier (not at the same time, although that might appeal to those interested in extreme sports), longtime friend and fellow smart mouth; unlike me, he had the good sense to give up golf years ago. He has had one book published and is working on his second; I suppose that is not surprising since he majored in English.

Larry Tom—Former Air Force navigator in KC-135 air refueling tankers; he is a very imaginative and creative person; he and Kathy made the tennis bugs (see Chapter 68); these days he is quite the community theater thespian and all-around handy man; quite an astute bridge player.

Kathy Tom—coincidentally married to Larry of the same last name; she is a very creative person; community theater thespian, director, and all-around handy man—er, woman; she is also noted for her cake baking and tennis bug (see Chapter 68) creations.

Fred Hudgin—computer programmer extraordinaire and professional author; he is my daughter's husband's father; not sure what relationship that makes us.

Donnie Johnson—retired US Army Colonel, fellow Vietnam veteran, earned (though not by choice) at least one Purple Heart; friend since the late 1950s.

Everett Sprous—former AC-119K Stinger Gunner, active in the

Gunship Association.

John Funk—former AC-119K Stinger Flight Engineer.

Craig Corbett—retired USAF CMSgt who was a gunner and one of seven survivors of a ten-man crew on a Stinger gunship that was shot down in South Vietnam while I was over there.

Barbara Steele—retired teacher, alto in our Chancel Choir; fellow wine apprecianado; volunteered to proofread this book for me, a chore made slightly easier since she is familiar with my personality as reflected herein.

Raegan Carmona—Manager of Permissions, Andrews McMeel Syndications; she was quite helpful in my acquisition of permission to use Bill Watterson's cartoon quote and Stephan Pastis's comic strip. She also made a suggestion, which I used, to disambiguate a certain paragraph.

Then there is my baby brother, Ronnie, two and a half years my junior (he will be seventy this year (2019); that makes me really old, which makes Bennett really, really old). He was in the Army, served in Vietnam, and became re-civilianized around the time frame that I began USAF pilot training. We have been there for each other for . . . our lifetimes.

My long-time step-father, Charles Maupin, or Charlie as we called him. That was before Andrea and I and Ronnie and his sweet wife, Cindy, became parents, thereby converting Charlie to Gramps. He served our country in the Army in WWII with a free, all-expenses-paid round trip to Europe. While there, he landed in Normandy the day after D-Day and lived to tell about. He would have been 100 years old in November 2019, but he died 16 days shy of 100. (Maybe I am not so old after all.)

Lastly, but who was actually first, is my mom, Marjorie McGill Freund Maupin. Mom strongly "encouraged" me to take Army Junior ROTC in high school, thereby creating my interest in a military career. She loved gardening; I always thought she could plant a pencil in the ground and make it grow. Mom had the good sense to remarry Charlie after they were divorced. If there are books in heaven, perhaps she will be able to read this Opus One.

PART 1

- PREFACE -

Not Quite the Way You Heard It in School…
or, Everything Is Relative

FEAR NOT, "Gentle Reader," as my favorite author, Isaac Asimov, used to refer to his Readers. What you are about to read will not harm you, should not offend you, but may entertain you. This book is *not* another documentary about and analysis of the United States military involvement in Vietnam. There are perhaps thousands of such sources available online, at your local library, your nearby college or university, or PBS television station. Rather, my forthcoming "scholarly treatise" will present to you one man's—i.e., my—up close and personal account of experiences more or less related to Vietnam. Most of it is laced with a humorous slant; just how humorous depends, of course, on your sense of humor. Forewarned, let us proceed.

Way back in the early 1960s when I was in high school, we studied, among other subjects, history. Hmm—that might perhaps not be quite accurate; I knew a number of fellow students who did not actually *study* history, or much of anything else for that matter in some cases. Neither can I say that they were taught; that would imply that they had learned. Let us say that we were all exposed to history, such as it was presented in those days. *There I was*, sitting in my standard wooden desk in the safety of the classroom. Remember, this was the 1960's; back then it did not occur to degenerates, psychopaths, and other mentally unstable types to enter schools and randomly open fire with automatic weapons, killing innocent non-combatants.

American history was, of course, history of the USA. It did not include Canada or Central or South America, except in those instances when there was brief mention of Leif Ericson or Amerigo Vespucci and other such intrepid explorers wandering around the "New World." So-called "World" history was full of European kings and queens and Machiavellian political intrigue and wars resulting in the same pieces of geography changing names so often that I was grateful for generally getting B"s in history. I was not really that interested or motivated in any courses that were not math and science.

And those history courses, I dare say, supposedly covered the history of Planet Earth. About six-billion-plus of the seven-billion-plus people currently populating the "other" areas of the world might have issues with the versions of "World" history we were taught—er, exposed to. China? Sure—when my younger brother and I did not finish our peas at supper, we heard about all the people that were starving in China. My wife got the same message when she was growing up in a family only two generations removed from Eastern Europe (or perhaps it was Western Asia; the Ukraine might be geographically considered a "swing" country), except that she was told about people starving in Europe, of course. But we knew about Europe. India? That was where Chris Columbus thought he wound up. Southern Rhodesia and Nyasaland? French Indo China? Someone just had to be making those names up.

Wars—we studied about wars: The Hundred Years War, The Spanish-American War, Tchaikovsky's War of 1812, and of course World War I, the "War to End All Wars." I am sure it was not referred to as World War One back when that war occurred and for a few years thereafter. There was no reason to start numbering world wars . . . yet. As human nature is so inclined, World War II was inevitably created. Most of us still around today (early 21st century) either heard about it from our fathers, uncles, and other relatives and friends who have first-hand knowledge, like my step-father, who waded ashore on Omaha Beach on D-Day Plus 1. My dad and father-in-law also were in WWII; all three of them were in the European theater, but I don't think they actually got to see many, if any, movies or live performances. Makes one wonder why such military operations are called theater; possibly that was a misnomer to make signing up for active duty seem more inviting to kids who were old enough to go fight for their country. ("Dear Mom and Dad and Aunt Matilda, I am somewhere in the Pacific Theater, but I haven't seen anything except training films.")

The Korean War came along during many of our lifetimes, and so it probably had not had sufficient time to mellow and mature into the history books yet. I remember first hearing about a place somewhere ten thousand miles away called Vietnam during Walter Cronkite's six o'clock news broadcasts on our thirteen-inch black-and-white TV. Little did I realize that in about a decade I would be there, sitting in the right seat in the cockpit of a gunship in Southeast Asia (SEA) dodging anti-aircraft artillery (AAA, or triple A).

About another two decades later, I was giving briefings and interviews about my experiences over there to junior high and high school students, including my own daughter, Allison, who were studying Vietnam in school of all places in social studies—which apparently includes history. Against my better judgement and without my consent, I had become a historical figure, someone who "was over there." Another dozen or so years later (it is amazing how rapidly and easily one can slip through time), I prepared and presented a slide briefing—there was no such thing as PowerPoint yet—to Civil Air Patrol cadets in Georgia squadrons. I called it "Vietnam According to Chick Freund" (that would be me); and as you might surmise, it was not exactly the same information that the youngsters were reading in school. This was the Real Thing - me telling it like it was, or at least as I experienced it as a United States Air Force (USAF) pilot, which was not quite the same as that experienced by my baby brother, Ronnie, who was an Army GI who worked his way through Vietnam hustling pool a couple of years before I got over there.

Now that I think about it, I need to ask him a bit more about that sometime. Where did the Army get pool tables in Vietnam anyway? Were they shipped over? If so, why? There was a war going on, or so I was told. He was sending home to our mother and step-father more money from hustling pool than he made as a one-striper private, and even more than I was being paid as first lieutenant on flying status. He used to be pretty good. When we played 8-ball together back home at Mom and Charlie's house, for me it was more like a spectator sport.

The Reader may on occasion find some of the forthcoming commentary biased toward the way I feel about things, but that is to be expected when reading any person's writings. What you are about to encounter on the succeeding pages are anecdotes, snippets, occasional detailed explanations and remembrances otherwise categorized however you wish of the war in Vietnam as I experienced it, which are out of necessity modified by my memory's accuracy thereof, or occasional lack thereof. I will cleverly (he said modestly) slip into corollary military experiences and disquisitions of disambiguating material as may be appropriate, or as the mood suits me at the time of writing.

Perhaps this kind of garden

My story-telling could be compared to ambling through a garden, any kind of garden—use your imagination; it will not affect the outcome whatsoever. I will essentially write about events in somewhat of a chronological order. However, as strolling through the garden one occasionally stops here and there to smell the roses or admire the Bonsai or meander down a different path where something has caught one's eye, I, too, will wander off course a bit. There is certainly a common thread throughout, and there really is a journey, so to speak, but if you are expecting to read of events going from point A directly to point B to point C, et cetera, you will be disappointed. However, if you have read to this point so far, you are starting to grasp my style. And, as you may have already determined, I tend to not take anything too seriously unless it involves an empty glass of Bordeaux or an absence of dark chocolate. Wait there a moment, please. . . . I need to refill my wine glass. . . .

AC-119K "Stinger" Gunship

- 1 -

A LITTLE HISTORY

There I was—all war stories begin that way—at 4500 feet AGL (Above Ground Level) over the Plain of Jars (PDJ) in Laos, sitting in the copilot's seat of an old AC-119K Stinger Gunship. What was I doing there?

Not all that long ago (EIR—Everything Is Relative—you will want to remember that acronym, as I will be referring to it often), as some of you who are no-longer-so-youthful may recall, there was a bit of ongoing non-friendly activity occurring in the mid-sixties in a slice of world geography generally known as Southeast Asia. You history buffs out there can delve into the details if you care to. We—my wife Andrea and I—have a rather tattered 1906 *Geography of the World* book which shows the name of that region to be part of China. I remember the territory being French Indochina in the 1950s, and the French already had been having "issues" there for a number of years. At some point that area of land changed names, as politicians, conquering generals, and other such entities tend to decide such things, and it became Vietnam. However, this new name, putting the country toward the end of the English alphabet, did little or nothing to mitigate the continuing unrest, and eventually there became a North Vietnam and a South Vietnam. Later, of course, it became plain old vanilla Vietnam again (actually, the Socialist Republic of Viet Nam). But we are getting ahead of the storyline. There is a storyline, nebulosity notwithstanding; that is the way these things are supposed to work, or so I understand.

Not being a historian myself, and at that time being immersed in more youthful concerns—girls, grades, cars, and girls—and even though I lived through the era when United States "involvement" in Vietnamese affairs began, I did not really care at that point in my life, so I do not remember exactly—or even approximately—why we were over there. It is my personal opinion that the vast majority of those in the upper echelons of the US political and military hierarchy at the time, also being non-historian academicians, came under the influence of the aphorism, "Those who fail to study history are destined to repeat it," or words to that effect. So, for whatever reasons (Oil? I don't think so. Minerals used to make transistors? Probably not. Something to do to give our younger military personnel some practical hands-on combat training and experience? Could be. Good excuse as any, from my perspective.), we—that is, those of us from the U.S. of A.—found ourselves over there, trying to succeed at—what?—where the French had failed for about ten years, plus or minus a couple of decades.

It was/is known as the War in Vietnam, or the Vietnam War. However, as I understand things, technically there never was a War in Vietnam, as Congress never officially made and the president never signed a declaration of war with Vietnam. It was only a "conflict" or "intrusion" or "prolonged skirmish" or "military intervention" or "police action" or whatever other sobriquet by which we chose to call this rose. I could be wrong; it is just that no one in all these years has corrected me.

So—*there I was.* . . .

. . . but I am once again getting ahead of myself. (We'll eventually get back to 4500 feet over the PDJ, I promise. . . .)

- 2 -

ARMY JROTC

My mother worked as a civilian secretary or clerk or in some sort of office job at Ft. Benning, Georgia, for over fifty years. When I became a sophomore in high school in Columbus, GA, she insisted that I take JROTC (Junior Reserve Officer Training Corps, a.k.a. Rotcy). That was the first year that a student was eligible to enroll; not surprisingly, considering that Ft. Benning was and still is a major Army post, Army JROTC was offered. All the high schools in Columbus (all six of them) offered JROTC. I don't remember if they were all Army; there might have been a school or two offering Navy JROTC, and I am almost certain (almost) there was no Air Force JROTC in Columbus in the early 1960s. It was not until 18 September 1947 that President Harry Truman signed the National Security Act which, among other things, established the US Air Force as a separate service, equal to the US Army and Navy. I was born in January 1947, so I am older than the whole USAF.

My baby brother, Ronnie—who was two-and-a-half years younger than I was, and even though he started collecting Social Security several years ago, he still qualifies as my baby brother— was not encouraged to consider a military career. However, he eventually did manage to get himself drafted into the Army and serve a tour in Vietnam. Incredibly, he got in trouble one night for firing his weapon while on guard duty. Go figure.

Although I had not planned to take JROTC, i.e., until my mother "encouraged" me to do so, I discovered that all that military stuff agreed with me and offered what I thought would make a good career choice. Some of my friends enrolled also. I joined the drill team, through which I became more proficient at "drill and ceremonies" than those only in the regular fifty-minute class each school day. I also learned how to disassemble and reassemble an M1 rifle and drill with it. Instead of just marching along, we drill team guys carried our M1s, learned to spin them and do some fancy moves with them. (Fancy for high school teenagers; not so much compared to, say, the very impressive USMC drill teams.)

One thing about the M1 I never became fond of, though, was inspections. We would be in formation, at attention, with the M1 on our right side. If you were left-handed, too bad. To be uniform, everyone did maneuvers the same way. When the drill team commander or other inspecting cadet or military officer approached in front of you, at the instant he completed his two-count left face, positioning himself directly in front of you an arm's length away, you would instantly initiate a sharp (if you were drill team) four-count maneuver of your M1 to port arms. The drawings below are extracted from an Army "Individual Drill with Weapons" manual, and they show the first two steps of port arms.

The rifle shown in the drawings is an M16 assault rifle. The older M1 had two more steps for inspection arms: Step 3) After grasping the rifle in the right hand, with the left thumb the bolt was pushed toward the right hand, opening the chamber for inspection while simultaneously tilting the head down briefly, like perhaps for .02 seconds, looking into the chamber to visually verify that the chamber was empty and safe for inspection. Step 4) The left hand was returned to the port arms position.

Marines at port arms

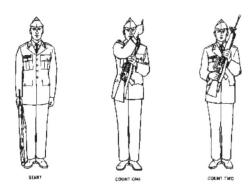

From Order Arms position to Port Arms position

The third count involved opening the chamber for inspection. Sometimes the inspecting officer would grab your weapon just below your left hand with a rapid one-handed slap/grip. If you did not react quickly enough releasing the M1, it would . . . create an awkward situation . . . for you. The inspector would check the M1 for cleanliness, especially inside the barrel where even tiny specks of dust particles would be easily visible. When he returned your M1 to you in the port arms position, you would take the weapon with your left hand with a rapid slap while maintaining it in the port arms position. You would then place the four fingers of your right hand in the chamber far enough for the fingertips to push down on the catch, releasing the spring-loaded chamber guard so it could close, applying a constant pressure squeezing against your fingers until you withdrew them.

When you withdrew your fingers, if you were too slow, you could suffer in one or both of two ways. One, you would suffer the indignation of embarrassment from the inspector's and your cadet mates' reactions to your loss of composure while you cringed and silently muttered #&*@%*!$! (or words to that effect) through gritted teeth.

When at the positions of Attention, Parade Rest, Port Arms, or Right or Left Shoulder Arms, eyes were kept straight ahead and there was to be no body movement; naturally, such times were when your nose or some other body part would start to itch or a gnat would decide to inspect the inside of your ear.

The second way you would suffer was then having to clean the blood out of the M1 afterwards while the other cadets were out on dates telling their girlfriends about the klutz during inspection that afternoon.

The chamber guard was always waiting, lurking as it were, ready to slam closed given the slightest encouragement. When the inspecting officer executed a right face to move on to the guy on your left, you would rapidly (for reasons stated above) withdraw your fingers from the chamber and resume a port arms position.

Nothing involving rocket surgery about that. However, during the interval between inserting your fingers to release the catch holding the chamber guard at abeyance and waiting for the officer to do his right face to inspect the cadet to your (ok, my) left, the threat of the evil, conniving chamber guard loomed ominously, especially if you were a skinny kid like me with limited hand strength.

During drill team inspections, this became a challenge between you and the drill team commander, who was a senior. As we underclassmen became proficient handling and drilling with the M1, it became somewhat of a game of challenges. Everything is done in cadence. For instance, while executing the four-step inspection arms movement, movements are done crisply: One! Two! Three! Four! and are not drawn out: Ooonnne, Twooo, Threeeee, Fooour. Some of us were sharper and snappier than others, but we were all sharper than most non-drill team cadets for the simple reasons that we drilled more and were "encouraged" to be so by the commander. We had more exacting standards expected of us. During inspection, if something as insignificant as an errant one-half-inch thread was noticed protruding from anywhere on the uniform, the commander would bark, "Cable! One demerit!" to his executive officer (second in command), who was following one step behind, and he would record it. I always found that humorous (except when it was said in reference to me, of course) – a tiny thread being called a "cable." A cable was something that ships laid along the bottom of the Atlantic Ocean to electronically connect the United States with Europe, or the braided wires from which the Golden Gate Bridge is suspended. But a tiny thread? Gimme a break.

Near the end of the school year the whole cadet corps was engaged in an inspection and drill competency review done by the active duty staff at school (actual US Army personnel assigned to the school) and some invited Army officers from Ft. Benning, after which we all marched in a Pass In Review, more or less "affectionately" referred to as "Piss In Your Shoe." But not during the parade ceremony, of course. I will not go into all of the details that might seem silly to a civilian, but briefly, the ceremony is one in which all of the cadet corps march by the Reviewing Stand where the commander and other dignitaries are gathered. You have no doubt seen videos, called "movies" back then, or "moovies" if you had a southern drawl, of large formations of troops passing in front of a general, president, or monarch.

At some point an announcement was made of the awards for Best Drilled Company (two platoons), Best Drilled Platoon (five or six squads), and Best Drilled Squad (seven or eight cadets). As luck would have it, I was a member of the best drilled squad in the best drilled platoon in the best drilled company. Three ribbons to pin on my uniform. Unfortunately, since I moved to Cincinnati that summer, I did not have long to wear them and show them off to other cadets.

- 3 -

AFROTC AT MIAMI UNIVERSITY

Upham Arch, Miami University, Oxford, Ohio

In June 1963, I moved to Cincinnati between my sophomore and junior years of high school to live with my dad; it was more of an experience than I expected. There were more high school *leagues* in Cincinnati than there were high schools back home in Columbus.

However, the high school district that I lived in had no JROTC. I don't think any of the schools in Cincinnati did. I suppose the South was still fighting the "War of Northern Aggression," in a (Southern) manner of speaking. When I went to register for school and plan my next two years of classes, it came as quite a surprise, and disappointment, that there was no JROTC offered. At first I thought the counsellor was kidding, but no such luck. Regardless, I had already decided to pursue a career in the military, so this was merely a minor setback.

After graduating from high school in 1965, I enrolled at Miami University, forty or so miles up the road in the small southwestern Ohio town of Oxford. I had my choice of Air Force or Navy ROTC. It was not really a choice for me since I wanted to be a pilot like my dad. Sure, the Navy has a formidable air force of its own, but as far as I was concerned, if you want to fly, go with the service that specializes in flying. I did not plan to be flying any boats.

Of course, I joined the AFROTC Blue Diamond Exhibition Drill Team. Apparently I was the only freshman that had any drill experience—I could already do an About Face without nearly falling over in the attempt. It is only a two-step movement, but it requires more practice than some of the other basic maneuvers, like

Right or Left Face. When learning to do an About Face, it is easy to flail your arms out and lean back and forth in an effort to maintain balance. Then add a rifle, and your balance changes. While other guys were still trying to not fall over, I could execute an About Face while at Port Arms with my 1903 Springfield bolt-action single-shot rifle. (Sounds like the Red Ryder BB gun that Ralphie wanted for Christmas in the movie *A Christmas Story*.) If it was referred to by name, it seemed that the rifle was always the 1903 Springfield, not just the Springfield. Not bragging; that is just the way it was. I had had a year of military drill and ceremonies experience while the military was new to the other Miami AFROTC freshmen. Six weeks into the trimester (pretty much like a regular semester in other colleges) I was promoted to staff sergeant (four stripes) because of my experience, although theoretically a freshman could only rise to the rank of airman first class (three stripes). Since then the Air Force has re-designated the titles of the four lowest ranks (see Appendix 2).

The same drill and marching maneuvers I had learned in Army JROTC pretty much held when I enrolled in AFROTC at Miami University. The uniforms were blue instead of green, but drill and ceremonies were the same. I believe the basic standards hold true for all of the uniformed services, but don't hold me to that.

At 8.69 pounds, the 1903 Springfield rifle weighed about a pound less than the M1 I had used in high school. The big plus, as far as I was concerned, was that opening the chamber was done by bolt action—no springs attached, no fingers scrunched. It is a single-shot weapon, meaning that it needs to be reloaded after each shot. We never fired live rounds, but we did perform at retreat ceremonies—the lowering of the Flag—on Tuesdays (uniform days) at 1700 hours (5:00 p.m. for the uninitiated), during which we fired blanks. It should have sounded like, "Ready! Aim! Fire!" Blam! (Blam is not part of the command; it is my onomatopoeic interpretation of the sound made by us firing the blanks. On occasion it actually sounded like that - Blam! But usually it sounded more like B-B-B-Blam!)

When military units, including ROTC, had to march across a road like we did at Miami, before marching into traffic, the commander would order, "Road guards, post!" The two cadets in designated positions in the formation would hustle out to the road and stop traffic in each direction by standing at port arms. Of course, we drill team weenies would take the opportunity to show off to the front cars by doing a few multiple spins and other maneuvers with the 1903 Springfields until the unit was safely across the road. When the commander ordered, "Road guards, recover!" the two road guards would come to port arms, maybe do another spin or two, do an About Face, and hustle back into position in the formation.

Our drill team would march along the sidewalk on the far side of the street from fraternity row, where some of the frat houses were located. The US military activities in Vietnam were very unpopular, to say the least. The frat guys would usually jeer at us and cast various aspersions du jour, but we were ordered to ignore them, which was just as well. It was not like we could load the 1903 Springfield rifles and take some shots in their direction. (I was at Miami U. in 1970 during the Kent State student clash with the Ohio National Guardsmen during which four KSU students were killed. I will write more about that later.) Eventually the frat guys got tired of getting no reaction from us, and they turned to other things—drugs, girls, or perhaps even studying. (Yeah, right.)

The AFROTC Detachment 640 at Miami was located in Van Voorhis Hall, an old, decrepit building next to the university administration building. It was a two-story building with creaky wooden floors. The first floor held the detachment offices and classrooms. The second floor was one large room, formerly a gymnasium. That is where the drill team practiced routines. During the year the Blue Diamonds were invited to drill team competitions at other colleges, so we would work on developing routines which complied with the time restrictions of the particular competition. Any one of us could suggest ideas to try out. There was a lot of rifle exchange between marching cadets executing various maneuvers, not unlike marching bands, except that band members do not exchange instruments while marching. Imagine trying to pass a tuba to a bass drummer or a piccolo player. The complex routines we practiced and performed were designed so that by the end of a routine, each cadet had recovered his own rifle.

Each drill team cadet was issued his own rifle, identified by a serial number. The care and cleaning of his rifle was each cadet's responsibility, and we took pride in our weapons. Our commander could form us into ranks and call an inspection at any time. There were extra 1903 Springfields packed in cosmoline in wooden boxes in the basement of Van Vooris Hall. Cosmoline is a rust inhibitor that is a viscous brown waxy substance when initially applied to the rifles, but after about sixty years or so it had solidified into a thick, sticky, waxy mass that was loads of fun to remove from a rifle. Guess who got to have all of this fun. Right—freshmen drill team cadets, or an occasional sophomore who joined late in life (EIR). It was almost like a party—well, a work party.

We went through rolls of paper towels getting the bulk of the cosmoline removed, then we used bunches of cloth rags when we got down to sticky metal and wood until we got enough off to start applying a non-corrosive solvent. When we reached the point where we could disassemble the rifle, we would clean each individual piece. Getting cosmoline out of the barrels was fun— trying to overcome the resistance of sixty-year-old waxy stuff packed into the barrel was a chore. Sometimes it took two of us to work on one barrel. Eventually we would finish by using special clean cloths which would not leave lint anywhere on the metal parts. That was the theory, anyway. Cleaning the wooden stocks was easier, as far as lint was concerned, but the wood had to have some kind of oil applied. I don't remember what kind of oil, though. I seem to remember that it started with an "S." Sesame? Sassafras? Silicon? Maybe not an "S" oil after all. No matter.

When each part was thoroughly cleaned, including a ramrod cleaning of the inside of the barrel, the rifle was then reassembled and wiped down again. Cosmoline is very clingy and hints of it can linger. Getting all the lint out of the barrel required special attention, because when the rifle was inspected, looking through the shiny surface inside, it was easy to see any recalcitrant specks. Too bad there was not a tank of some solution that we could have just put the entire rifle into for a couple of minutes, then taken it out, and Voilà! All done.

Some of our drill routine maneuvers involved tossing the rifle with a 360° end-over-end flip to the cadet marching behind, who simultaneously tossed his rifle to the cadet behind. When practicing those tosses, it was not uncommon for a rifle to be missed or dropped. Since we practiced on a wooden floor, the only harm to the rifle was to the wooden stock. They would crack or chip or even break sufficiently to be rendered useless, except as firewood kindling perhaps. Once I even got an old rifle (old as in its condition; they were all old) that had a stock that would not pass muster in competition, or even in a daily inspection. I sometimes practiced the backward flip/toss, but with no one behind me to catch it. That was generally not a good idea, but that particular stock was already headed for the scrap pile anyway.

Checking online now as I write, I see a number of 1903 Springfields for sale—for as much as $6,000! Perhaps I should have been a little more diligent.

The forward gunsight was at the front end of the barrel, which is where a front gunsight should be. It had a shark-fin shape which proved to be unsafe for exhibition drilling such as what we were performing. I can still see a faint scar on my right wrist from when one of those shark fins reached out and attacked. It did not take long for our commander to call for the removal of the front sight on all of our rifles. If the sight was gripped with pliers or vise grips and encouraged—meaning gently tapped—with a hammer, it would slide out of its groove in the barrel and thus draw no more blood.

The commander had several tricks available to him while we were in formation for inspection. He would take a step and place himself in front of whichever cadet was to be inspected. For ease of orientation, let us say that it was me. He would move down the line from our right to left. He took a step to be in front of me and halted, in cadence, of course: Step-Halt. Then he would do his two-count

Left Face in cadence: Left-Face. Together it was four sharp, distinct, and separate movements: Step-Halt-Left-Face. You notice the cadence. That was drill team. None of that slurred and sloppy Steeep-Haalt-Leeeft-Faaaace. Our movements resembled something more like robots. Or were supposed to.

As soon as his heels came together completing the left face, facing me, I would immediately and sharply execute the four steps in that same cadence: Port-Arms-Inspection-Arms. His face would be serious; mine would be frozen, my eyes looking straight ahead, unmoving, my 1903 Springfield—and the rest of me—ready for inspection.

That was the way things were *supposed* to go. Commander: Step-Halt-Left-Face. Me: Port-Arms-Inspection-Arms, all in cadence. Occasionally the commander would be in a mischievous mood. If I was too slow getting to inspection arms, it would result in pushups or some other not-so-fun behavior modification activity designed to prevent a recurrence of my lackadaisicalness. I could see him with my peripheral vision, since my eyes were focused straight ahead. When he turned from the cadet to my right and stepped to face me, I was spring-loaded ready. Step-Halt-Left-... Port-... oops. He had paused after turning left, intentionally not completing his Left Face, but I, in keeping cadence, reactively began bringing my rifle up to port arms before he had finished his maneuver. The commander would have a bit of a smirk as he then finished his Left Face. I thought, *Okay. You got me that time, but wait until next time . . . Sir!* Or words to that effect.

As we became more educated in the ways of the drill team and of our commander, that little game got down to a matter of our not flinching at all, not even ever-so-slightly. The better we got at not falling for his little deception, he would fake a slight movement toward -Face. Usually when he pulled that little stunt and we maintained strict attention, still frozen like a statue, he would have a fleeting little smile as if to say, "Well done, Cadet. You're learning." He would not actually say that to us, of course. He did not have to. It was something to talk about later.

Another "game" could occur just after I came to inspection arms. The commander would usually stand there looking me over, trying to find the infamous cables, any spots of uncleanliness, hair touching the ears, facial hair not trimmed to strict compliance, a tiny smudge on uniform brass, the 1903 Springfield not being held to perfect inspection arms position, or an imperfect gig line—the line made by the vertical edge of the uniform shirt, the edge of the highly-polished belt buckle, and the vertical edge of the trousers (trou, for short) zipper cover. The slightest degree of misalignment of the vertical line of all three rated a negative comment. Satisfied, he might move on to the cadet to my left.

He also might or might not inspect the rifle. If he chose to inspect mine, I did not simply hand him my weapon. He would snatch it from me with a rapid slap/grasp—just as the JROTC commander had done in high school. If I held on to the rifle a hair too long, we could both be pulled slightly off balance, as if we were fighting for it. I never knew when or even if he would take my 1903 Springfield, but if he did, he would strike out like a snake snagging its prey, and I had to be ready to release it. He might take it right away, or he might do so after looking me over for discrepancies. Or sometimes he would make his move while still otherwise looking me over, trying to catch me by surprise.

The "game" involved the initial exchange of the rifle during inspection. Whenever he decided to take it, the commander would try to do so as quickly as he could. I would try to release it as quickly as I could. At his first hint of a movement to take my rifle, I would release it.

It was all about reaction time, like in Major League Baseball. The pitcher's mound is 60.5 feet from home plate. When a pitcher throws the ball at 100 miles an hour over the plate, by working with a few differential equations, spherical trigonometry, and p-brane time-space configurations, it is easy to translate that to 146.7 feet per second. This means the batter has less than half of a second (for the persnickety Reader, that's about 0.41 seconds) to analyze the flight of the ball, the type of pitch - fast ball, curve ball, slider, knuckle ball, spit ball (!), et cetera—decide whether or not he is going to swing at it, and if so, his visual perception as related to the brain must be converted via nerve synapses at the rate of about 272 miles per hour into signals to body muscles, which must then react accordingly so that the path of the swinging bat intersects with the speeding ball within a very narrow angular margin of error. Piece of cake.

Back to rifle inspection. When I released my rifle, it would be immediately subject to the accelerating influence of gravity in a direction toward the ground at a rate of 32.174 fps^2 (feet per second squared (feet per second per second)). If it hit the ground from my error, I would get the demerits and also have to clean my weapon once we were back inside. If it was blatantly his fault, I would still be the one to retrieve it from the ground and resume port arms, but at least I would not get demerits. However, I would still be the one that had to clean it. Any bets on whose fault it would likely be at any given time? I didn't think so.

Early in the school year the commander would make a faint move with his right shoulder or right hand as if he were going for the rifle, but then not complete his fake. Of course, being ever diligent and ready to demonstrate my sharp reflexes and impeccable timing, I would release my 1903 Springfield the instant I noted his move, after which said rifle would drop to the ground, or floor if inside. Naturally, it would be my fault that the rifle fell. After recovering my rifle and resuming Port Arms, he again may or may not inspect it. If he did, then when he returned the rifle to my port arms position, I would strike with my left hand to secure it without changing the attitude of the rifle. (I'll bet you didn't know old rifles could have an attitude.) When he did a Right Face to move on to the next cadet, I would do a four-count movement, closing the bolt and returning to attention, rifle at my right side.

After a few weeks of training, during which time we freshmen learned what to expect, the rifle never hit the ground. Then the game became more equal. If both the inspector and the inspectee coordinated our reflexes, the rifle would remain at the inspection arms position in the same three-dimensional space, but in the commander's right hand rather than in my hands, and I would be standing at attention, arms back at my side, fingers curled, and thumbs along the outside seams of my trousers. It was a matter of pride for each of us to have executed a perfect exchange of the rifle. There would usually be a hint of a smile on each of our faces. His smile would mean, "Well done, Cadet, but wait until next time!" My smile meant, "Nice try, Commander. And I'll be ready for you next time, too!"

The commander had another trick he could play. When returning the 1903 Springfield, he would hand it over in a position other than inspection arms, including his having closed the bolt while he was inspecting the rifle. That was a no-no. The weapon was to be returned in the same condition and position as when taken. If it was not returned that way, I was not to accept it. Initially, most of the other cadets could be caught accepting the rifle with the bolt closed. Remember, I had the advantage of having had a year of drill team in high school. However, it only took once or twice for a fellow cadet to learn that little detail.

A fun "exercise" to occupy the time for some of us was to develop proficiency in spinning the rifle with the right hand. Some parts of our competition routines involved spinning it once in one 360° rotation and sometimes twice in one 720° rotation while marching in and out of various formations. Just for kicks, some of us taught ourselves how to spin it continuously. Once you got the hand and rifle combination into a balanced spin, you could keep it going for a while, rather like a baton twirler, except with a nearly nine-pound rifle instead. While practicing to build up to more and more spins, there was the occasional, and inevitable "OOPS!" We broke a few of the stocks from some of the older rifles (EIR); "older" in this case meaning rifles that had been in use longer, as opposed to those *new* 1903 Springfields recently exhumed from their beds of cosmoline. Of course, that meant we had to clean the cosmoline off of another stock, but that would have had to have been done anyway. (Hmm—a seven-word verb phrase.) We also became proficient at spinning a 360° right-hand spin into the left hand, reversing the spin direction into the right hand, et cetera ad nauseam.

Many of my friends were in AFROTC. I had a roommate my sophomore year who was in Navy ROTC. He was the only NROTC person I knew. There was not much interaction with or between the two units, which was sad. There should have been more. However, in the fall there was a football game between AFROTC cadets and NROTC midshipmen in the Miami Redskin's stadium. I will probably always remember—at least as long as I am able to remember anything at all—a cheer the NROTC band hollered at us from across the field:

"Rah rah ree, Kick 'em in the knee.

Rah Rah rass, Kick 'em in the other knee."

Miami University was a very conservative school. We affectionately (more or less) referred to it as Mother Miami.

- 4 -

THE BLIND DATE

In February of 1966 during my freshman year the AFROTC Military Ball was held in the stereotypically decorated Gymnasium. Military balls are formal affairs. The active duty staff at our detachment all wore what is called the mess dress uniform. Nonmilitary Readers may well be wondering why a "mess" is as associated with its military meaning. Herewith the light of wisdom (okay, research): "Mess" refers to an area or facility where military personnel socialize and eat. Accordingly, mess might be an appropriate term for it, especially after excessive quantities of alcoholic beverages have been consumed.

But I doubt if one military person in a thousand can tell the derivation of this particular term. I include myself in with the other 999, so after decades of military association, I figured it was about time I found out for your, and my, enlightenment. According to Wikipedia, the root of *mess* is from the Old French *mes*, meaning *portion of food*, the original sense being *a course of a meal put on the table.* The term *mess* was often used in thirteenth century England, referring to cooked or liquid dishes in particular, as in a *mess of pottage* (porridge or soup). So now we all know, more than anyone ever cared to know. It is the modern military usage to which I will be referring.

Since as cadets, and in particular first- and second-year cadets, we had only the regular blue uniforms that were issued to us, it was acceptable for us—i.e., required of us—to substitute a white dress shirt and black bow tie for the usual light-blue shirt and dark-blue tie to wear to the military ball, usually referred to more colloquially as the mil ball. At Miami University, the Air Force Military Ball was THE affair for a young lady to be invited to. I just now asked my wife, nearly forty-eight years after the fact, if it had been considered an honor to have been invited. Her immediate reply, "Oh, God yes!"

For us cadets, preparation meant getting the uniform cleaned and pressed, all insignia on and aligned precisely, a high polish on the low-quarter shoes (plain black lace-up uniform shoes) and belt buckle, and a haircut. Perhaps a white dress shirt and black bow tie might have been needed to be purchased, borrowed, or otherwise scrounged if we did not already have one at school. Naturally a corsage of tasteful presentation was ordered a few days beforehand, just like for a high school prom.

I suppose preparation for the military ball was a tiny bit more involved for our lady guests. I do not pretend to know all the details of the mad scrambles they went through, but I suspect it involved hours of shopping for a formal dress (not a mess dress—a girly dress) and matching accessories. Then, of course, there were the hours spent on getting hair, makeup, and nails done just so, and whatever else was felt required in preparation for such an occasion.

That military ball was my second experience at a formal co-ed military function. Peggy, the girl that I asked to be my date, was the daughter of an Air Force full colonel, so she was not new to military ways.

I suppose that, since I was evil enough to blatantly imply a first mil ball in my experience, I am bound to briefly explain my first such event. Back at Columbus (GA) High School, there was a mil ball that I attended. I was only fifteen and only had a learner's permit to drive, so one of my parents drove my date Susan and me to and from the ball. Susan wore a white furry over-the-shoulder type thingy—a shawl perhaps? My JROTC uniform was the Army O.D. green wool Ike jacket (Ike as in Eisenhower) and trousers. Turned out that the white furry over-the-shoulder type thingy surrendered about a third of its white hairs to my O.D. green military jacket. And that is about all can I remember of that night.

The AFROTC Military Ball at Miami that year was on a Friday evening. The Tuesday beforehand I got a call from one of Peggy's dormitory friends. Peggy was in the university infirmary with measles. However, not to worry, they had already arranged another girl for me. I was given her phone number so we could go on a blind "date" to meet each other. That evening I met Andi (as she was introduced to me, and as she—Andrea—was known back then) at her dorm, and we walked to the Res, a.k.a. the student union, for a Coke date (the bubbly liquid kind, not the illicit kind). Since I managed not to offend her, she accepted my last-minute (not my fault!) invitation to accompany me to the Ball.

That Tuesday was a misty, somewhat drizzly evening. Andi was wearing what she called a swamp coat—an olive drab, rain-proof coat something in between a regular coat and a full-fledged rain-coat. Not at all memorable, one would think. So why do I remember these little details over a half-century later? It all has to do with Happy Tuesdays, which is a topic for another time.

The next day, Peggy's dorm mates called me back to announce that Peggy did not have the measles after all and that she could go to the Ball with me. That gave me two dates for the same event, but it was a dilemma realized by the dorm mates. They took care of explaining the situation to Andi, so Peggy was the one who accompanied me that Friday evening. Although she and I dated for a few weeks afterward, other cosmic forces were at play in the universe, or at least in the southwest Ohio part of it.

- 5 -

FINAL EXAM IN POETRY

Look familiar?
(This is actually a later edition;
I could not find a photo of the old edition.)

During a period of nebulosity in my long-range educational progress, I had planned to transfer to the University of Cincinnati, known in Cincinnati as UC, although I am not aware of any other Universities of Cincinnati. At the end of each trimester, Miami U. would send our grades to us, printed on an adhesive-backed label that we were to put into our red M Books—booklets that were given to each freshman with pertinent details about everything a student new to the campus should know. There were blank pages in the back onto which we were to attach our grade labels. I carefully placed mine from the first trimester nicely and neatly aligned onto the first blank page. By the time the next trimester ended, I had already applied to and been accepted to the Aerospace Engineering (ASE) program at UC beginning the upcoming fall semester. Therefore, since I did not plan to be attending Miami afterwards, I slapped my grade label rather devil-may-care haphazardly on the page with my previously neatly-placed grade label.

Although there were plusses and minuses resulting from my decision that lasted for the next school year, in the long run it had turned out to be a mistake. The year itself was enjoyable enough; perhaps it was too enjoyable, as it resulted in adding a year to my graduation date. With Vietnam in full bloom (okay, admittedly not the best of metaphors), promotion in the US Army and Air Force from second lieutenant to first lieutenant had been reduced to one year. Likewise, another year for promotion from first lieutenant to captain. Not long after the cessation of hostilities, each of those years was changed back to one and a half years, making it three years total to captain rather than two. A quirky adjustment— quirky, in my humble opinion (a phrase that Dave, a retired Air

Force friend of mine, likes to use—rather insincerely, I might add!) was applied to those of us between promotions. The number of months one had remaining until his or her date of promotion was then doubled. In my case, since I had been expecting to be promoted to captain in eight months, I then faced an additional eight months as a first lieutenant. That equated to eight fewer months of time in grade as captain and eight fewer months of captain's pay. That change in the promotion structure was unforeseeable, at least to me in 1966, a time when the Vietnam situation looked like it would be ongoing indefinitely. However, the year I spent at UC pushed me out of the two-year-to-captain time frame.

But again I am getting just a wee bit ahead of the storyline.

That spring trimester at Miami in 1966, finals week began on a lovely sunny Saturday in mid-April. As serendipitous events are wont to occur, Andi and I happened to have the same professor for freshman English Composition and Literature, though we had not been in the same class. However, our two classes were taking the final exam together in the same classroom early that Saturday afternoon. I think serendipity was aided somewhat that day by Andi as she happened to be sitting at a desk in front of me. Planned on her part? I don't know, and she's not saying. She also happened to have placed some papers with her name on them under her seat, conveniently in my line of vision. Also planned? I don't know that either. What guy really knows the machinations that churn and evolve inside the mind of a woman? Anyone who says he does is lying and probably has something to hide. I think it is an inherent trait females are born with and which develops at an early age—no later than age two would be my guess.

I am not one to remember names particularly well, no better nor worse than average I would guess, but on occasion factors intervene to assist. That clever juxtapositioning by Cupid was one of these assisted occasions. Andi's last name was Daskivich. Andi Daskivich. Not that common of a name, or at least not to a boy raised in the South. However, she lived in Euclid, Ohio, a suburb of Cleveland in northeastern Ohio, an area noted for its Eastern European ethnicity. Seeing her name on her papers (how could I not?), I remembered her—she was the girl I almost took to the military ball a couple of months prior when Peggy was in the infirmary. About the time her name dawned on me, the final exam started, so I had missed an opportunity to speak to her.

That second trimester of English Lit was mostly poetry. I am not now nor ever have been particularly fond of any poetry exceeding the intellectual requirements of something to the tune of

There once was a boy of Bagdad,
An inquisitive sort of a lad.
He said, "I will see
If a sting has a bee."
And he very soon found that it had.

I do not know who the author of this bit of "poetry" was or even what grade I was in school when we studied limericks. I think I might have come across that little ditty in seventh or eighth grade, which for me was in the late 1950s. Of all the "literature" I have been exposed to since then, I cannot explain why that particular bit of intellectual pursuit has remained with me, nor am I interested in any psychological analysis.

So, after laboriously slogging my way through the first half of the final exam, I came to the poem we were to analyze and comment upon. After reading it through the first time, I knew I was a goner. I spent the last half of the time allowed for the exam reading and rereading that stupid poem. That (stupid poem) is my commentary here, not what I wrote in my blue book at the time. It was one of those poems with lots of didactic pentameter (whatever that happens to be) symbolism, obviously referencing foreshadowed mysteries unknown but predestined. I was in agony. Good thing I was transferring into the ASE program at UC—science, numbers; real concrete stuff. None of these flights of fancy of a drugged-out (probably), unemployed poet. I was entirely out of my element and I knew it.

And time ran out. Andi had finished her exam and turned in her blue book long before. In desperation, I hastily wrote in my blue book:

"I know there are deep, secret, hidden meanings in this poem, but I haven't a clue what they are."

Surprisingly, that was still sufficient for me to get a B for the trimester. I think the old professor must have liked me—or else he felt sorry for me.

Even more surprising was that when I turned in my blue book, gathered my papers and things, and walked out of the room . . . Andi was there, waiting . . .

. . . for me.

- 6 -

GETTING TO KNOW YOU

I saw her as soon as I walked outside the testing room. Although I did not know it at that moment, she had waited so that I could not help but notice her. We greeted each other and chatted as we walked back to our dorms together. Reid Hall and Symmes Hall were freshmen women dorms and men dorms, respectively, in the East Quad. I walked Andi to her dorm. She was fascinating— beautiful, charming, sharp sense of humor, intelligent . . . how was it that I had not taken her to the mil ball? I suppose that was rather out of my hands and in those of the girls' dorm occupants. As soon as I got back to my room, I called her and asked if she would like to go out with me. Tonight. After dinner; we ate in a common mess—er, dining hall. She said yes.

I don't remember what we did—went to a movie, or uptown, or to Tuffy's for a Hershey sandwich. When I got back to my room that night, I called her again. After talking a little while, I asked her if she wanted to go out again.

She asked, "When?"

"Now."

"Now?"

"Yes, now."

It was a romantic evening . . .

It was a lovely, clear spring night. We just went walking, nowhere special, just us being together. Somewhere in the Formal Gardens we stopped and gazed up at the stars in the night sky. I stood closely behind her, my left arm around her waist, and pointed up over her shoulder with my right arm, telling her about Ursa Major, the Big Bear, a.k.a the Big Dipper. I have been interested in astronomy since I was a little kid. I told her how she could follow along the pointer stars, as I was pointing them out to her, about five lengths to find Polaris, the North Star, at the end of the handle of the Little Dipper.

For me I was just sharing with Andi one of my joys. But I had never before experienced the joy I felt at that moment. Many years later, and by many, I mean decades, she happened to mention to me how she thought that I was really romantic at that moment with my arm over her shoulder. I had not thought about that moment over those same decades, but I remembered it well. The feeling brings warmth to me even as I type. . . .

And so it went for the next five days and nights. I don't remember much of what she and I did that week except stroll, and talk, and kiss . . . it was euphoric magic. Fairy tale magic, like something Walt Disney would create. We spent all that week together as much as we could, interrupted occasionally for some studying and to take final exams when we had to. We each had our last final exam that Friday morning. In a short time, we had grown quite smitten with each other. "Fond" would have been a more romantic word for it, but "smitten" is more accurate. Fond occurs while growing over time. Smitten happens right now.

Our last date was Thursday night. I still had to get back and "read" the fifteen chapters in my psych book that I had managed to neglect all trimester. But I called Andi again when I got back to my room and asked her if she wanted to go for one last walk in the morning before our exams. We made a date for 0600. That's 6:00. In the morning.

It was another beautiful spring morning in Oxford. We went walking in the Formal Gardens behind our dorms. She was not a smoker, but though she had tried to hide it, I could taste that she had had a cigarette. She said she was nervous about her last exam. I gently—for me—chastised her for it, and to my knowledge she has never smoked since. It was one of those bittersweet mornings. At the end of the school year, I had found a girl perfectly suited to me, and for some reason she seemed to feel the same about me. In that week (during finals of all times), a fondness between us had grown, which had made it really difficult for me. On the solitary hour drive home to Cincinnati after my last final exam, I was a bit on the depressed side. Our last morning walk was to be our last time together. . . .

- 7 -

A TALE OF TWO CITIES—AND TWO GIRLS

Don't go away yet; that is not the end of the story. Andi went home to Euclid in the northeast corner of Ohio, and I went home to Cincinnati in the southwest corner of Ohio. We began corresponding over the summer. Actual hand-written letters, with a pen and paper, delivered by the United States Post Office or, as the process is now referred to, snail mail. 1966 was way before personal cell phones, email, texting, Facebook, and all the other social media communicating systems. Her letters to me were a reflection of the same humor and wit that I had started enjoying before our departure from each other. Those letters managed to keep the embers of attraction glowing over the summer, so much so that we planned to get together after she returned to Miami in September. Miami was only about forty miles from my dad's house. I made the one-hour trip to be with her for a marvelous weekend. I don't remember doing anything special; just being with Andi was special. At night I slept in a men's dorm in the room of a friend whose roommate had gone home that weekend.

Andi and I continued writing each other after I went back to Cincinnati, and we planned another weekend together, four weekends after my first visit. Our next two rendezvous were three weeks apart, then two weeks, and then two weekends in a row before finals week began.

In the interim, I had met Kathy during a fraternity rush week party at UC that fall. We met and began talking while in a line for dinner. As it turned out, she was quite gregarious, and we monopolized each other the rest of the evening. She had just moved with her parents from California to Cincinnati. We spent about three hours getting to know each other. Among other things, she talked about the boyfriend she had left in California and I talked about Miami and Andi. After the party was over, I drove her and two of her classmates to their nurse's dorm, which was a part of UC but off of the main campus. She and I started dating on the weekends that I did not go to Miami, so that semester I saw more of Kathy than I did of Andi, although the gap was narrowing.

Andi was not aware of Kathy. That I was also dating Kathy was no secret that I was withholding, but there was never an occasion nor a need for the subject to come up. Andi and I were not going steady—that is what "exclusive" was called back in the day. It had not occurred to either of us yet, considering our obviously differing geography and universities. I suppose that if I had thought about it I would have realized there was no reason for Andi not to be dating other guys. However, I did not think about it.

Decades later, Andi and I were invited to spend a few days at a time-share condo in North Myrtle Beach, South Carolina, with our good college friends Roger and Carol. While reminiscing about college days, I found out that Andi and Roger had dated some—or at least once. It got to be a topic of hilarity as Carol and I kidded Andi and Roger about it as they kidded us back by remaining completely reticent. They definitely had the upper hand.

As that fall encroached upon winter, I was both fortunate and conflicted simultaneously. I liked both girls and was growing to care for each of them the more I got to know them. They were quite different from each other, not that that factored into the equation, but they shared some of the same characteristics—intelligence, attractiveness, keen wit, sense of humor. And they both liked me.

Somehow I knew I was eventually going to have to make a decision about one girl or the other, and although I was seriously drawn to each of them, I think I knew in my heart which way I was leaning. Kathy was local, but I was willing and eager to drive the hour to be with Andi.

The decision came one cold December night in Cincinnati. I had taken Kathy to her dorm after our date. We sat on a couch in the lobby still talking, prolonging the end of our evening together. At last she told me about the Christmas party she was planning at her home, expecting that naturally I would come as her date.

BLAM! There it was—critical mass. Rather than my having to make a decision at some indefinite time in the future, the decision was suddenly thrust upon me. I knew the party was important to Kathy, and it would have been important to me—except . . . I had to reply to her, "I am so sorry. . . . I will be out of town that weekend."

Kathy knew exactly what that meant—that I was going up to Oxford to be with Andi.

With little else left to say at that point, I departed to go home. When I got into my car, there on the front seat were Kathy's gloves that she had left behind. It was cold outside, and I knew she would be needing them, so I took them back inside to her. When I opened the door to the lobby, I saw Kathy still sitting on the couch where I had just left her . . . and she was crying. Unwittingly, I had apparently broken her heart. I really felt terrible about it, but what else could I say then? When I had left for my car a couple of minutes earlier, I knew she was disappointed. When I saw her sitting there crying, I knew she was more than disappointed; she was hurting inside. Something had suddenly and unexpectedly just been lost between us—a loss for both of us.

It may have been possible for me to rearrange or somehow adjust my plans to go see Andi so that I could go to Kathy's party and possibly get up to Miami also. That might have possibly salvaged our friendship, but it was not to be. I was deeply saddened, for her sudden loss of our relationship—as well as for mine. But I still had Andi. It was at that ethereal moment in time that I realized I had made a major decision in my life. . . .

Andi . . . .

Too much of other stuff and not enough studying left me unprepared for ASE. I re-applied to Miami that spring.

- 8 -

THE BLIND DATE REVISITED

The Next Military Ball

Although I was not yet re-enrolled back at Miami, I asked Andi to the AFROTC Mil Ball to be held there in February 1967. Remember all the "stuff" I wrote about that girls did to get ready for these formal occasions? This next episode is really why I even brought up the subject in the first place. Andrea, a.k.a. Andi, thinks I need to get over it; I said I will as soon as I finish writing about it. She is not going to be overly pleased with my rendition.

One of the procedures at a military ball is the Receiving Line. It is indeed possible, although highly unlikely, that I did not properly brief Andi on expectations. Or maybe I just did not sufficiently emphasize timeliness to her. Or perhaps I lost her attention after she said yes and her mind immediately jumped ahead to making mental lists and planning whatever it is that girls plan under such circumstances.

Since girls seem to start planning for these types of events the moment they accept an invitation, it behooves the males of our species to give the ladies sufficient notice—i.e., I would guess at least a few months—to prepare themselves. Apparently getting ready in a timely fashion, or even in a semi-timely fashion, was not a restriction to be considered if she were to be properly presentable . . .

. . . which just so happens to be a convenient segue into the next topic of the story —timeliness. In the military, being on time means being five minutes early. Not to sound sexist, but I don't know how female-type women ever manage to succeed in the military; perhaps they come from military families and were indoctrinated from early childhood on the importance of temporal cognizance, or possibly the advent of digital chronology and LED displays helped. At this point, one might well wonder why I belabor this point. After all, it was just a dance, wasn't it? (No; but that is my humble opinion.)

I must admit that I am not noted for being overly punctual myself. In planning, I note the time I need to be at any particular meeting, function, performance, et cetera, and work my way backwards from there to calculate the time I need to leave: getting myself appropriately ready, driving time to destination, including estimated traffic conditions (especially rush hour), time for asking directions when I get lost—er, I mean, when I get temporarily spatially disoriented; time to park and walk to wherever it is I need to be, including time to ask for directions again; time to ask directions from somebody else that actually knows; and time to be where I am supposed to be when I am supposed to be there. With time needed plus another ten per-

cent for miscellany calculated, I work further backwards to figure how long it will take me to be ready to leave—shower, shave,
et cetera if needed: dress, time to eat before leaving. Thus, I
have calculated the exact time I need to begin preparations for
a timely arrival.

Except that it usually does not work out quite that way. Often
I manage to "fiddillyfart around" (to borrow an expression from
my friend Bennett) doing other "important" things that take me
beyond my initial start time. Then it is play catch-up and, of
course, any of a multitude of factors intervene to thwart my pre-
cisely-timed schedule.

However, that has nothing to do with the night of the Mil
Ball because I was at Andi's dorm in plenty of time to escort her
to the gym where it was being held. Apparently my arrival was
not sufficient impetus to inspire her and her assorted roommates
(I am just guessing here—girls seem to require a bevy of support
for proper preparation) to come even close to any semblance of
timeliness for her grand entrance. We are not talking a mere five
or ten minutes late. It was more like half an hour or forty-five
minutes late.

But have you seen the Rex Harrison and Audrey Hepburn
movie *My Fair Lady*? Remember the scene when Liza Doolittle
first comes down the stairs before going to the queen's big affair,
and a few movie minutes later when she is presented at the ball?
It could have been Andi—Andrea—that night when she came
into the lobby where I had been impatiently waiting. The room
glowed with the reflection of her regalness. And she was MY date!

Still, though we missed the Reception Line entirely, it was not
an unforgivable faux pas. How could it be? Some things are worth

waiting for. As we immersed ourselves into the evening, and as she held my arm, I proudly introduced Andrea to the active duty staff and other honored guests as we milled around. She was more than just a trophy date. Andrea was elegance personified.

At the AFROTC Military Ball, Miami University, 1967

- 9 -

LOVE BLOOMS

As a result of having spent too much time pledging a fraternity, dating Kathy, and going to see Andi, I did not successfully make it past the first semester of ASE at UC. Oops. Plan B.

Actually, there was no plan B, so I had to make one. I took some optional courses at UC the next semester while I reapplied to Miami. Needless to say, I continued making weekend trips to see Andi as often as our schedules permitted. I was definitely past being smitten. I had thoughts of love, but I was only twenty years old. What did I know? I had no frame of reference for what love was really supposed to feel like. Sure, we all go through puppy love and school kid infatuations, but how does one really know? Poets write about love, songs are sung about love, love makes the world go 'round. But how does one really know? I asked myself that question more and more often that spring of 1967. When I was eighteen I made a rather mature (for me) decision. While listening to some lyrics of a popular song at the time, "When I fall in love, it will be forever." I decided that that was the philosophy for me. The next time I said "I love you" to a girl, she would be the girl that I would marry. And thus it came to pass.

Love blooms

Andi took a couple of courses at Miami during the first six-week summer term. In June I received notification from Miami that I had been accepted for re-admission. I drove up to Miami to see Andi again before she went home for the summer. She was staying in Richard Hall in the South quad. I was waiting for her in the lobby; men were not allowed out of the lobby area in a women's dorm at Mother Miami. It was another bright, sunny, late spring day. Final exams were over. When she came to me in the lobby and we greeted each other—use your imagination—as I held her I told her of my re-admission to the University. Her overwhelming joy at the news overwhelmed *me*. She was more than just happy that I would be back; she was ecstatic. Could that mean . . .?

Without thinking further about it, I clumsily blurted out, "I think I am falling in love with you." She was speechless. Literally. I wasn't sure if she was happy speechless or concerned speechless. I thought—hoped—it was the former. She seemed to be the former, as far as I could tell.

It was in June 1967, on a Tuesday.

That day I went with her back to Cleveland. On Friday, three days later, we were on a date in her parents' grey 1964 Ford Galaxy. She was driving, since she knew her way around, and we went to a park somewhere before we headed back to her parents' house. It was there that Andi told me that she had been thinking about what I had said to her back at Richard Hall. Neither of us had spoken about the awkward profession of my love for her since I had uttered it those three days prior.

"I love you, too," she told me.

Back at Miami a couple of months later, I asked her to accept a gold GDI (gamma delta iota) lavalier. Of course she was delighted. We were in love.

That was the afternoon of 29 August 1967 . . . a Tuesday.

Fast forward a few months to 2 April 1968, yet another lovely spring afternoon at Miami. All of those pleasant sunny days really were—pleasant and sunny; I am not just remembering them this way for convenience. Andi and I were strolling in the Formal Gardens, as we were wont to do on occasion, happy and light-hearted. The Formal Gardens at Miami were quite a pleasant place to stroll when one is happy and light-hearted and in love. We stopped on a path between two spruce trees whose lower limbs were encroaching over the path and conveniently providing a little quasi-privacy. I took off my uniform wheel hat and laid it on an extended tree branch so it—my hat—wouldn't fall off when we kissed. Suddenly, without preamble or forethought, I heard myself ask, "Andi, will you marry me?"

Without the slightest hesitation she said, "Yes, I will."

Wow. I could not have planned a more romantic setting and moment. And surprise—for each of us.

That year, April 2 just so happened to fall on . . . a Tuesday.

A day or so later we went uptown to Oxford (a trip of about two blocks) to the jewelry store to explore the world of diamonds. The jeweler educated us on the five C's of buying a diamond: color, cut, carat, clarity, and cost. He showed us a number of different diamonds as illustration. Andi and I decided that we liked the marquis cut, which looks something like:

If I shrank the photo copy to match this font point size, it would just look like a tiny smudge. Then I went to downtown Cincinnati to the jewelry store where my dad's wife, Louie, worked. Her name was Mary Lou, but we called her Louie. I selected a marquis cut diamond in my price range, including Louie's employee discount, and had it put in a white gold setting with a matching wedding band.

On 11 April at Andi's parents' house, I asked her rather domineering father for his daughter's hand in marriage. If truth be told, I really wanted her whole body, intact.

"Have you asked her yet?" he asked me.

I said, "Yes, sir."

"What did she say?"

"She said, 'Yes.'"

"Then what are you asking me for? Do you have a ring yet?"

"Yes, sir."

"Then why don't you give it to her?"

And I did. It was the first time she had seen it.

A month or two later, while we were both enrolled in a summer term, one of the courses I was taking was Public Speaking. I had been told it would be a skill I would need to acquire if I expected to be successful in just about any career. The course itself was not difficult; however, writing and giving two-minute speeches were not such an easy task for me—especially one in particular. We were to emphasize the attention step. I had the not-so-bright idea to do a speech on diamonds. I knew where I thought I could borrow one for my attention-grabbing step.

That was the hard part. Andi's sparkling shiny new engagement ring was still bright and shiny on her left-hand ring finger. She had not yet even had time to develop a pale, untanned area under it. And, it was certainly the kind of thing a young woman in her betrothed condition likes to proudly show off to other friends, particularly those of the female persuasion. Girl-friends would express proper "OOH'S!" and "AH'S!" We guys would be less enthusiastic about such things: "Oh. Nice ring."

And I needed to borrow it for my attention step. Andi was naturally reluctant to part with her ring even for the couple of hours I would need it. I suppose I could have used her whole person with the ring still in place as my attention step, but, as fate schedules such things, she had a conflicting class. With about fourteen promises that I would guard it with my life, not let it get separated from my personage for even a moment, cross my heart and hope to die, and give it back to her as soon as my class was over, she finally but not very happily consented to grant me very temporary custody of her ring. I did not think it was like the one J.R.R. Tolkien wrote about in his famous trilogy, but "Everything Is Relative"—it certainly was to her. Actually, I was happy that she was so attached to it that a momentary detachment was of such concern to her. After all, she was going to be my trophy bride!

The speech went okay, and I returned the ring to Andi's anxiously-awaiting naked fourth finger on her left hand once again. There were sighs of relief from both of us—her for getting her ring back undamaged and in one piece, me for being relieved of the huge responsibility for its safekeeping.

Andi and her mother decided on a wedding date of 10 May 1969, about thirteen months away; not away from now, of course, but away from then.

- 10 -

THE BLIND DATE—EPILOGUE

Incredible as it may seem to friends who know me, that lady is still my bride over half of a century hence. . . .

Even more incredible is that we met on a blind date.

The tie that binds

HAPPY TUESDAY

For those curious Readers, and even for the rest of you, below is a brief explanation of my apparent fixation on Tuesdays.

A number of years ago Andrea and I got to reminiscing about college days and realized that, purely coincidentally and serendipitously, several happy events between us had happened on Tuesdays. We first met on a blind date on a Tuesday; I first told her that I love her on a Tuesday; I gave her a lavalier on a Tuesday; I proposed on a Tuesday. For over fifty years now, wherever we each may be in the world, every Tuesday we wish each other a Happy Tuesday. It still works: our daughter Allison was born on a Tuesday, our son Ian almost was, the difference being that he was born in Pacific Daylight Savings time, and so it continues. . . .

PART 2

- 11 -

ACTIVE DUTY

After graduating from college (back then it was college; since I earned my MBA a few years later, "college" has become "undergrad school." (It's a snob appeal type thing, I suppose.)) My first USAF active duty assignment was to what some people called the armpit of Texas —Laughlin Air Force Base (AFB) for Undergraduate Pilot Training (UPT). We affectionately, or sometimes not so affectionately, referred to it as Laugh-In AFB, a bit of an easy pun and often a double entendre named after the popular TV variety show of the time, *Rowen and Martin's Laugh-In.* Actually, even though Laughlin AFB was outside the remote city of Del Rio on the Rio Grande River in the southwest corner of Texas, my wife and I enjoyed our fourteen months there. (The Mexicans just across the river in Ciudad Acuña probably wondered why we Gringos referred to it redundantly in its translation—River Large River. Wasn't Rio Grande enough?) Of course, we knew it was just a temporary first stepping stone of the anticipated exotic locations to which we could expect to be assigned during my Air Force career. There was the river and the Lake Amistad backwater created by the dam, which was especially nice if you knew someone with a boat. San Antonio was only 150 miles due east—about an hour and a half drive, unless you got stopped by the Brackettville police. (No comment. . . .)

Occasionally we would drive to one of the major Air Force bases in the city (San Antonio, not Brackettville; the "-ville" could have been considered a euphemism) for dinner. Our destination would be to the Officers Club at either Randolph AFB or Lackland AFB. Randolph, itself a UPT base, was the location for the headquarters of Air Training Command, the umbrella under which pilot training and a plethora of other types of training operated, and Lackland was/is a large base which could be considered the Air Force's equivalent to the US Army's Fort Benning, Georgia. New Air Force recruits (as opposed to old recruits? (perhaps I am guilty of a bit of redundancy)) would go through basic training there, as did aspiring officers as they went through Officer Training School (OTS). The Army equivalent at Fort Benning was/is Officer Candidate School (OCS). Besides Brackettville, on the way to and from San Antonio we also drove through Hondo, Texas, which had signs up at either end of the highway that went through the "city" limits that read, "This is God's country. Please don't drive through it like hell."

There was a sign like this at each end of town

At this point you may well be wondering, and rightly so, why anyone would drive an hour and a half, each way (okay, so maybe two hours if we caught the one traffic light in Hondo red), just to go to dinner. Consider this: Del Rio was a metropolitan area of about 26,000 people at the time. When the first "chain" restaurant of any kind - in this case a Dairy Queen—was built there in 1970 or '71, it was the leading DQ in the country after its first year of operation. Does that help put things in perspective for you? Besides, dinner at the Officers Clubs at both Lackland and Randolph were superb. For example, at Lackland my wife and I would sometimes order the chateaubriand-for-two dinner, which included a humongous salad bar—which included fresh fruit embedded in an enormous volcanic-shaped mound of whipping cream, of which I had at least two or three helpings . . . I was young (EIR), trim (EIR), and could afford the calories at the time,

71

plus a couple of side dishes and dessert. This was a few years before my "wine period" began. Actually, it could more properly be referred to as my "wine ellipsis"—you know—those three dots . . . that you see occasionally that imply an ongoing and as yet unended situation.

The bill for the dinner was $7.50; no sales tax.

Sometimes we would spend the night in the Visiting Officers Quarters (VOQ) at Randolph. Compared to the duplex that we lived in in Del Rio, the VOQ at Randolph was très chic, uptown, quite elegant, and otherwise very nice. We never saw any nasty critters at the Q, as the VOQ is often referred to when the name Visiting Officers Quarters being reduced to VOQ is still not short enough. On the other hand, at our abode in Del Rio, my wife, of course, was the one who found, at different times, fortunately, the scorpion, the tarantula, and the snake. I don't remember what kind of snake it was—probably a boa cobra or a coral rattlemoccasin. All snakes are poisonous as far as I am concerned. And of course (again) it was the job of her dauntless and intrepid husband, the United States Air Force Second Lieutenant Killer Pilot (trainee)—well, okay, me—to remove any and all threats of this nature, thus securing the safety of the premises for posterity. That is, if I ever had any hopes of having any posterity.

- 12 -

UNDERGRADUATE PILOT TRAINING

Okay, now, where was I? Oh, yes—there I was at 4500 feet over—no, wait—that comes still a bit later.

Student pilot in front of a T-37B

Pilot training: There are a few elementary—or, in many cases, not so elementary— subject areas with which a student pilot must become familiar before he (this is in no way a sexist provocation on my part; I refer to "he" since there were no "she" type Air Force pilots at the time) ever touches the Cessna 150, Piper Cub, or whatever basic type of machine he will begin training in: weather, navigation, FARs (Federal Aviation [Administration] Regulations), VFR—Visual Flight Rules, Basic IFR—Instrument Flight Rules, basic aerodynamics, basic thermodynamics, radio communication, etc. The list goes on.

In aviation there is a "language" and structure, the use of which are fairly rigid. English is the internationally agreed-upon language used in aviation, and there are a plethora of stories involving various international accents . . .

. . . a quick one here: In UPT we had an Iranian student in my class (different time, different century, different world). I think he was to be admired, going through all this training and in what was to him a foreign language. It was hard enough even for those whose native language was English. His English was not as polished as that of our Norwegian student, and his accent manifested itself in interesting ways. The first jet trainers we flew in the Air Force were the T-37Bs. The T-37B is a small, two-seat side-by-side jet trainer . . . a 6,000 pound two-engine machine for converting fuel into screaming noise; it was more or less fondly referred to as "The Tweet." However, my computer does not have a large enough font to accurately represent the size of this misnomer.

Part of the flying training included pattern work—i.e., doing touch-and-go landings: takeoff, fly along the essentially rectangular flight pattern around the runway in use, touch down (land), lower the nose to the runway, immediately apply power to takeoff again, repeat until reaching bingo—minimum fuel. The different segments of the flight pattern have names, and the final segment before landing is called—this may come as a surprise to some of you—Final Approach, or Final. Since it was a pilot *training* base, there was always a Supervisor of Flying (SOF) on duty who was an instructor pilot. He was in a small building, a.k.a. the "shack," that provided visibility to either end of the runway. The prevailing wind direction determined the direction of the runway being used (and still does, except in those instances where local geography mandates otherwise). Each student was assigned a specific call sign which he used during his T-37 training. When a student pilot was coming in for a landing, he would make the required radio call, "Bravo One Three final approach gear check." This radio call would alert the SOF to use his binoculars to locate the aircraft (hopefully it was somewhere at least in the general lateral and vertical vicinity of where it should be), and visually confirm that the student did indeed have his landing gear hanging down, which is an excellent orientation for the landing gear to be in at that particular time of any flight. For his final landing of the training flight the student would call, "Bravo One Three final approach gear check full stop." Everyone flying around the pattern, or sitting in the control tower, or watching from the SOF building, was monitoring the assigned airfield radio frequency. We would all know when it was our Iranian student: "Bravo One Afour finahpproach geahcheck fool astop." (Even so, his English was far superior to my Farsi, which was and still is zero.)

Now, back to the story . . . resuming pilot training:

Some of the Ground School had to be completed before flying; some of it continued throughout the flying phase. While learning how to actually fly each type of airplane, a pilot also has to become intimately familiar with all the characteristics, procedures, systems, and a myriad of other things about the aircraft. Each type of aircraft is different in size, shape, speed, performance, cockpit layout, number of engines, normal procedures, emergency procedures, aircraft systems (electrical, hydraulics, fuel, flight controls, pneumatics, engines, communications . . .), operating procedures, and all the details in between, as well as preparation before and debriefings after each flight. On more modern aircraft (EIR; my last pilot logbook entry is dated 4 June 1996), pilots spent more time learning to program the Electronic Flight Instrument System (EFIS) than learning aircraft systems. On even more modern aircraft, pilots just enter into the Flight Management System (FMS) computer the flight number, destination, and date, and the computer then downloads all the flight data into the EFIS. Pilots still have to learn aircraft systems and flight characteristics, but the systems are much more automated and designed to provide necessary information to the cockpit.

- 13 -

BASIC WATER SURVIVAL

"Parting is such sweet sorrow. . . ."
(Romeo and Juliet, Act 2, scene 2)

Andi, my wife of nearly two and a half years at the time, pinned my first pair of Air Force pilot wings on my uniform at the conclusion of the Undergraduate Pilot Training graduation ceremony in September 1971, thirteen months after we had arrived at Laughlin AFB. From there it took another seven months of various types of training before I arrived in Southeast Asia for my next permanent change of station (PCS) assignment. There were several temporary duty (TDY) itinerary deviations along the way for these further training requirements, of course.

First I will present a sketch of the abridged version of the journey: enroute to my assigned base in Vietnam, I went from Texas to Florida to Texas to Ohio to Florida to Ohio to Florida to Washington (state) to California to the Philippines and finally to Nakhon Phanom RTAFB (Na-KON Fa-NOM Royal Thai Air Force Base). Sometime during the TDYs, my SEA assignment was changed from Phan Rang Air Base in Vietnam to Nakhon Phanom, a.k.a NKP, a.k.a Naked Fanny, in northeast Thailand. Not exactly the direct rhumb line route, but, as I said, I needed a bit more training first to prepare me for an environment totally outside any frame of reference I had at the time. Now to fill in a few details.

Basic Water Survival, Homestead AFB, FL

In October 1971, I flew as a passenger on a commercial airline to Homestead AFB, Florida, located a little north of Key Largo, for Basic Water Survival training. Even though pilot training is about flying airplanes, there is a lot more to it than just "stick and rudder," as in the "olden days" prior to WWII. (If I have to explain what WWII stands for, perhaps you should put down that glass of cabernet sauvignon which you are too young to be drinking anyway and ask your grandfather about it before continuing.)

In UPT we also received a smattering of training for a variety of situations we might encounter should we happen to experience an unscheduled and otherwise unpleasant event immediately following a flight that terminated prematurely under less-than-optimal conditions, territory, and location. Water survival, for instance. During UPT we spent one sunny day at the base swimming pool, in our flight suits, learning how to tread water for twenty minutes by trapping air in pockets of flight suit material. If done successfully, one could trap enough air to make an improvised, albeit soggy, cushion that could support one's head above water and possibly allow a cat nap; at least until your buddy decided that you looked entirely too comfortable.

The Basic Water Survival Course at Homestead lasted three days. Most of the first day was spent in the classroom; no surprise about that. We were instructed in the use of the various pieces of water survival equipment we would most likely be issued at our next PCS base, which we would certainly be learning to use for real in a couple of days. I do not recall what we did the second day— it was probably an advanced version of what we experienced during pilot training. The big decision we students had to make was what to have for dinner at the Officers Club each night. I clearly remember the last day, though. It was actually the most fun.

We were taken out a little way into the bay on a large boat (large for the Air Force (EIR); Navy types are permitted to snicker here). By "a little way," I mean far enough out from land to be out of the way of any recreational or other activities closer in along the coast, a distance of perhaps two or three miles. We were provided with all the equipment that "Those Who Knew of Such Matters" felt we might find handy to have available should we find ourselves in water, whereas just moments before we had been high and dry in the cockpit of whichever Air Force aerospace vehicle we had been flying. I say that in semi-jest, but the necessary water survival gear was determined and revised on occasion by unfortunate aircrew members, and no doubt Navy and Marine sea and aircrew members, who survived their experiences. They with such experiences constituted "Those Who Knew of Such Matters." They probably had a bit of constraining input from military accountants in the Pentagon, however.

We were provided with a Mae West flotation device (ask your grandfather, or maybe even your great-grandfather, why they are called Mae West life preservers). If you have ever flown commercially and actually paid any attention whatsoever to the pre-flight safety briefing given by the flight attendants (or a video of such shown throughout the passenger cabin, starring absolutely gorgeous flight attendants (not the ones on your flight)), then you are at least somewhat familiar with a Mae West. It is designed to inflate automatically. I do not know if the ones used by the military are the same as the civilian ones, but if not, the differences are relatively minor (EIR—it's everywhere!). Supposedly a person could pull the cord and the two halves of the bright yellow Mae West would self-inflate—which was definitely not gonna happen in a training situation. For those of you who paid attention to the flight attendant briefing and/or classroom instruction, you were made aware of how to manually inflate the Mae West, giving the sharks more time to find you thrashing around in the water.

We were each issued a mesh life vest outfitted with various pockets which contained a collection of basic accoutrements which could be useful in a water survival situation. These items included one or two day/night flares, shark repellant (yeah, right), a Very pistol (a.k.a. flare gun, named after its inventor, Navy Lt. E. W. Very), eye glare diffuser (the black stuff you see athletes in some outdoor sports wearing smudged under their eyes), a smidgen of sun block, sea water dye (so the sharks could find you easier), water purification tablets, metal signal mirror, et cetera. There was also a selection of other convenient items in the survival pack that came with your seat cushion, all of which accompanied you on your way down. It would be rather useless to anyone if it stayed with the airplane, which could easily crash and submerge miles away before you ever hit the water. The survival pack included a basic medical kit, fishing hook and line, life raft repair kit, solar water purifier, sea anchor, and other assorted items. We may have been wearing our own flight suits and boots, or they may have been provided from the school's re-supply; I do not remember. (You may have noticed by now that I do not remember a lot of stuff. Gimme a break—it was over four decades ago (although in 1960 I did memorize—and still remember—Pi to seventy decimal places, a feat useful only for barroom betting, I suppose, but hardly helpful while floating in the middle of shark-infested waters).) As you can see, considerable thought had been given in determining which equipment items were to be included.

- 14 -

DISQUISITION ON PARACHUTES

The Air Force boat (that sounds a bit oxymoronic) had a flat, open deck on top with a large vertical screen behind it. The function of the screen was to support an open parachute, one exactly like the kind we would be wearing in an aircraft, unopened until needed, of course. The screen allowed the parachute to be attached to a student without his being dragged backwards off of the boat. These were not of the modern (again, EIR), highly maneuverable type parachutes that the skydiving housewife next door uses to land touching down on one foot in stride while carrying a bag of groceries and sipping her chardonnay. We had the old "cut four" parachute; for directional guidance, we would use the hooked blade of our survival knife to cut a certain four lines to the parachute canopy. This action would result in a small pocket forming on the rear edge of the canopy, allowing some air to escape, thereby providing a bit of Newtonian action/reaction propulsion to guide us to exactly where we wanted to land.

Theoretically speaking, of course. Over land, this activity, employed by an adrenalin-induced first-time user in an actual emergency situation during which a sudden departure from the comfort (?) and safety (?) of his (former) aerospace vehicle, would be guaranteed to place the aforementioned user in the top of the only tree visible within a fourteen-mile radius. Being the only such tree, and it having no competition from other trees, it would have grown to 217 feet high. (Murphy's Law? Never knew the guy.)

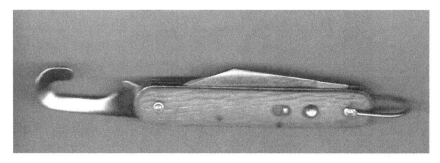

Air Force survival knife with hooked blade open—smaller than actual size.

You might be wondering how, in such a situation, the descending parachutist could manage to visually find that one tree to avoid, locate his survival knife, get it out of his pocket without dropping it, and get the hooked blade open. I'm just speculating here, but probably someone in the past who did not have all the pre-planned advantages that we had but who had miraculously survived by landing in a huge haystack (somewhere in Oklahoma during the filming of the movie version of the play named after that state) thought about all of these things as he made his way not-so-gently toward Planet Earth: "What if I had had a knife? With a hooked blade. That was kept open. In a knife-shaped pocket so it could be easily removed. Somewhere convenient but out of the way. Like on the inside of my left thigh, since, as most people, I am right-handed. Held in place with a snap. And attached to my flight suit by a lanyard (small cord) in case I dropped it—er, in case the wind blew it out of my hand." Now there is an idea that should fly! (Sorry—too hard to resist not writing that one.)

That is conjectural probability if the parachutist (not his prior occupation until about nineteen seconds ago) happened to be flying over a large tract of *land* when his aerial mishap . . . occurred. However, there is always the distinct possibility that our human projectile, hurtling toward Earth at a terminal velocity of about 125 miles per hour, give or take a mile or two, depending on the degree of his particular svelteness, might encounter some part of the other seventy percent of the Earth's surface that just happens to be covered in water (or snow or ice, as the case may be, but since no self-respecting Air Force aircrew member on his way to SEA would ever be likely to find himself over water in its unmelted form, we need not consider those possibilities). One good thing about landing on water: no trees to contend with. No lions or tigers or bears either. Fifty-foot-high ocean swells, perhaps, and maybe a great white shark or two, but we were issued a parcel of shark repellant in our overwater survival vest. However, we were advised to never open it, as the shark repellant attracted sharks. I did not make this up; I am not that imaginative. Another nice thing about landing in water is that, compared to landing on land (except haystacks), water is soft. (Need I say it? EIR.)

Just keep in mind what it feels like the next time you do a belly flop off of the low diving board.

Returning once again to the top deck of the large Air Force boat—this top deck and parachute-supporting screen did indeed serve a purpose. Each of us basic water survival students was strapped, one at a time, into one of the parachute harnesses, and the instructors would open and spread out over the large vertical screen one of the parachutes pretty much like the one just described. However, unlike in the movies, there was no dramatic checking of the altimeter to determine when one was below 10,000 feet (especially since we were only about twenty feet above sea level). There was no grabbing the ripcord handle and pulling it, thereby releasing the small pilot chute, which was attached to the main chute. And no pilot chute which, upon entering the 125-miles-per-hour jet stream through which it (the pilot chute) was being dragged above its human projectile (the pilot or other human) hurtling vertically in a downward direction, it (the pilot chute) deploys (the technical term for "pulls out") the main chute, which in turn pops fully open (hopefully), *suddenly slowing* said human projectile to a more reasonable and somewhat more controllable descent rate of perhaps ten or fifteen miles per hour. Nope; none of that excitement.

As pleasant as that may sound, keep in mind that the parachute harness in which we were secured was attached to the parachute by about 24 or maybe 739 nylon shroud lines, called risers (nylon cords – probably some number in between 24 and 739, and certainly much closer to the smaller number than the larger, except after you had landed either on land with gale force winds trying to drag you along before you could release the harness, or after you entered the water and the parachute landed right over you with its nicely-tangled jungle of risers all around you, you would swear there were at least 739 lines).

The "suddenly slowing" part mentioned above manifested itself most vehemently via the nylon harness straps which were snuggly routed around and between each upper thigh. This routing obviously was designed to prevent the human occupant from slipping out the bottom and resuming his or her 125 miles per hour plunge, unaccompanied by further safety devices, but in so doing it also conformed to Newtonian Laws of Physics, which are everywhere, except where the Einsteinian laws of the time-space continuum and the laws of quantum physics apply.

Newton's Second Law, the vector sum of a force, is represented mathematically by his famous formula, $F = ma$, where $F =$ force (the force applied to the body when the parachute suddenly pops open); $m =$ mass, which is essentially the weight of the parachutist (parachuter?) and accompanying accoutrements; and $a =$ acceleration, 125 miles per hour in our discussion. (Technically, 125 miles per hour is a velocity, whereas acceleration is a velocity change over time; but we need not concern ourselves with such mundane distractions while Planet Earth rapidly approacheth.) Now, according to Sir Isaac's Third Law, forces reacting in equal and opposite directions, the "ma" (mass times acceleration, not someone's mother) just before the "suddenly slowing" part must equal the "ma" immediately after it. The 125 miles per hour works out to be 183.33 feet per second. If we assume a weight for the parachutist and equipment to be 200 pounds, then 200 pounds x 183.33 feet per second equals a force of 36,667 foot-pounds per second. If the post-chute deployment descent rate is fifteen miles per hour, that is now a descending force of 4,400 foot-pounds per second (into that "soft" water still a few thousand feet below). That other 32,267 foot-pounds of energy had to go somewhere, however briefly. . . .

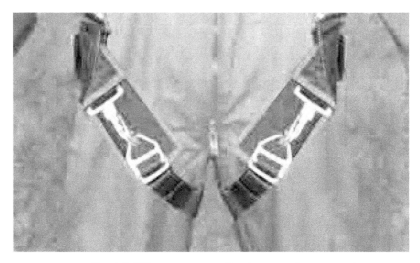

. . . Ooph! (Photo courtesy Butlerparachutes.com)

We will not even go into the theory of entropy here. You can read Stephen Hawking or Isaac Asimov for further disambiguation if you are so inclined; I would recommend Asimov unless you are overly scientifically cerebral.

- 15 -

PARASAILING, PT. 1

Back at Homestead again, still day three—ready to launch. . . .

Meanwhile, back on the top deck of the large Air Force boat again—we are getting really close to departure now, I promise. Maybe.

Recalling the situation: My turn has come for parasailing, and I am on the top deck, parachute harness strapped on tightly, water survival gear hanging behind me on the deck floor, my parachute already opened against the screen behind me, and attached to my chest strap is a long rope. An eight-hundred-foot-long rope. This in itself is not a concern. The real concern is what is attached to the other end of the rope . . . a 65,000 (give or take a few dozen thousand) horsepower motor boat with a couple of hairy, grinning NCOs (non-commissioned officers—i.e., sergeants) anxiously waiting to shove their boat throttle forward and pull us young officers and some other sergeants to our impending doom.

Actually, it was not quite like that. The motor boat would start out fairly slowly until the slack in the rope was taken up, and *then* it would accelerate quickly.

My first time parasailing had been in pilot training a few months earlier, but at that time we were attached to an Air Force blue pickup truck, and we were over land. On the boat, I had watched as other guys were readied by the instructors, attached to the rope, and, at a coordinated signal, the motor boat started away pulling the attached student with it. The student took two or three steps forward until the parachute behind him caught the wind and the student was pulled into the air. The boat accelerated until the student was about 600 feet above the water. Then, with a visual signal to the crew on the motor boat, the student para-sailer released the rope and began to float gently down into the warm shark-infested waters of the Atlantic Ocean.

Truth be told (there is always a first time), I don't think anyone ever saw any sharks in the area at all. The Air Force accountants were not about to waste the $1,000,000 (really) spent on training each pilot to get this wings by allowing one of them to become dinner for a denizen of the deep.

We cheered as each guy got airborne and on his way. That is, until Marvin's turn came. Marvin was a guy whose size was just about the maximum allowed by the Air Force to fit into its current inventory of aircraft cockpits at the time, which included the super-giant, 800,000+ pound C-5A cargo plane.

As a bit of interesting trivia, according to Wikipedia, the cargo hold of the C-5A is one foot longer than the entire length of the first powered flight by the Wright Brothers at Kitty Hawk. This, of course, is an exaggeration; even Wikipedia articles are written by people who occasionally get by with some fun. FYI, that landmark flight was 852 feet.

We watched as Marvin was secured and readied for his turn. The signal was given to the motor boat crew, and it proceeded normally.

Mistake.

Marvin took two or three steps. His chute was open, as it was supposed to be, and Marvin kept taking steps on the deck—he did not have a choice, being attached to the motor boat with the monster motor—but he did not magically float up into the air as the others before him had done. He kept taking steps until he reached the end of the boat's deck, at which point he descended below our view until we all heard the splash.

Marvin was recovered unharmed and the poor guy was hooked up again. The motor boat crew assured the instructors on the deck that this time they would him get him airborne or, by god, they would buy the beer. That time we heard a significantly louder roar from the motor boat as it pulled away with determination—and with Marvin.

Marvin did indeed get airborne before the end of the deck and floated up and along on his merry way, although not quite so delicately as the rest of us. I only weighed maybe 135 pounds at the time, so I had no concerns about a premature splash when my turn came. I was airborne after about two steps.

- 16 -

PARASAILING, PT. 2

In case you've never been parasailing before. . . .

Back at Homestead—parasailing at last.

I was going from about twenty feet above sea level up about
another 600 feet; so the above mini-dissertation did not come
into play, although in a real-life bailout situation, the aircrew

member would most likely have been wearing an oxygen mask that attaches to the helmet. "What was it they said in class about gauging the size of ocean swells on the way down? I wish I hadn't dozed off during that instruction on overwater bailouts. . . . "

The instructors had me all strapped in and hooked up at both ends—parachute behind me, motor-boat in front of and below me. I listened—attentively, of course; I did not need any accidents or war scars before even getting to the war—to last minute instructions, the same ones that the instructors had given every other guy before me. The adrenalin started to take effect as they asked if I was ready. I gave a thumbs up—actually, just one thumb. They stepped back and signaled the motor-boat. No time to change my mind at this point; I was committed. Actually, I was committed whether I wanted to be or not, but I did not mind. I knew that it was going to be a new experience and mostly fun— or a bit fun at least—rather like a ride at an amusement park. A really, really high ride.

I felt the tug on the rope and stepped forward—the only direction I could go. I took about two or three steps and then I felt the exhilaration as I was lifted into the air. I mechanically took another two or three steps without thinking about it; one does it for two reasons: 1) It is instinctive to do so, and 2) It is a safety factor in case for any reason one momentarily settles back onto the deck. My 135 or so pounds were not going to deter the outlandish horsepower of the motor-boat nor neutralize the principles of aeronautics, so reason number two was pretty much not applicable in my case. I had a B.S. degree in Aeronautics—still have, in fact; academic degrees do not just disappear—and I had watched the preceding dozen or so guys about my size as they were pulled up, up, and away. Not exactly like Superman or Mighty Mouse, but up, up, and away nonetheless. We were not going to Vietnam to "to save the day" particularly, but we definitely were going over to fight "for truth, justice, and the American way."

If you have ever been parasailing, then you know something of the feeling and experience, except that you probably were not wearing combat boots and a flight suit with water survival gear hanging under you. Your general impression was hopefully the same as mine—a mixture of awe at semi-floating in air; wonderment at the view from that new, elevated perspective; and maybe a tinge of anxiety about your eventual return to Earth—either on dry land, in warm water, in a boat, on a sandy beach, wherever. I was running through my mind some of the techniques we were taught in class, hoping that I had learned them. I was also hanging on to the shroud lines, waiting for the red flag signal from the motor-boat crew. One might have thought it would have been a green flag, the accepted color for "go" at traffic lights, drag races, and many other situations. However, looking down from 600 feet toward a small boat (from 600 feet up it was a small boat) on a large blue-green body of water, the red flag was much more visible.

As far as that point goes, the human eye is most readily attracted to light wavelengths we call yellow, so an introspective Reader, or writer in my case, might justifiably wonder why a yellow flag was not used instead. I was neither consulted nor briefed on the topic.

When I saw the red flag waving, I knew that it was "Show Time." I pulled the rope release and felt another immediate adrenalin rush as I floated free, no longer connected to the Earth by anything but gravity and a 600-foot cushion of air. The rope disappeared beneath me as it fell away; the darkened, water-soaked color of the rope made it invisible against the background of tiny rippling waves below. Besides, I had other matters foremost in my attention at that time, and I was completely unconcerned about the rope. It was still attached to the boat and would be reeled in to be used for the next guy. The boat crew sped back around for the next human aerial performance, and I was a free spirit for a while. The motor-boat crew were careful not to release us so that we would all wind up on top of each other. We were fairly spread out in the ocean waters when each of us landed.

As I think about it, had we been over land, we would have landed; it only follows as logical then that since we were over water, we should have watered. Who knows? Perhaps when the rope was released a couple of guys just might have "watered," so to speak. But we need not speculate further.

- 17 -

DISQUISITION ON AIR, OXYGEN, AND THE ATMOSPHERE

Backing up just a couple of minutes, my turn finally came to step up to the plate, as it were. Since I had been parasailing once before in UPT, I anticipated the "flight" with a little excitement since, although it was supposed to be a training situation, there was still a major element of fun in doing it. Later on I would find out that people actually paid money to go parasailing. I was getting another heretofore unexpected and un-proclaimed fringe benefit to a career as an Air Force pilot. Go figure. However, on the other hand, it was a mixed feeling, as I admit to a slight degree of trepidation. I was going to be hauled up six hundred feet in the air.

Technically, of course the atmosphere is the term applied to the layer of air covering the earth from the surface up to about six hundred miles (not feet). There is no definitive line or other demarcation indicating the outer "edge;" the layers of the atmosphere get thinner and thinner the higher it extends above the surface, although rate of change of the thinning is not a direct linear correlation. But it does get thinner and thinner and thinner and thinner. . . . The thinning rate varies due to certain geophysical and solar effects. Half of our atmosphere is not within the lower three hundred miles of the earth's surface, as linear thinking might tend to deduce. The lower half only goes up to about 18,000 *feet*, or about three and a half miles; the other half is in the other six hundred miles. Do not go trying to do any math here and subtract *about* three and a half from *about* six hundred. The difference is so minuscule as to be a non-issue. If you are making some spaghetti sauce and the recipe calls for two cups of red wine, which you measure out with a reasonable precision, and if you put your finger in the wine and remove a drop for a taste, you certainly are not concerned about that one missing drop affecting your anticipated gastronomic pleasure.

Federal Aviation [Administration] Regulations require the pilot to "be on"—i.e., breathing—supplemental oxygen after thirty minutes above 12,500 feet and up to 14,000 feet. Supplemental oxygen is required at all times for the pilot above 14,000 feet. Oxygen is required for everyone on board above 15,000 feet. These restrictions apply to cabin pressure altitude as found in non-pressurized aircraft, like perhaps your local Cessna 150 or AC-119K Gunship. The air pressure inside the cockpit is the same as the air pressure on the outside of it. In pressurized aircraft, such as just about any commercial jet airliner and high-performance aircraft, the air pressure inside the plane is maintained at a significantly higher pressure than outside, effectively keeping the pressurized areas inside at an "altitude" that would be found at the lower altitudes complying ing with FAA regulations. That explains why Goldfinger gets sucked through a window of his corporate jet when the window gets shot out, creating a rapid de-compression. Realistically, most people would be unable to fit through most pressurized aircraft windows, and certainly not anyone the size of Goldfinger. Of course, FAA regulations do not apply to any pilot, or anyone else, climbing up Denali (formerly known as Mt. McKinley) since he or she is not operating or riding in an aircraft.

- 18 -

ON MY WAY DOWN

Once I had run through a mental checklist to assure myself everything was as it should be, I had nothing much left to do except enjoy the ride down to the water. It really was quite pleasant by that time, both physically and emotionally. The sunny afternoon was warm, and the Florida coast was in sight, so there was a little scenery to admire . . .

. . . until the beckoning water got almost within reach. Then the tricky part began. You were not supposed to release from your parachute until you were about ten feet above the water. It was not an Olympic flight-suit-and-combat-boots diving competition, so any distance of more than about ten feet would result in an acceleration to an undesirable impact velocity. Also, and more importantly, you did not want to drag the parachute down on top of yourself, creating an undesirable situation—water below, a 35-foot diameter pile of nylon above, and a couple of dozen (or 739 maybe) 25-foot-long risers tangled in a massive Gordian knot all around your body.

Have you ever noticed that, during diving events such as those from the Olympic ten-meter diving platform, there is a spray over the surface of the water below the divers? The spray provides a visual reference to aid the divers' ability to gauge the distance to the water's surface. I would imagine that after a completing a double somersault, half gainer, triple axel, double Nelson dive, it might be important for the diver to have an idea of how many meters he or she had remaining to get into a minimal body arrow shape before piercing neatly into the water.

We did not have a convenient spray for us on the undulating water below. It would not have mattered if we did. Judging distances over water is difficult, even standing still, and doing so while descending over water at about twenty-three feet per second is even more difficult. You did not want to hit the water still holding on to the risers attached to your parachute. On the other hand, you did not want to release the parachute too soon; the acceleration due to gravity acting on your body is 32.174 feet per second per second. The higher above the water you release, the greater your speed at the time of water impact. Needless to say, estimating when you are ten feet above the water is a sporty proposition at best. I believe I may have been a bit higher than ten feet when I released. Maybe eleven feet, or seventeen-and-a-half feet, or whatever. The impact with the water was nothing more than one would experience jumping off the ten-foot diving board at one's local swimming emporium. In fact, it was more than likely a bit less "traumatic" than at the pool. People at swimming pools, public ones, anyway, usually wear some sort of swim-suit. I personally do not recall seeing any bikini-clad beauties briefly slipping the surly bonds from the high dive and making a pencil point entry into the water below. I am sure I would have remembered as they climbed out of the pool. . . . However, we water survival school trainees were protected by our flight suits, and even more so with our aqueous feet-first entry while still wearing combat boots. Regardless, my fellow water survival students and I all did. Survive.

The three days of preparation apparently worked.

- 19 -

IN THE WATER

If, after finding yourself comfortably submerged in the water and, in spite of having carefully followed all training precautions, you happened to look up and, instead of blue sky, you saw only orange and white nylon—lots and lots of it, in every direction—an astute observer would quickly determine that the parachute canopy had followed you down to the water anyway. Without proper training, such a situation could easily trigger a tiny bit of anxiety, or even panic, which could be hazardous to your health. However, all you had to remember to do was to start pulling on the canopy until you found a seam, the size of which made it easily noticeable, and just start pulling along that seam. It did not matter which direction you pulled; sooner or later you would come to the edge of the canopy (sooner if you happened to be fortunate enough to choose the shorter direction; just a little later if not) and voilà!— blue sky above. Wow—that training stuff really worked. Now you could concentrate on other minor details, like how to remain above water with your self-inflating Mae West and entertain yourself for the next hour until the instructors came by and "rescued" you.

If you are fortunate enough to have a Mae West from an airline, that is.

Naturally, none of our Mae Wests would inflate by themselves. That would be way too easy in a training situation. As you no doubt recall from previous preflight briefings, the Mae West can be inflated orally via a manual inflation tube with a one-way check valve. This latter inflation method was deemed by those who designed the Air Force Basic Water Survival Course to be the preferred method to afford students the maximum benefit from classroom training. Quite considerate of them indeed.

After successfully inflating the Mae West and no longer having to strenuously tread water, I was feeling more confident that I was indeed not going to die just yet, just as our instructors had hinted. The next procedure on the agenda was to direct attention to the yellow, rubber one-man life raft that had accompanied each of us on our "trip" so far. To be honest, I cannot remember if there was a pull cord attached to a pressurized air canister that would inflate the raft in seconds or if I had to blow it up manually as well. We probably had the canister; even the Air Force would not think we needed to spend the entire hour we were scheduled to be in the water exercising our lungs and the less savory shades of our vocabulary.

One would think that getting up into the life raft would be no big deal. Just reach up and pull yourself over the inflated side. Good luck with that. The raft was not anchored down. It also was not inclined to just remain stationary on the gently rolling waves (according to satellite photos from hundreds of miles overhead) while you valiantly struggled to climb inside, much like, I can only assume, that of a cowboy trying to mount a wild stallion that had never been ridden before. However, thousands of taxpayer dollars had been invested in getting each one of us to the culmination of the course, and getting up into that recalcitrant life raft was the very next step. If only there had been an actual step somewhere nearby, or maybe even two. That step would have been much easier if there actually *had* been a step. If you have ever tried to climb from the water into an inner tube from a large truck tire with no one holding the other side, you know what I mean. We had been instructed in a technique for getting ourselves up, over the side, and into the life raft while it tries to escape and evade (E&E) our best efforts. The technique was to hold on with one arm, pull yourself sideways along the raft, swing a leg up and over the side—easier said than done—and then work the rest of your body over without puncturing the raft with your survival knife or anything else sharp. It still was not particularly easy or elegant, but it was doable. Sometimes it took a couple of tries, and maybe even a couple more.

Once inside the raft, basically we were done except for waiting an hour for rescue. Different guys did different things to occupy themselves. Most of us checked out the various toys—er, survival gear—and actually used some of them. I mentioned some of the items earlier. We had it relatively easy (EIR) since we were leisurely floating in a life raft on a lovely fall day just off the coast of southern Florida. Our training environment was slightly less traumatic than real-life episodes where one moment you are flying along fat, dumb, and happy – that's just an expression – all pilots and, to a lesser degree, other aircrew members, are Gentleman's Quarterly trim, smarter than the ave-er-age bear, and, well, happy. The next moment you are hurtling through space in a reverse direction, like a meteor, toward the vast expanses of wetness covering Planet Earth, except a tad slower than 30,000 miles per hour, in which case you really would be a meteor with no hope of becoming a meteorite.

Under actual bailout circumstances, obviously a high-pressure situation, having printed directions for all the various survival toys was undoubtedly helpful. They also happened to be appreciated even by us leisure "survivors." We had sunscreen, a camouflage stick, and day and night flares. One end of the flare was knobby and the other was smooth. One end produced red smoke for daylight signaling, and the other end was a bright flare light. The knobs were so you could identify which end was which in the dark. Using the smoke at night did not enhance your chances of survival in an actual combat or a just-lost-in-the-woods situation. Of course, you had to remember which one—smoke or light—was at which end. It was written on the side of the flare; you just had to remember it at night. Were the three knobs representing Tango Uniform for night, or . . . ?

Among the survival gear there was a small, shiny, flat, metal plate about three inches square with a hole in the center about the diameter of a pencil. This was a signal mirror, and it could work very effectively, at least when the sun was shining. Not so much at night. The hole in the middle was so that you could see where the reflected light was hitting. Everyone knows, or should know, Morse Code for S O S: ...- - -... (dot dot dot dash dash dash dot dot dot, or, if you were a telegraph operator, didididadadadididi).

SOS actually does NOT stand for "Save Our Souls" or "Save Our Ship" or anything else. It is just the internationally agreed-upon emergency signal, quick and easy to remember.

One thing we all did was deploy the sea anchor -a tough plastic bag that you filled with sea water, attached to a lanyard, and put overboard to help stabilize the raft. Had there been sufficient time, we also had a fresh water filtration kit, but desalinating a gallon of water using the kit was a very slow process. However, some of us did manage to process a few drops of salt water into fresh water from it.

There was also fishing equipment—the proverbial hook, line, and sinker. One of the guys in my class actually caught a small fish. Not sure what he used for bait—probably a piece of sandwich or Hershey bar or whatever he had managed to have with him. Having absolutely no interest whatsoever in fishing myself, after satisfying my curiosity about the other toys, I took a bit of a practice nap.

Eventually the "rescue" guys arrived in the area to start rounding up all of us guys scattered around bobbing in our bright yellow one-man life rafts. We were not hard to find on the surface of the blue-green water. I believe our radios were actually operational, just in case. Sometime after arriving back on land at the training facility we had a debriefing, and we completed the ubiquitous course critique sheet endemic in every Air Force training course.

And that, Gentle Readers, brings us to the end of the three days of my first TDY after pilot training; that still leaves essentially the other whole seven months remaining prior to my arrival in Southeast Asia.

- 20 -

BACK TO TEXAS, THEN OHIO

After successfully completing the Basic Water Survival training course and hoping I would never have occasion to draw upon my newly-acquired aquatic skills, I caught a commercial flight back to Del Rio. Andrea and I packed some clothes, toiletries, and such for our drive to my next assignment, which was in Ohio. We also gathered the things we thought we would need for the next few months of living in temporary quarters: clothing, some pots and pans (probably *a* pot and *a* pan), and other kitchen items, etc., up to the six-hundred-pound allowance that the Air Force would pay for. The Consolidated Base Personnel Office (CBPO—I don't know what it was consolidated from, so if you ask me, you would be asking the wrong person) arranged to have our things packed up and shipped by a commercial moving company to wherever we would be in Ohio. The CBPO also arranged to have all the rest of our household goods (that is the official term for our "stuff") packed up by another commercial moving company and stored somewhere unknown to us for the next year and a half. By "have our household goods packed up" I mean our (my and Andi's) job was to stay out of the way while the movers did everything. Literally. Every. Thing. That was a military perk we would sorely miss in our moves subsequent to my leaving active duty. Anyone who has ever packed and completely loaded a twenty-eight-foot Ryder truck so that there was no more room for even so much as a toothpick, hitched a car-tow trailer to it, and had the wife follow all the way across this vast country of ours in the other car with the two kidlets, one of whom was still in diapers, and then had to undo everything at the destination, knows of which I speaketh.

Since we did not have any more stuff in Del Rio, and since I had orders to report to my next TDY assignment, we loaded all of our "take with" things in our sierra yellow 1970 Pontiac Lemans and drove to Lockbourne AFB (now Rickenbacker AFB) in Columbus, Ohio. By then it was late October or early November, and Ohio generally tends to be a little chillier than southwest Texas at that time of year. Fortunately, we did not encounter any snow on the highways. I suppose it was still a little early in the season for that particular winter phenomenon to manifest itself upon us in unpleasant ways, so the trip was pretty much uneventful. It must have been so, since neither Andi nor I can even remember making the trip. But we must have done so; our car, all of our clothes and other necessities in it, and the two of us arrived at the VOQ at Lockbourne centuries before Scottie could have beamed us there.

Why, one might reasonably ponder, would the Air Force send me to the middle of Ohio when I was supposed to be headed (eventually) to Southeast Asia? Ohio was (and still is, by all accounts) northeast of Texas, whereas Southeast Asia was south-ish-west. Wright-Patterson was and still is a major AFB in Dayton, but it was not on my orders. There were also some other less-than-notable military installations scattered about in the state. At least Lockbourne had some name recognition and, as it turned out, it also had an Ohio Air National Guard (OANG) unit there as a tenant, sharing the Columbus airport. As luck would have it, the OANG had some C-119G aircraft around and instructors to train people in the various aircrew positions—pilot, co-pilot, navigator, flight engineer, and loadmaster. The aircraft and instructors being there was quite serendipitous—perhaps more fortuitous than serendipitous—since my next assignment was introductory training as a copilot on those very C-119Gs. Maybe it was just a coincidence. Or, perhaps the Air Force assignment schedulers at Randolph AFB in San Antonio actually knew that those C-119s were in Ohio and that I needed training in them, and they connected the dots. (Okay, so I may be a little bit sarcastic once in a while; I have had years of practice.)

For those of you unfamiliar with US military aircraft nomenclature, a little disambiguation might be helpful. The "C" stands for cargo. The "119" is an aircraft designation, but who decided on that number, I have no clue. The "G" is the model of the aircraft; generally, the further down the alphabet the letter is, the newer the model of the aircraft, based on whatever major changes and modifications have been made to the basic airplane. (I use plane, airplane, aircraft, and aerospace vehicle interchangeably, the latter usually slightly more tongue-in-cheekishly). The "s" is just added as a plural indicator and is not part of the aircraft designation. The C-119 was more commonly known as the Flying Boxcar because of its design shape and its function—carrying cargo and troops, including paratroopers. Some of you may remember seeing MovieTone Newsreels of hundreds of paratroopers jumping out the back ends of a whole herd of C-119s during the Korean War; some of you may have been among those guys yourselves. Others of you probably have no clue what a MovieTone Newsreel was. If you are curious, ask your parents (or grandparents), or Google it. Personally, I think parasailing is about as close as I want to come to actually jumping out of a perfectly good airplane, although I will admit to a morbid curiosity in wanting to have experienced the excitement. But not with enemy fighters buzzing around the skies like they were at a duck shoot and with more guys on the ground doing their version of the same thing.

For the Readers' benefit, I have included an appendix on aircraft nomenclature, including my ubiquitous commentary.

- 21 -

AT LOCKBOURNE, AFB, OHIO

While in Ohio I flew a C-119 on a cross country trip to another "hardship" destination at Patrick AFB in Cocoa Beach, Florida for a couple of days. (The FAA defines a "cross country" flight as one of at least fifty nautical miles in which the aircraft lands at a different destination from which it departed. While training in a Cessna 150 to get my private pilot license in college, one requirement was to complete a solo three-leg cross country flight. Several years later, flying a KC-135 tanker on a six-hour 2,200 nautical mile mission and landing at the same base from which we took off did not count as cross country time, as far as the FAA was concerned. Fortunately, commercial airline hiring department personnel were quite familiar with the minor distinction.)

The Florida trip was basically the last part of C-119G training we had to do. It was mostly training for the navigator, although we did do some approaches and landings and pattern work—takeoff, fly around the airport traffic pattern, do a touch-and-go landing, repeat. The Reader might recall from chapter eleven a little more description of pattern work. After those two or three days in sunny Florida, we flew back to Ohio (join the Air Force and see the world . . .) where, being early January, it had gotten a bit nippy. It is an odd thing, but try as I might, for some reason I cannot remember where we spent Thanksgiving, Christmas, or New Year's that year.

Andi does not remember either, and she usually remembers things like that. Her parents lived about two and a half hours away in Euclid, Ohio, on the east side of Cleveland in northeast Ohio, and my dad lived two hours away in Cincinnati in southwest Ohio. (Cincinnati had, and maybe it still has, a good-sized German population. In the mid1960s, Dick Perry, a Cincinnati native, wrote a book entitled "Vas You Ever In Zinzinnati? [sic]". I never read the book, but I remember seeing it in a store window.) We may have had Thanksgiving with my dad and his last (fourth) wife, Christmas in Cleveland, and New Year's Eve somewhere in Columbus (Ohio). We have an ongoing joke about that with some friends who had lived there, although we did not know them at that time, as I am from Columbus (Georgia). Anytime one of us mentions the city name it is always "Columbus (slight pause) Georgia." Or "Columbus (slight pause) Ohio." Still, it is vexing that neither Andi nor I can remember. . . .

- 22 -

BACK TO FLORIDA AGAIN—HURLBURT FIELD

Once again it was time to pack up our "carry with" things, load them in the car, and head on to my next TDY assignment . . . which happened to be in Florida. There are many places to be assigned that are much less desirable than on a coast where palm trees grow and you can play golf in January. The pristine white sandy beaches were relatively uncrowded; not so anymore, sadly. Hurlburt AFB, a.k.a. Hurlburt Field, a.k.a. Eglin AFB Auxiliary Field #9, is located just west of Mary Esther, Florida, which is just west of Destin, Florida. Pensacola is about sixty miles along the coast to the west and Panama City Beach is about eighty miles to the east. The average January temperatures are 45° to 61°. We could, and did, manage quite well to live with that. It was a bit too chilly for a plunge into the Gulf but warm enough for bare-foot walks on those beautiful beaches and for playing a little golf.

Sunshine, sand, golf, flying occasionally—not a bad way to spend a few winter and early spring months. That was at a time (early 1972) before everyone discovered those pristine white sandy beaches and drove up the prices of all the real estate. Andi and I rented what we came to call Toad Trailer—an old silver Airstream in a trailer park with sandy roads and very sulfur-y water. She tolerated the stinky water, but to brush my teeth I had to use water that had been boiled first. I guess Andi was more manly (manlier?) about it than I was. From our bed you (well, Andi and I; you weren't there) could easily touch the walls on either side without getting out of bed. Cozy. Still, the beaches and sand dunes were really nice—if you could keep the sand out of the bed.

Coincidentally, we found that some good friends from my UPT class, Rick and Ginny Hanson and "Eve Baby," were there also. Rick had been training in a C-7 Caribou, which was a USAF cargo plane, as the Reader may have guessed immediately upon seeing the "C" designation. That plane just plain (couldn't resist the temptation) looked funny. Not ha-ha funny so much—well, as I think about it, yes, ha-ha funny as well. The fuselage bent twice. It was actually designed that way.

C-7 Caribou (Photo: airpowerworld.info)

See? You didn't believe me, did you? For whatever reason, which I do not remember just now, before completing training in the C-7, Rick was reassigned to the C-123, another cargo plane that was not folded up twice and then stretched back out like the C-7. And as it serendipitously happened, the C-123 training was at Hurlburt Field.

Although her name is Katherine Yvonne Hanson, or was before she eventually got married, Andrea and I have always referred to her as "Eve Baby." Even now, whenever we chat or get together with the Hansons, we ask how Eve Baby is doing. A bunch of years after Hurlburt Field, she graduated from the Air Force Academy (AFA), but she is still Eve Baby to us; we have not actually seen Eve Baby since Eve Baby actually was a baby, however. And the Academy was not accepting infant babies at that time, nor even old babies.

There was a par three golf course at Hurlburt Field where the three Hansons and we chose to abuse golf balls on occasion. Eve Baby came along for the fresh air, deciding she wanted to learn the game. Actually, watching all of us play, she could have learned how not to play. Okay, so perhaps EB didn't really watch us play from her little padded baby-carrying thingy. But we all took turns carrying her by the baby-carrying thingy handle. When whoever was carrying her was next to use a golf club weapon, he or she would put EB on the ground to make the shot. Someone else would carry her to the next ball to be ~~abused~~ hit, and so on. We had a good time. I think EB slept through most of it. Just as well. I don't believe some of the golf language we used would have been appropriate for a baby. Or in church.

At Rickenbacker AFB we had our shipment of the things we needed while TDY—things like clothes, uniforms, pots and pans, etc.—packed up and shipped to Mary Esther, Florida, on the gulf coast. We lived there in the aptly-named Toad Trailer for about two months while I went through AC-119K gunship training. Not a bad place to spend the coldest part of winter, I must say.

Note: do not be concerned if you do not follow some of the next four paragraphs. There are more detailed explanations of all that stuff in a later chapter, including some neat pictures.

As with most other military training, initial instruction began in the classroom. I cannot say I remember any of it at this point in my life. One does not usually remember the mundane. However, I do remember the missions, flying out over the Gulf of Mexico to an airspace restricted for military use—restricted for good reason. The restricted areas contained some water-based targets. I assume the targets were unmanned; they never shot back at us. On at least two or three missions we copilots got to fly in the left seat—the seat that had the trigger button on the yoke. The purpose was not merely to give copilots a chance to have some fun actually doing the shooting. The reason was to let the copilot experience what the pilot had to contend with while getting the aircraft positioned and aligned in the firing circle.

The table nav got us to the target. The NOS and FLIR operators acquired the target in their scopes. The flight engineer set and synchronized the reciprocating engines. The gunners set the alignment of the guns for our altitude, loaded the gun belts into the gun canisters, and cleared any jams that occasionally occurred during firing, especially during training. The illuminator operator launched the flares or controlled the spotlight to shed some light on the subject. The copilot maintained airspeed with the jet engine toggles and also maintained altitude by applying appropriate pressure forward or aft on the middle of the yoke. Instead of a "stick" to control aircraft movement such as what is usually found in fighter aircraft, in most cargo planes that function is done via a yoke, which is rather like a half of a steering wheel. The pilot controlled the aircraft angle of bank to align the two quarter-sized HUD (head-up display) gunsight reticles by applying small turning inputs to the yoke handles. When everything was configured, coordinated, and ready to go and the reticles were aligned, he "pulled the trigger," so to speak. Actually, he pushed the button on the yoke that connected electrically through the table nav's switch, the selected targeting scope, and the gunners' switches.

Simple enough.

Under ideal, no-wind conditions, the gunship could fire from anywhere along the firing orbit. Once in a while winds at altitude would actually be calm or very light. Most of the time, however, there was some degree of wind to have to compensate for, generally resulting in two shooting opportunities on opposite sides of the firing circle. The higher the wind speed, the less time was available for shooting. The remainder of the time in orbit was spent maneuvering the airplane to stay on target, which in turn required "flying" the aircraft. Of course we were always flying the plane, but the introduction of winds necessitated bank angle changes and airspeed changes. In the tailwind segment of the circle, airspeed had to be reduced to counteract an increased ground speed; the bank angle had to be increased more sharply on the first crosswind portion of the turn to keep from being blown past the optimal target distance, and vice versa during the headwind portion.

Somewhere along the way, optimal aircraft angles and speeds were able to be maintained, however briefly. The pilot would be looking out to his left, sighting through the reticles, trying to keep them aligned as much as possible. There is a natural tendency for a pilot to pull back on the yoke (or stick in fighter-type planes) when making a turn to offset the increased drag and decreased lift coefficients incurred during a turn. I will not try to make a pilot out of you here (if you are not already one) by introducing all the aerodynamic forces at work. Just trust me on this (ever heard that anywhere before?). The copilot was responsible for maintaining altitude in the firing circle. Unless a pilot and copilot had flown together enough to be comfortable with each other, occasions could momentarily arise when the two could be inadvertently "fighting" each other on the yoke—i.e., one pulling and the other pushing. The copilot, watching the altimeter, would be applying input to the yoke and the pilot, watching the reticles, might be applying opposite pressure. It was a "feel of the yoke and seat of your pants" type thing. More likely than not, it would be the less experienced copilot having the trouble, a situation easily remedied by them briefly talking about coordination of effort.

After we settled into Toad Trailer, Andrea got a job teaching at a middle school. It would last until the end of the school year, after which she would move back to Cleveland to live with her parents. In mid-March of 1972, she and I parted. At this point in our journey, I packed everything I thought I would need to take with me to SEA for the next twelve and a half months because I would not be returning to Florida. I was headed to Basic Survival Training at Fairchild AFB in Spokane, Washington. Have you noticed that everything I have been assigned to in the Air Force up to this point—and still beyond—has been training for this, training for that, or training for something else? Every Air Force person that was headed for that less-than-fabulous, no-frills, most-expenses-paid vacation on the other side of the Pacific spent two weeks at Fairchild before going over. Part of my self-taught survival training there was to clandestinely ration out the pound or so of scrumdiddlyumptious (amazingly, spell check did not object to that word) homemade fudge Andi had made for me so that it would last the whole two weeks. Yeah, right. Like that was going to happen.

- 23 -

THE C-119 FLYING BOXCAR

C-119 "Flying Boxcar"

After earning my USAF Pilot wings in in September 1971, I was assigned to be a copilot on an AC-119K Gunship. (That might explain all the rhetoric so far about gunships and SEA.) About the only people around Laughlin AFB in good ol' Del Rio—made dubiously famous in a cowboy movie when John Wayne mentioned something about heading "south to Del Rio"—who had ever heard of such a contraption were aviation veterans of Vietnam. At that point in time, that classification did not include me; I also had never heard of it. But I was going to fly one, whatever it was, and in a war zone no less.

The basic airplane was the C-119; refer to Appendix 3 "Aircraft Nomenclature" for a dubious attempt to make some sense out of the muddled numbering system. The famous Flying Boxcar was noted for droves of paratroopers jumping out of the back end and equipment being offloaded by parachutes, so many they nearly blotted out the sun, except for night jumps, which did not show up very well at all during the MovieTone newsreels.

US Paratroopers dropping into a war zone

Equipment being offloaded

The "AC" of AC-119K referred to the gunship versions: Attack Cargo. Does the term oxymoron come to mind? One even stranger USAF aircraft designation "over there" was the QU–22B, which sounds funky and which was a military version of the civilian Beechcraft Bonanza, sometimes known as the doctor's airplane because it was relatively (EIR) expensive. I will cover my "association" with it a little later (I know you can't wait).

So, it was a mere two more months later before I set foot on the other side of the Pacific. Talk about a slow boat to China. . . . No, of course I didn't go by boat. We were way past WWII. Besides, I was an Air Force pilot. In the interim between graduating from UPT and arriving "in country," as being in the operational theater was called (South Vietnam, North Vietnam, Thailand, Laos, Cambodia—oops . . . disregard; we were never in Cambodia; the Secretary disavows all knowledge of . . .), I was assigned to a few other stops along the way (as covered earlier) for further training in various and sundry activities deemed necessary for a successful round trip. Sadly, too many Americans wound up with a one-way ticket. . . . I still had two more training stops before finally arriving at NKP RTAFB.

The Fairchild C-119 made its first flight in November 1947. I was born in January 1947. Do the math. I was going to war in an airplane nearly as old as I was. Scary thought, that. And as far as I know, *I, for one*, was not built by the lowest bidder.

- 24 -

EARLY GUNSHIP TRAINING

And now, back to this tale of adventure, more or less…

WHEN UNINVITED GUEST DROP IN CALL FOR

18 S. O. S.

A Fly By Night Organization

We Provide :
Lighting for
All Occasions
Beaucoup 7.62
& 20 mm Truck
& Mortar Suppression

We Defend :
Special Forces Camps
Air Bases
Outposts
Troops in Contract
We Also Stop
Truck, Sampan and
other Traffic

DANANG VIETNAM   N.K.P. THAILAND

(Larger than actual size)
Someone had these "business cards" printed and naturally I acquired a few.

Our call sign was "Stinger," and we —the aircraft, the aircrews, and the squadron—were known as Stingers. We had a crew of ten men, including five officers: pilot, copilot (our local hero), table navigator (nav), FLIR (Forward-Looking Infrared Radar) operator (also a nav), and NOS (Night Operation Sensor) operator (also a nav); and five enlisted troops (airmen and non-commissioned officers (NCOs)): flight engineer (FE), three gunners (gunner), and an illuminator operator (IO). The pilot, who was the aircraft commander (AC—no, not the same AC as in Attack Cargo, but you are to be commended for noticing), was indeed the commander of the aircraft. He was responsible for the equipment, meaning the airplane and everything in it; the crew; and the mission. Most of the ACs were captains, with an occasional major or lieutenant colonel (lt col). Most of table navs were majors and lt cols, and although they usually outranked the AC, the AC was still the commander during the mission and thus "outranked" everyone else on board. As every officer except shiny new second lieutenants knows, senior non-commissioned officers—the ones with lot of stripes on their upper arm sleeves who were in the service before the rest of us were born—actually outranked everybody, but by tradition they let us officers believe we were in charge.

Now, some of you who are still awake at this point may recall that we were last at Hurlburt Field, Florida, for training in the AC-119K "Stinger" gunship. Including instructors, we had a crew of not just ten, but of . . . a bunch. There was one instructor pilot, an instructor for each of the three navs, one for the FE, one for the IO, and I don't remember how many gunner instructors—at least one but not more than three. And quite frankly, I don't remember how everybody fit. There just was not that much room in the cockpit, and the "back end" where the guns and such were got a bit crowded also. However, somehow we all got trained and were eventually sent on our merry ways.

I do remember one of my first flights on the gunship. The whole gaggle of us—trainees and instructors—were walking toward the aircraft we were scheduled to fly (and I do indeed use the term aircraft loosely—but affectionately). It was early evening, and daylight was still available. The maintenance crew was doing an engine runup on one of the recips (reciprocating engine, as opposed to a turbine (jet) engine, a.k.a. as a turbojet), checking it out after some maintenance had been done on it. I was a young first lieutenant (1lt, like there were any OLD first looies?). The instructor pilot was a grizzly old lt col (to a young 1lt, all lt cols were old and grizzly). We stood a respectable distance from the plane and watched as the engine huffed and puffed. The right wing seemed to rotate in a circle. The left wing seemed to rotate in a circle in the opposite direction. The fuselage —the main body of the airplane—seemed to be swaying from side to side. The boom—the tail section attached to the wings on the boxcar, not to the fuselage —seemed to be wobbling up and down.

I would have bet money right then and there that the plane was going to disintegrate before our very eyes into a pile of smoking rubble, when about that time the engine was shut down and all was quiet. The plane somehow miraculously escaped becoming my envisioned collection of scrap metal.

Then the maintenance chief climbed out of the aerospace vehicle, walked over to the Colonel, and said to him, "Here's the key, Colonel," (there wasn't really a key) and the Colonel then said to the rest of us, "Let's go." I was incredulous! We were actually expected to "slip the surly bonds of earth" (from "High

Flight" by John Gillespie Magee, Jr.) in THAT? You gotta be kiddin' me. I dutifully expressed my concerns to the Colonel, perhaps not using quite that exact phraseology. After all, he was a combat veteran and may have been experiencing whatever name they called whatever combat veterans experienced back then.

The very fact that you are reading this now is sufficient evidence of my naiveté at the time and proof that we lived to tell about the subsequent uneventful training flight.

This is not the best photo of an AC-119, but the minimal photo quality adds emphasis to my early concerns about its air worthiness.

While we are comparing the thrill ride nature of different aircraft, I hope any Reader who has not flown a T-38A Talon supersonic jet trainer like we flew in UPT can vicariously feel the thrill of acceleration and the adrenalin rush as I put you behind my eyes for a moment . . . .

- 25 -

RIDING THE WHITE ROCKET

T-38A Talon—"White Rocket"

Flying from the front seat of the T-38A is like flying on the front tip of a nicely-sharpened supersonic pencil—at over Mach 1 (which is about 761 miles per hour at sea level on a "standard day," which is 29.92 inches of mercury atmospheric pressure (essentially sea level) and a temperature of 59° F. I could do another disquisition on the standard day; perhaps some other time.). All you can see of the jet outside the cockpit is the pitot (pee-toe; I did not misspell "pilot") tube—the pointy thingy centered up front and visible at the bottom of the windscreen. It is too bad everyone does not get the opportunity to experience flying, or at least riding up front in, the T-38 at least once in his/her life. It should be a bucket list item for sure.

"Inca Two Five you are cleared for takeoff left turn to zero one zero afterburner climb to flight level one eight zero [18,000 feet]."

(If the careful Reader is wondering why there are no commas in the radio clearance above, it is because language over the radios is kept short.)

"Roger Inca Two Five cleared for takeoff heading zero one zero burner climb to flight level one eight zero."

As you pull out onto the active runway there is nothing quite like the adrenalin rush of being strapped in near the front of a supersonic pencil with 5,800 pounds of thrust just three or four feet behind you straining to be set free as you stop, line up on the runway centerline, firmly press down on the brakes, smoothly move the two throttles in your gloved left hand forward to military power (100% rpm), run a quick scan over the engine gauges—all needles pointing where they should—release the brakes, advance the throttles over the detent into afterburner, and YEEE HAAH! . . . you feel yourself slammed into the back of the seat as the White Rocket accelerates straight down the runway centerline like a banshee on fire, except much faster . . . within seconds you scream through S1, the go/no go speed at 124 knots (about 143 miles per hour) . . . and a second or so later you see 155 knots (about 179 miles per hour) on the airspeed indicator . . . you pull back gently but firmly and smoothly on the control stick in your right hand to a five-degree pitch up attitude. . . . a glance at your Vertical Velocity Indicator (VVI) shows that you are climbing . . . you immediately raise the landing gear lever so that you do not overspeed the gear at 184 knots . . . three green lights, the gear are all up and locked . . . you hold the five-degree pitch angle as you accelerate to 280 knots in a climbing left turn . . . you clear left visually as you pull back on the stick to maintain 280 knots . . . the VVI is showing a climb rate of 18,000 feet per minute—that's three and a half miles per minute—*UP* . . . until you pass through 17,000 feet . . . you have to push forward on the stick now to lower the nose of your thrill machine over toward level flight so that you do not soar through FL180 feet (easy to do), the altitude you were cleared to, and you accelerate to 500 knots. . . .

Just a little over a minute ago you were sitting at the end of a runway 18,000 feet below, a mere earth-bound mortal, waiting for takeoff clearance.

Life Is Good—and they paid us to do it!

- 26 -

THE GUNSHIP CONCEPT

Perhaps now a brief (EIR) explanation of the gunship concept would be appropriate for your disambiguation and enlightenment. As is my style, I will insert a little levity to maintain your interest.

After viewing actual aerial war footage over the years—either during Movietone Newsreels or historical war documentaries on PBS, or the glorified and gorified Hollywood versions, or perhaps from personal experience (I salute your service to our country), you have seen how the fighter aircraft "cruise" along at 15,000 feet plus or minus a few thousand feet looking for either planned targets or "targets of opportunity" ("Flight Two, Flight Lead. Ten o'clock low. Trucks making a run for it. Let's go git 'em!"), bravely disregarding the dangerous and deadly flak from bursting triple A shells (AAA does not stand just for the American Automobile Association or the American Academy of Audiology. (I had to look that one up now that I find myself needing hearing aids, according to my family and a few friends.) It also refers to Antiaircraft Artillery, the one I will be referring to henceforth.)

Then the fighters break off into a dive to the lower left (ten o'clock would be to the left, for those of you young enough to not have any clue of spatial orientation defined in terms of an analog clock) and make strafing passes at the trucks or trains or tanks (Oh my!), or soldiers or oil refineries or ball-bearing factories or whatever. In doing so they begin shooting as they approach close enough to the targets on the ground until they whiz past, then they climb back out and circle around to come back again for another strafing pass, if there is anything left of the target worth making another pass.

In the early 1960s, the gunship concept was developed for use in unconventional warfare. The theory had been known for years beforehand, but the idea was finally developed into actual weapon systems. (Notice how these days everything is a "system"? When I was a kid, we had windows in our house; now we have window systems.) The AC-47 was developed from the affectionately named C-47 "Gooney Bird." The gunship version call sign was "Spooky," a.k.a. "Puff the Magic Dragon," a.k.a. "Puff." The AC-119G call sign was "Shadow," the AC-119K "Stinger," and later the AC-130 "Specter," and indeed it was that - a specter. All of these gunships have left-side-mounted guns and the aircraft fly in a left-hand circle around the ground target, because that is the side the guns are on (duh), but also because that is the side the pilot is on. They can loiter over the target until they run out of either ammunition, fuel, or time, or until the target has been disposed of in a less-than-friendly (from the target's perspective) manner, or unless the target begins shooting back with quad 23 mm guns or SA-7 missiles. (The "mm" is an abbreviation for millimeter and is used in this book mostly to refer to bullet diameter. There are 25.4 mm per inch.) The original AC-47 Spooky Gunship had three mini-guns, the AC-119G Shadow had four miniguns, and we Stingers were equipped with four mini-guns and two 20 mm Vulcan cannons. The AC-130, which flew at an operating altitude of around 10,500 feet, plus or minus a foot or two, as opposed to the 3,500 - 4,500 feet where the rest of us operated, had two 20 mm Vulcans and two 40 mm guns ("40 mike mike"; saying millimeters is four syllables; mike mike is only two.; when you are in a hurry, it matters). You may be more familiar with these 40 mm guns as the name they were known by on WWII warships: pompom guns, because of the sound they make when firing. The 40 mm shell casing base has a 2.37 inch diameter (about the size a bit farther up the forearm from the wrist) and is over twelve inches long. Being the astute observer that you no doubt are, you have noticed that the AC-130 had no miniguns. Beyond about 5,000 feet, the 7.62 mm rounds would begin to tumble in flight, thereby losing accuracy and efficacy.

Toward the end of the "war" a newer and much more effective version of the AC-130 gunship began to see action. In addition to the aforementioned armament, it was equipped with a 105 mm recoilless howitzer toward the rear of the fuselage. That shell is over four inches in diameter. The Howitzer barrel had to be retracted for takeoff and landing so it would not drag on the runway. Now we're talking biceps, baby! The crews that flew those machines would brag, truthfully, "One truck, one bullet."

40 mm

105 mm

*Cross-sectional area of the size of ammunition fired from the AC-130
Specter gunships*

[If you care to read more about gunships, a good reference is "Development and Employment of Fixed-Wing Gunships 1962—1972" by Lt. Col. Jack S. Ballard (Ret). Also, at Hurlburt Field, Mary Esther, FL, where the HQ Air Force Special Operations Command is located, just inside the main gate you can see on display most of the aircraft used in Special Ops. Just inside the gate there is an AC-119G on display painted shiny black instead of flat black for some reason; perhaps that is the way the G-models were painted. However, you will not see an AC-119K. None of them were returned to the United States. They were all turned over to the South Vietnamese Air Force. If you happen go on a vacation to Vietnam or know where a K-model might be lurking in the US, one that was possibly back here at the time for maintenance or repairs, I would certainly appreciate you letting me know. Maybe send a photo of the tail number. I probably spent some "fun" hours in it.]

- 27 -

THE AC-119K "STINGER" GUNSHIP

AC-119K Gunship
(This coincidentally was the very first tail number I flew
at Hurlburt Airfield on 14 January 1972)

The gunship was more fun to fly than the basic C-119, for several reasons. The C-119 has two large reciprocating engines driving the propellers. Because of all the extra weight added to the gunship version, the AC-119K gunship was equipped with two J-85 jet engines in addition to the two recips. These are relatively small jet engines, as jet engines go, but they were sufficient to do the job. They were the same engines that were on the T-38A Talon, the USAF's sleek white supersonic White Rocket jet trainer that I flew in Undergraduate Pilot Training.

During pilot training we each got one opportunity to go supersonic. We had to get clearance ahead of time from air traffic control (ATC) to do so (so that the Federal Aviation Administration would know who to blame just in case the shock wave broke a window or disturbed a farmer's chickens on the ground – hardly likely in southwest Texas in that small airplane). In the T-38, going supersonic was no big deal. There was no loud bang (as opposed to a quiet bang?), no acceleration surge, and no airplane shaking, rattling, and rolling as portrayed in a Hollywood movie about breaking the sound barrier in a Bell X-15. We (student in the front seat, instructor in the back seat) would merely sit there in the cockpit and watch the Mach meter needle climb and pass through Mach 1.0 to 1.1 or 1.2. That was the only indication we had that we were supersonic. But it was a "rite of passage," as it were—most likely the first time any of us students had ever been supersonic. This experience afforded us the commensurate bragging rights over those students still in the very sub-sonic T-37 training phase and, of course, our wives, girlfriends, and any other civilians willing to endure the bravado.

Curious civilian friends, having little or no frame of reference, have asked me for more details about all this—stuff—so I will elaborate a bit on a few things. As I just mentioned, one reason for the two added jet engines on the AC-119K was so that, while rolling down the runway for takeoff, the old and no longer quite so aerodynamic gunship could actually become airborne before reaching the end of the pavement, which, if you happen to be inside the airplane at the time, was always a good thing. There was a second purpose for these auxiliary jet engines, but I will go into detail about that in a later chapter.

So, how did the USAF make a slow, lumbering ox of a cargo airplane into a fearsome attack aircraft? It (the USAF) added guns, sensors, and other equipment, cut holes in one side of the airframe to accommodate these guns, sensors, and other things, and painted it flat black. The reason for the flat black was because the primary mission was designed for the aircraft to fly low and slow at night. That was similar stealth technology in one respect that was applied to the SR-71 "secret" spy planes. The flat black paint was about as stealthy as it was going to get for the gunships.

If the T-38A were a Jaguar XKE, the AC-119K would be a Model T.

The airplanes originally had one of those large Slow Moving Vehicle (SMV) signs painted on the back, but they were painted over so as not to confuse the enemy. Okay, I admit that perhaps I exaggerate just a little once in a while. There never were any large SMV signs on the airplanes.

The signs were small.

We were not the only ones in Vietnam with guns. As it turned out, the North Vietnamese Army (NVA—not to be confused with the NBA, as if the five-foot tall Vietnamese would ever be mistaken for the eight-foot tall NBA players) "bad guys" (EIR) had some nasty guns of their own, like the quad 23 mm—a four-barreled ground-based anti-aircraft gun that fired shells about a third of the diameter of your wrist, assuming you are not a petite young thing or Andre the Giant. (More about the quad 23mm later in one of my two more serious chapters uninflected with any attempts at humor.) The 23 mm is the diameter of the actual bullets many of the NVA anti-aircraft guns fired at US aircraft. Perhaps this will give you a better visual image of the cross-sectional areas of the various ammunition I will be referring to as we go along; the shell casings for each have a little larger diameter to accommodate the actual bullet:

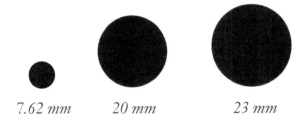

7.62 mm   *20 mm*   *23 mm*

They also had some to-be-avoided-at-all-costs radar-guided SA2 and SA7 (Surface to Air) missiles that went about Mach 5 or so. We were flying at about Mach 0.2. That's zero point two—so laughably slow that the AC-119K speed is not measured by Mach number. Relative to an SA7, we were basically sitting still in the sky – almost literally sitting ducks. As a matter of fact, one of our aircraft—I don't remember the tail number—was fondly named Black Killer Duck.

To be an attack aircraft requires the capability to some degree to inflict aggression in a convincing manner. To qualify for the "A" in AC-119K, the plane was armed with guns. Among other items mentioned earlier, it had four mini-guns. You may have heard of mini-guns before, but you may not be quite sure exactly what they are. The term "mini-" is definitely misleading. Designed and manufactured by General Electric in 1962, the "mini-" designation is relative to larger guns of similar design, such as the 20 mm Vulcan cannon, two of which were also part of the AC-119K arsenal. The mini-gun itself weighs in at 85 pounds and is 31½ inches long. Personally, that hardly fits my definition of "mini-", and it is most definitely not a hand-held weapon. But EIR.

The general design is a little like the old Gatling guns you may have seen in spaghetti western movies starring Clint Eastwood. The mini-gun, which you have probably seen shooting out the sides of helicopters in movies like *Apocalypse Now*, fires 7.62 mm rounds (7.62 mm is NATO standard (NATO: North Atlantic Treaty Organization)), which are very close in size to .308 Winchester rounds. I have never actually seen a .308 Winchester round, or even a .308 Winchester, but I have seen beaucoup 7.62. Those are about the size of your little finger. The ammunition is belt-fed into the gun and expelled at high velocity (2,800 feet per second, for those curious Readers) through its six barrels, which revolve rather quickly. By rather quickly, I mean quickly enough to fire 6,000 rounds per minute. That is *one hundred bullets per second*. When a mini-gun is firing, it is noisy; but it does not go *rat-a-tat-tat* like the old Gatlin guns. It goes *hmmmmmm* but loudly. More like ***HMMMMMM!***

Paths made visible by tracer rounds formed solid lines of light in the night sky—yet incredibly only every ninth bullet was a tracer.

*Time-lapse photo of a Stinger firing about seven miles south of Da Nang; every ninth round was a tracer, so what you do **not** see are the other 25,700 rounds per minute.*

Time-lapse photo of a Stinger showing part of the path of the firing circle

At one point in my seven months of SEA preparation I saw a training film about the mini-gun. The video showed a ground-mounted mini-gun aiming at a cinder block wall. The mini-gun was fired for about a two-second burst. The effect was as if a bomb had hit; the cinder block wall disintegrated. I was impressed—and glad I would not be on the receiving end.

We carried four of these bad boys in the -119. That came to 24,000 hunks of hot lead per minute shrieking to wreak holy hell on targets on the ground.

But wait! There's more!

The first -119 gunships, the AC-119G, were equipped with just the four mini-guns. The later K-models that I flew (maybe kids these days would refer to it as Version 2.1) had been up-graded a bit. We also had at our disposal two Vulcan cannons. These were just like the mini-guns, except they were bigger: 248 pounds each and six feet long. They fired 20 mm rounds—the shell casing is about 1¼ inches diameter for the .787-inch diameter projectile and seven inches long. Many fighter aircraft employ Vulcan cannons, which are set to fire at a rate of 7,200 rounds per minute. Those on the Stinger gunships were geared down to 2,500 rounds per minute because the rounds could be placed in a much smaller target area while flying in a circle than from a fighter coming onto a target from over 10,000 feet and travelling at Mach whatever.

Now we're talking about our hulky attack cargo plane putting down 29,000 rounds per minute of pure hellfire terror onto ground targets.

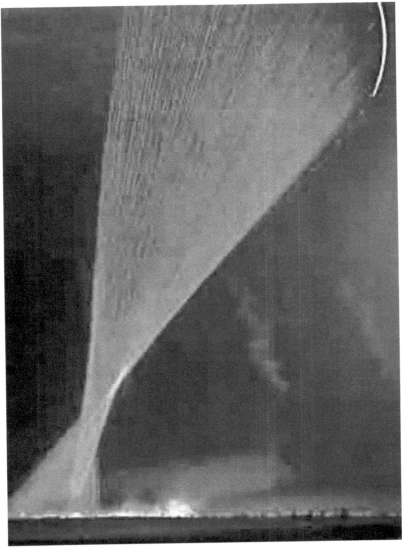

A really impressive time-lapse photo of a Stinger firing on a target

As a side note (actually, I suppose a lot of what you are reading are side notes), we only carried about five plus-or-minus minutes of ammunition on our typical 3.3-hour missions. The guns were necessarily only fired in two- to four-second bursts. Longer than that and they would overheat, as you can imagine, and develop undesirable operating issues. The three gunners in the plane, whose job it was to keep the guns loaded, adjusted, and operating smoothly, would be a little on the unhappy side when such pilot-induced errors occurred. Sometimes, however, with mechanical parts moving as they were at mini-gun speed, problems would manifest themselves without any human assistance.

Military intel (yes, we are all familiar with the cliché that military intelligence is an oxymoron; moving right along . . .) reported that many North Vietnamese Army truck drivers hauling supplies south along the Ho Chi Minh and other trails had actually been chained to their trucks. This information came from friendly ground forces reconnoitering target areas, after the fact, of course, and reporting battle damage assessment (BDA). Once the sound of the gunships became "familiar" to the drivers and they were made cognizant of our willingness to rain the End of the World upon them, many would desert their trucks and cargo whenever they heard a gunship overhead. Ergo the chains.

I remember seeing a cartoon drawing in a military magazine or newspaper showing two NVA truck drivers looking up to see a gunship overhead. One guy says to the other, "I hear their pilots are chained to the airplane."

Besides the four 7.62 mm mini-guns, the two 20 mm Vulcan cannons, and lots of ammunition for each gun, the -119 was further equipped with a low-light night observation sensor (NOS), a forward-looking infrared (FLIR) scope, a flare launcher, and a search light illuminator. The flare launcher could launch out the side of the aircraft up to 24 flares which would suspend from parachutes and light up the ground. Each flare was 500,000 candle power, which is approximately equivalent to the light output of 4,063 one-hundred-watt light bulbs all in a very tight space.

The 1,500,000 candlepower (12,189 light bulbs) search light illuminator was like a low power Klieg light, which were around 9,000,000 candlepower. Today you can buy a 7,000,000 candle-power handheld light for about $140.

The Stinger gunship carried a crew of ten men. Earlier I mentioned holes being cut in the side of the airplane. Each of the four mini-guns needed a hole to protrude through, as did each of the two Vulcan cannons (indeed a necessity to prevent us from shooting ourselves down). The NOS needed an opening large enough for the NOS operator (also called NOS, as in, "Hey, NOS, see if you can track those trucks") to have a sufficient range of motion of the scope to operate efficiently. Likewise, it was incumbent upon the flare launcher to be able to launch the flares outside the airplane. Otherwise, everyone's rhodopsin, a.k.a. visual purple, would get momentarily bleached out, resulting in the temporary loss of night vision. The illuminator also needed a hole to shine through. When the illuminator was not needed for target acquisition, the illuminator operator (called eye-oh) would strap in, well-connected to the aircraft, and hang about half-way outside the plane looking for triple-A.

The AC-119K aircraft was certainly neither airtight nor waterproof.

- 28 -

FERRYING THE GUNSHIPS

Speaking of waterproof, what absolute dreariness it must have been for the crews who ferried these gunships from Maryland to the West Coast and then continued on across the utter vastness of the Pacific Ocean. Thousands and thousands of miles—at 160 miles per hour. Much more time was spent over water than over land. Of course, they were hardly non-stop trips, not even across the US. They had to make at least two stops stateside before beginning the island hopping trek across the Pacific. I would imagine the crews probably discovered some mechanical issues with the aircraft when they happened upon a nice little tropical island big enough to support a runway, some coconut trees, and possibly a few nubile young native girls right out of a James H. Michener novel. Then, after a sufficiently long enough delay for some rest and relaxation (R&R), but not so long as to stimulate the wrath of their commanders—on either side of the ocean—the mechanical difficulties would "mysteriously" manage to fix themselves.

A possible communication exchange might have been something like: SEA commander to Stateside commander: "Where are those darn (or words to that effect) gunships I'm supposed to be getting?" Reply: "Aren't they there yet? They should have been there last week."

Of course, this is purely conjecture on my part. I am almost certainly nearly positive it probably perhaps never actually really happened that way. Very often. Probably.

- 29 -

HOW TO FIRE A GUN(SHIP)

To actually get the ammunition to depart the mini-guns and/or Vulcan cannons onto targets on the ground required the coordination of all ten aircrew men. Working from the back of the rear cabin forward, the illuminator operator (IO) had to have the flare launcher and/or spotlight ready; the table nav passed the aircraft elevation above the terrain to the gunners, who then adjusted the guns to be set for proper aircraft elevation; one or both sensor operators had to be tracking the target/s; the table nav had to confirm the target, select the optimal sensor, and connect it to the fire control system (FCS), then activate access to the "trigger" button on the pilot's yoke; the flight engineer (FE) resynced the recips; the copilot maintained aircraft altitude and airspeed; and the pilot had to have the target/aircraft reticles aligned. Then everything was ready for the pilot to push the trigger button. All this activity was occurring at the same time, and when all was accomplished, the table nav advised the pilot that we were cleared to fire. Button pushed, bullets flew.

Of course, we had to have clearance from higher up—figuratively, of course—to wreak vengeance on our selected targets. Usually we had blanket clearance to fire upon any targets within a specified area or areas. Without prior approval, meaning when we found "targets of opportunity" outside our pre-approved target areas, or previously unspecified targets, we had to initiate by previously-arranged FM (fox-mike) radio frequency a request for clearance to engage the target. More about such requests in a later chapter about the 18th SOS Detachment at Da Nang AB in northern South Vietnam. (I have also seen it online spelled Danang.)

The night observation sensor (NOS) was a low-light telescope apparatus manned by the junior navigator on the crew, who was accordingly referred to and addressed as the NOS; no connection to Jimmy Durante. He (the NOS, not Jimmy Durante) was strapped to a harness because the NOS telescope protruded about half-way out the airplane. The view presented was like watching the "snowy" low resolution black-and-white TV after the station went off the air for the night at 11:00 P.M. or midnight. Many of you "younger" folks (EIR) have no experience with a black-and-white TV, with only three channels to choose from, but you can get an idea of it by watching some of the 1930s and 1940s black-and-white movies on your local Turner Classic Movies channel. I highly recommend you watch *"Casablanca"* when you get a chance.

Back to the NOS: Movement on the ground could be distinguished even though it might appear a little snowy without overly sharp resolution. The forward-looking infrared radar (FLIR) was operated via a joystick by the middle ranking navigator, who was called the FLIR (who'd a guessed?). The FLIR resolution and tracking was a little more accurate than the NOS. Both the NOS and the FLIR devices fed target tracking information to the aircraft fire control system.

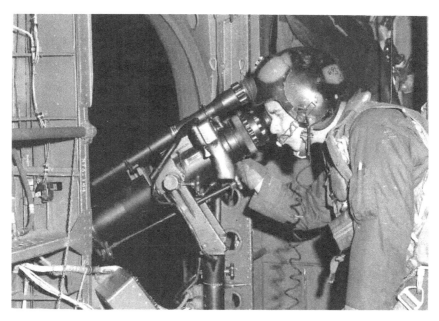

"NOS"—Night Observation Sensor; also, the officer operating it

The Table Nav was usually the senior navigator on board; he was called Nav, or "Hey, Nav" if you really wanted to get his attention. Among his other duties, he basically coordinated which sensor to provide target data input to the FCS, depending on which scope was providing the best data at any given moment. The NOS and FLIR could each be focused on different targets at the same time, or at the same target. Weather, moonlight brightness or lack thereof, terrain, aircraft angle of bank, and other factors all had influence on which scope to use. Computers were involved, but this was late 1960's technology. Those computers were not exactly up to flying-a-drone-over-Afghanistan-from-a-comfy-chair-in-an-air-conditioned-building-in-Nevada-while-sipping-a-Perrier standards, or your iPhone capabilities, or even Windows 95. But they sufficed at the time. The FCS also received input from aircraft bank angle, from height above ground, from which guns were "on line," and probably from a few other necessary sources that I do not remember.

This amalgamated data was reflected on the pilot's display reticles to his left. These were basically two circular rows of dots, rather like two floating clock faces but without numbers clogging up the display. They were about the size of a quarter, or maybe a half dollar (remember those?). One reticle represented the target selected by the Nav and it "floated" on the Head Up Display (HUD) in relation to the other "fixed" reticle, which represented where the aircraft was "aiming." Not aiming as in where it was heading, which was essentially a circle around the selected target or some semblance thereof, but where the calculated impact point of the bullets would be. Both dotted circles seemed to drift around, reflecting aircraft movements and target sensor movements. The targets, usually NVA personnel engaged in various nefarious activities (from our perspective) and/or supply trucks, tended to not remain in the same place when they heard us overhead. When altitude, airspeed, and bank angle were correct, and when the appropriate guns in back were selected and put on line by the gunners, and when the NOS and/or FLIR had a good track on the target, then the Nav flipped a control switch connecting the FCS with the pilot's HUD, enabling the pilot to fire the guns, and when the two circles of dots in the gunsight display floated together and coincided, the pilot squeezed the trigger (er, pressed the button) on his yoke . . . and it was SHOWTIME!

The mini-guns and/or Vulcan cannons ramped up to full speed immediately and started their blurred spinning, spitting out beaucoup 7.62 ("bo coo 7-6-2") and 20 mike-mike ammunition. It got noisy, especially in the back where expended brass casings were ejected by the thousands. This cacophony was over and above the noise from the four six-barrel mini-guns each spinning at 6000 revolutions per minute, the two Vulcan barrels whirling at nearly half that speed, the two large reciprocating engines, the two jet engines, all the earphone chatter from seven radios plus intercom, and the wind rushing by and into various openings in the aircraft. Then, about two to three seconds later, the noise the guns and brass made ceased as the pilot released the trigger. Besides possibly overheating, the guns also needed a few seconds to spool down - i.e., stop spinning. Otherwise, if they had not stopped fully and were activated again too soon, they tended to jam very easily, necessitating the gunners to rectify the situation by un-jamming them. I imagine that at such times the gunners had thoughts something like, "Darn pilots," or perhaps other expletives to that effect.

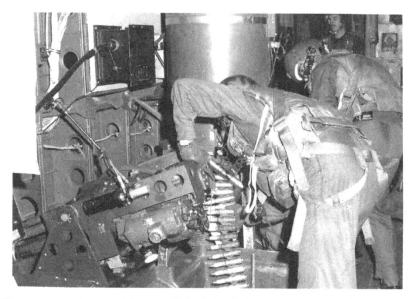

Gunners working with one of the belt-fed 20 mm Vulcan cannons

The dry season varied depending on the specific geographic location—essentially on the coastal belt east of the mountains, or on the other side, which, for the spatially unenhanced, would be the west side. The visual results from all the 20 mm high explosive incendiary (HEI) projectiles impacting the ground were more spectacular during the dry season than during monsoon season, for obvious reasons. Soft mud was more absorbent and less resistant to incoming hard objects than hard ground was. We carried three types of 20 mm rounds—standard (hunk of lead), armor-piercing (hardened), and high explosive incendiary. When the HEI hit the ground and trucks, it produced what was called "sparkle," the effect produced by all those hundreds of tiny explosions. They were usually visible through the NOS or FLIR scopes. Unless they hit a truck. Then it did not matter whether it was rainy season or dry, those explosions were visible to the whole crew, and you could hear cheers throughout the airplane.

Once the target had been sufficiently "neutralized," to use today's TV espionage vocabulary, the NOS and FLIR would look for other targets in the area, or the Nav would direct us to other reported and/or approved target areas. This was our modus operandi until we ran out of ammunition, until we started taking accurate incoming triple-A (not a good thing), until we heard from the next Stinger that was enroute to the target area to replace us, or until we reached bingo. Bingo meant we were down to the amount of fuel remaining necessary to return to base (RTB).

And that, Gentle Reader, is the simplified version (really) of how to fire a gun(ship).

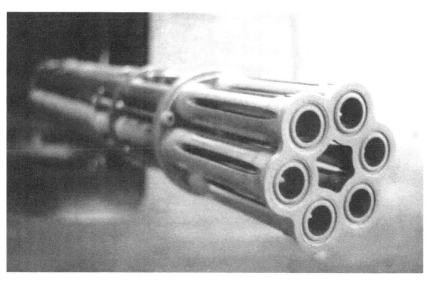

The business end of a Vulcan cannon

We're talking guns…

- 30 -

TOGGLING THE JETS

The two J-85 jet engines were necessary for takeoff and in the firing circle, when tight airspeed control was needed. It made systems a little more complicated, but I had been used to jets in pilot training, and to these engines in particular. On the other hand, the recips had not only throttle levers to control propeller rotation speed, but also mixture control levers, which regulated the fuel/air ratio going into the engines, and propeller feathering levers, which rotated the angle of the propellers in relation to the incoming air. Feathering the props turned the propeller blades so that they stopped and no longer rotated, even though the engine was still running. There was a flight engineer who sat on an ammunition can—unpadded, of course—between the pilots' seats and aft of the center console located between the pilots' seats. Among other things, he would synchronize the propeller speeds. It was easy to tell when the props were out of sync—i.e., not rotating at the same speed: the vibration in the plane and in your ears was definitely noticeable—and annoying. If you have ever driven a car at highway speeds with the windows asymmetrically down just enough for the wind to be obstreperously noisy, then you have a partial idea of what I am describing. Highway speeds for you may be 55; for me, just a tad faster: "Yes, officer, I might have been 'flying along,' but I have a pilot's license . . . ." Believe it or not, that actually got my dad out of a speeding ticket in New Jersey once.

The two jet engines were controlled by toggle switches rather than with the usual larger throttle levers found on nearly all jets, and the engines spooled up or down (increased or decreased engine rpm) very rapidly. To change their rpm by 1 percent, which would need to be done frequently while in the firing circle (I'll explain firing circle later), the copilot (in my case that would be me) would have to "flick" the toggles up (or down) twice and then an even shorter "flick" back down (or up). That's how fast those J-85 engines reacted. Up 3 percent, down 2 percent.

Of course, having guns to shoot - in this case, six of them, firing 29,000 rounds of ammunition per minute when all six guns were put "on line"—made the AC-119K version of the C-119 more fun than the basic cargo airplane. That is, at least when we were shooting at inanimate targets over the Gulf of Mexico just off the Florida coast—targets that did not shoot back.

In the war zone—not so much fun.

- 31 -

ON TO FAIRCHILD AFB—BASIC SURVIVAL TRAINING

As a refresher, in our story-line so far, I was preparing to leave sunny Florida and catch a flight to Fairchild AFB, Spokane, Washington, to begin the two-week Basic Survival School. Any Readers who have been through the Fairchild experience your-selves during the Vietnam "War" era can easily skip ahead to the next section without missing anything—except perhaps the eru-dite (he wrote modestly) retelling of the two-week saga as I ex-perienced it in March 1972.

As I am beginning to write this section, it has only just now oc-curred to me, over four decades after the fact, to wonder why the state of Washington was chosen as the site to host, as it were, Air Force Basic Survival Training for preparing us troops for the rigors we might perchance encounter overseas. Let us examine and com-pare some highlights of the geographies of the two locations. (That phraseology sounds like a question on a high school or college ge-ography final exam: "Compare and contrast everything you can possibly conceive of, or imagine if you do not remember, or if you could not stay awake in class, or might have ever possibly been even subliminally exposed to during your lifetime, including prenatally. . . . You have six hours or until you faint from hunger to finish the exam.")

Fairchild AFB is near Spokane in the far eastern side of Washington in the high desert plain. The field elevation at Fairchild is 2,462 feet (average), just under a half of a mile above sea level. Being situated east of the coastal range, the climate there is relatively (EIR) dry, averaging about sixteen inches of rain per year. Seattle, on the other hand, on the other side of the mountains, is in the path of the moisture-laden westerly winds from the Pacific. (In case you are wondering about which direction westerly is, or easterly, or similarly with the other points on the compass, such as NEbE, which translates to northeast by east(erly), there is a fairly simple explanation which even I cannot, probably, un-dis-ambiguate. If westerly refers to the direction a wind is blowing, it is the *direction from which* the wind is blowing. If it is the direction of travel (via walking, motor scooter, space shuttle, et cetera), it is the *direction in which* one is heading.) Topologically situated as it is, Seattle thus soaks up most of the moisture in the form of rain or snow before some of it can manage to escape over the mountains and scatter itself on its way to Spokane. During the wintery months in Spokane, the clouds deposit on average forty-one inches of snow annually. The entire country of Vietnam averages . . . hold on while I calculate it . . . let's see . . . multiply by the square root of the last eight digits of Pi, carry the two, divide by the square root of negative one . . . . Ah, yes: zero inches of snow per year. I could almost have figured that out in my head. Almost.

Obviously, climate acclimatization was not a reason for selecting Fairchild, especially in the winter. As you may recall, I left for the Great Northwest in the middle of March when the daily low temperatures there average right about freezing and the daily high temperatures are not much higher. Ole' dopey me, it never occurred to me to haul along a parka and thermal underwear enroute to the tropical climes of the Philippine Islands (my next training assignment) and subsequently, finally, to nearly-tropical Southeast Asia. Fortunately, the Powers That Be thought of this beforehand and had a supply of cold weather gear to issue us on a temporary basis.

I cannot imagine that the thermal underwear was a "temporary" issue—at least I hope that it wasn't—not that it matters in the least to me anymore. However, I do not remember what I/we did with it after finishing training, and I certainly do not remember taking mine on to SEA. Perhaps I gave it to my wife to take back home when I met her later in San Francisco before I headed west(erly).

The two weeks of Basic Survival Training at Fairchild were divided into two segments: one week of training to survive in the elements—meaning, in this case, the mountains about sixty miles north of the base—and a week of training how to survive being a prisoner of war (POW) in Vietnam. As always, there were a couple of days of classroom instruction before we were sent out into the wilderness or sent out to become a student POW. During the time period I went through Fairchild, massive numbers of military troops were being filtered through the training system there. My class had about two or three hundred students, which was pretty typical then. Accordingly, each class was divided into two sections. One section went through the POW training the first week while the other section went through training for what was known as the trek. As an astute Reader might surmise, during the second week the survivors of the first week swapped training schedules.

Hang on; there is no cause for alarm. Nearly every student survived all the training. Warm, healthy bodies were needed overseas by the truckload, planeload, and boatload. Those who did not "survive" from the occasional injury on the trek or from psychological issues from the POW camp were merely rescheduled into a subsequent training class. I never heard of anyone actually dying from anything related to the training. The accountants in the Pentagon would not look upon any such loss with any sense of financial comfort; it cost too much to recruit and train anyone, regardless of his or her Air Force Specialty Code (AFSC)—i.e., job title.

- 32 -

THE TREK

My half of the class had the trek first, which, depending on one's perspective, was either good or not so good. The trek was essentially three days of classroom instruction and four days of camping. I liked camping. My dad and baby brother and I used to go tent camping as kids. Andi and I also used to go on camping trips both before and after our Southeast Asia experience. But I had always camped in warm or reasonably warm weather. Where we were on the trek, in the mountains in eastern Washington State in mid-March, even though the northern hemisphere was rapidly approaching the Vernal Equinox, there was still three feet of crusty snow on most of the ground. Not my idea of ideal camping weather. We were divided into elements of nine or ten, mostly men, but there were a few female military types in the class also. None of them were in my element. I call it my element because, having recently pinned on my silver First Lieutenant bars, I was the ranking officer of our little group and was otherwise expected to be its fearless leader. Each element also had an instructor to give us our training, assignments, et cetera, and lead us on the trek on the third day. I will explain what is meant by "the trek" in a moment.

On the last day of classroom instruction we were given decommissioned parachutes and were each told to make one item from parts of it to take with us on the trek. Not being a particularly imaginative sort of person, I made myself a pillow. It was not a pillow such as one might encounter in a five-star hotel, or even a three star hotel, or even in a Motel 6, but it was small, firm, and lightweight. It served me well on our three nights on the trek. Our instructor, a staff sergeant who was based at Fairchild AFB, asked if he could have my pillow after we had finished the trek. I was flattered and, since I did not anticipate needing it any longer and did not want to haul it across the Pacific, I gladly gave it to him when we got back to the base.

Part of the trip from Fairchild to the trek area was via an HH-53 Super Jolly Green, as I recall. It could have been a smaller helicopter, but I have ridden in Jolly Greens enough times that let's just say I have the nomenclature close enough in this instance. It could have been a CH-53, but not having seen them side-by-side, I don't really know the difference. Regardless, it does not matter here one iota (which has most likely already occurred to the Reader). When the mass of the elements going on the trek had assembled at our staging point, we hiked into the woods to the area where we were to set up camp. Each element cleared its own area as necessary, cutting small evergreen branches and saplings to create shelters. The saplings supplied poles, and the evergreen branches provided some cover and protection from the elements.

Each of us selected a spot to build a basic one-man shelter in our designated area, not too far from the campfire. Even with all the snow on the ground nearby, there was plenty of dry firewood around. At least we did not have to sleep on the snow, although if we had had to we would have had at least a couple of options: 1) Put plenty of greenery underneath, and/or 2) Build a makeshift cot out of sapling poles and greenery. The sleeping bags were the one ~~man~~ person variety, so they were fairly snug and airtight, sorta.

Each element was issued some basic food items, like a hunk of beef and a live bunny rabbit. The first night we used half of our beef ration, cut it into strips, and made it into beef jerky. We built a smoke tent to go over our campfire for the night, and we set up a "watch" schedule to keep the fire smoking and turn the jerky as needed. The jerky took all night to smoke, but it was worth it. Better than what you could buy at a convenience store, and fresh out of the smoke. The next night, after we tried making some kind of boiled concoction out of the other half of the beef, we all wished we had made jerky out of the whole thing.

Next time.

There was one instance during the trek where I actually had to "pull rank." Remember the cute little bunny rabbit? Our instructor demonstrated how to kill and prepare it for cooking. I will avoid any gory details, because there weren't really any (EIR). However, according to the instructor, the eyeballs were supposed to be a delicacy with the consistency of oysters. He demonstrated the first one—just popped in it and swallowed it down. He then asked who wanted to try the other eye. We all backed up a half a step or so, thereby indicating a willingness to let someone else do it. Seeing that he had no takers, the instructor - a staff sergeant, remember—said to me something to the effect of, "Lieutenant, you're the ranking officer here. Why don't you try it?" Let me interject here and mention that I was not then nor ever have been what one would call an adventuresome practitioner of the culinary arts. I said something like, "As the ranking officer here, I would rather not. Anyone else up to it?" Fortunately for me, anyway, a 2nd lieutenant navigator stepped up to the challenge and suffered no apparent ill effects.

When it was time to bed down for the night (by "bed down" I am using the term very loosely) when I could still see my breath frosting in the air, getting undressed and zipped up into a sleeping bag was done as quickly as possible. Maybe any guys from Minot AFB in northern North Dakota thought it was spring already, but, being a cold weather wimp from Georgia, I would have had to take issue with them. Twenty-two degrees outside is just plain cold. Except maybe in Antarctica. In the winter. EIR. It only took a few minutes to get warmed up—once the sleeping bag was zipped so that my face was all that was exposed, and usually by then I had fallen asleep anyway.

I don't know about you, but I, for one, have never relished the experience of waking up at oh-dark-thirty inside a warm and comfy winter sleeping bag inside a lean to, knowing that I had to leave my cocoon and brave the cold (not chilly—cold!) new world merely inches away. Truth be told, I have never relished waking up at oh-dark-thirty for anything. The temperature outside was somewhere in the freezing range, plus or minus a few degrees. We kept our clothes inside the sleeping bag with us overnight, which helped the situation somewhat. I managed to get dressed while still lying inside the sleeping bag, although I had to unzip it, but only as little as possible. I finally had to get the rest of the way out to put on my combat boots, which had managed to chill during the night (no surprise there). At least my socks were still warm. I was going to have to speak to the management about this arrangement. There wasn't even any room service to order a cup of hot chocolate.

Whoever in our element managed to get up and moving first got the campfire going and started heating some water for coffee. I have never cared for coffee myself, except when my baby brother and I were kids and our parents would let us have it— half coffee, half milk, and half sugar. But when it was cold, any-thing warm was welcome. However big the campfire was, I felt it necessary to add more wood. I was not interested in a campfire. I wanted a campFIRE. Get warm NOW. These days instant grat-ification is a term used to describe it. When we had first selected the location for our campfire, I ensured that there was at least fifty feet of clearance over the fire pit to the lowest tree branches. It was seriously cold, and I was seriously not messing around with any puny fire.

On the morning of the third day we actually went out on "The Trek." We broke camp, policed the area (I don't know why this procedure is called "policing," but for those of you who may not be familiar with the term, it simply means cleaning up, dis-posing of all trash, and leaving the area as nature would have preferred), packed up everything, and headed out. Our instruc-tor led the way. We would be hiking most of the day to some prearranged spot where all the elements would gather in a cen-tral area that evening—still in the forest. All the elements had gone out in separate directions; we never saw or heard any of them while we were out and about.

We also came upon no previous tracks—at least no tracks from another element anyway. We encountered tracks from deer, rabbits, and lions and tigers and bears (oh my) and other such wild creatures, of course. Procedurally, we swapped out the point man—the troop in front leading the way—about each half hour or so. The instructor gave directions to the point man, like, "Continue forward over that hill towards the tall, dead tree visible beyond it." Most of the time we were struggling through crotch-deep snow. The pace was slow, as you might imagine. Sometimes the snow was still soft and not very much fun to plow through step by step, raising one leg out of the hole in the snow track and stepping down into the next one. That is why we changed out the point man every so often. He was the one who had to plow through the snow; the rest of us would try to step into the same leg holes he had made rather than create new ones.

Well, that we did, except when the lead managed to take a step only to discover—completely unintentionally, of course—that the surface at the bottom of his next step held a surprise. It might have been sufficiently lower than the previous steps had been, or have been uneven, or on a rock or root so as to cause a loss of balance, and he would make an impression in the snow. We are not talking snow angels here. We were going to be doing this for several hours, and no one wanted to get hurt or any damper than we already were. Sometimes the snow was crusted on top and thick enough to be walked upon. That made the going a little easier, except when we found places where it suddenly stopped being crusty enough and the next step went through to the ground again. That happened to our instructor a couple or three hours into the trek. Although he was not looking for it, he found a little stream under the crust and fell. Being tired and cold was bad enough, but being tired and cold and wet was not fun at all. We were all in a position to empathize.

There were two positive outcomes to his fall. The little stream was pure mountain snow run-off. Unlike the so-called mountain spring bottled water of today, this water was the real thing. We filled out canteens with it. I cannot describe how water can be tasty—water is water—but indeed it was. It just tasted clean and refreshing and smooth, like a 2006 vintage Bordeaux. That was the first positive.

The second positive was that although we were to rendezvous with the other elements at a certain time a couple of hours hence, the instructor was naturally not particularly inclined to continue slogging, and for him sloshing as well, through the snow. Furthermore, he knew where we were and where the rendezvous area was. He also knew we could take a short-cut and trek for about another half hour to a spot not far from the rendezvous point where we could wait until the designated hour. We rested there, fairly quietly so as to not be heard by anyone of authority who might question our presence so near so early. I believe our element learned and experienced everything we needed to learn and experience from three hours on the trek, so a fourth hour would only add to discomfort, a decreased learning receptivity, and therefore a declining marginal utility value.

When our instructor determined it would be okay to do so, we headed to the rendezvous area, where we set up another campsite. That night our instructor told us we all had to shave. To this day I still don't know the logic for this. If I were in an actual survival situation, shaving would not be something I would aspire to each morning—or any morning. I had only used an electric shaver ever since I first started shaving at age fifteen (once a week back then—or maybe once a season). After I determined he was not kidding about the shaving thing, even though he could give me no explanation other than we had to shave, I asked him if there was a tree nearby where I could plug in my shaver. Sure—like I had brought it with me. He was unsympathetic to my "delicate" conditioning and told me to borrow someone else's razor, which I did. One of my troops let me borrow his razor, and he told me how to use it.

I don't recall if there was any blood—probably some but not enough to call for a medic. I do remember that it was quite uncomfortable. Cold water and soap was not ideal, I now realize, but back then I had no frame of reference. I also think that particular razor blade was not freshly out of its packaging. It certainly was not like the ones in the TV commercials, and I certainly wasn't smiling as I attempted to shave with it. I thought the blade was supposed to smoothly trim the whiskers right at the outside of the skin level; I did not know that the blade was supposed to pull each whisker out by the root. At least that's what it felt like it was doing. Like I said, how was I to know any differently? I did what I could, under the circumstances, but since I had a low pain threshold to begin with and had not yet developed any masochistic tendencies, I was satisfied by doing only a rudimentary shaving job. After all, I had no plans to be kissing anyone until I met my wife in San Francisco after survival training.

So much for the excitement of The Trek. I would no doubt have enjoyed the whole thing had it been in June. But by June I would have been remembering the time on The Trek when it wasn't so hot and humid. I guess the phrase, "There is no pleasing some people," could have applied to me.

- 33 -

POW SURVIVAL TRAINING CAMP

The trip back to Fairchild was pretty much the reverse of the trip out to the trek area—hike, helicopter, ground transport. When I got back to my VOQ room, that nice hot shower felt mighty luxurious. I also had some of the fudge my wife had made and packed for me.

Week two: As the Week One POW trainees were preparing for the trek phase, we began the Week Two POW Survival training. We had all heard stories about both the trek and the POW parts. I, for one, was not looking forward for to it, but I realized it was necessary. No one wanted to become a prisoner of war, especially in North Vietnam, but if fortune shined unfavorably, one wanted to at least have some idea of expectations and training in how to best deal with the probable adversities one could encounter.

The POW training would be different from any other training I had encountered in the Air Force or anywhere else. In fact, it was different from any training I have been exposed to since. That suits me just fine, as my memories of it are mostly of the unpleasant variety. Of course, it started with academics in the classroom, as always. At this point in our program we were presumed to have already been trained in the classroom apropos Escape and Evasion (E&E) situations during which we WOULD be captured, taken prisoner, and interrogated. During our "captivity" we would be expected to attempt to escape.

Although I do not remember any names or specifics, in the academic phase we had one or two briefings from guys that had actually survived having been shot down. In fact, all of our survival training course curricula, from basic water survival at Homestead AFB, Florida, to the POW camp at Fairchild AFB, Washington, to Jungle Survival at Clark Air Base in the Philippines (coming up shortly) was designed with the help of those who had already been through the actual experiences in hostile situations. As our service men and women were returned to safety from their various "unscheduled" detours from their assigned missions, they were asked to give detailed debriefings on their actions which led to their eventual successful recovery. Each new "telling of the tale" provided input to the various survival course designers.

One story I do remember was told by a fighter pilot who had been shot down. For purposes of retelling his story, let us refer to him as the Captain. After bailing out of his mortally crippled aircraft, probably an F-4 Phantom or an F-105 Wild Weasel, he found himself in a tall tree in the jungle. In many areas in the jungles of Southeast Asia, the trees form a canopy two to three hundred feet above the jungle floor. We were taught techniques to get ourselves down to the safety (ha) of the ground below using equipment supplied in our survival kits. However, in the Captain's situation, getting himself down at the moment was not an option.

He could hear gunfire and Vietnamese voices below. The probability of being rescued was the greatest if you could be recovered within the first twenty-four hours after going down. Generally, the longer a downed airman had to survive on his own, the more his chances of successful recovery diminished. The Captain knew that little fact also; he had been through an iteration of survival training himself before heading across the Pond.

A little background information is necessary at this point. One of the important pieces of paperwork that we all completed before heading into a war zone was our personal security code information card. This information consisted of a set of six questions that you made up and your corresponding answers. These sets of six Qs & As were supposed to be designed so they could be easily remembered under high stress situations. This set of information was included with your records so that it could be readily accessed and given to rescue crews should the occasion require it. It was one card that everyone concerned hoped would never have to be used. However, if the emergency situation did arise, as it did all too frequently, the questions and answers would be used by rescue crews in a challenge-response format to verify that the voice on the other end of the radio was in fact the downed airman.

We all were issued and taught to use battery-powered hand-held survival radios. They were carried in a mesh survival vest, along with various and sundry other items which could be found useful in unpleasant situations. Such items included spare batteries for the radio (not your everyday Eveready D-cell type batteries; these were designed specifically to fit and power the radio); a non-reflective camouflage stick; and other items mentioned earlier in the Water Survival chapter. Also included were an area topological map and a pointee-talkie booklet which had a number of words and phrases in English and corresponding equivalents in several languages, depending on the region of the world one happened to have found oneself wandering around in while being non-conversant in the local language. You would point to an English phrase, and the person with whom you were attempting to communicate could read a reply in their language, i.e., assuming they were literate in their own language. That person could respond by pointing to a phrase in their language which would have the English interpretation for you. Ergo, pointee-talkie (whew!). The most significant of the other survival items in the vest was a loaded 38 caliber, six-shot military-issue pistol and forty extra rounds of ammunition, including six tracer rounds.

The tracer rounds were intended to be used for signaling potential rescuers, all the while hoping that any unfriendly persons out looking for you had poor night vision and would not be able to see or hear the source—i.e., you—of the tracers. No one I knew really wanted a pistol. As if we were going to get ourselves into a gunfight with a search patrol of NVA carrying Russian-made AK-47 machine guns (Russian: Avtomat Kalashnikova 1947. Translation: Automatic Kalashnikova 1947, a Kalashnikova being the weapon designer's name). And when we ran out of regular rounds, we could load and fire our tracer rounds as if to say, "Hey, bad guys, I'm over here." Right. What we really wanted was a second radio and more batteries. But by the time I got back to the States to tell someone, the "war" was over. Bad timing on my part.

Experience and feedback had shown that the NVA were not dummies. They had learned they could use a captured hand-held survival radio like we all carried and lure rescue aircrews into a trap. The survival radio emitted a continuous radio beacon on certain preset frequencies as long as the radio was turned on. You may wonder why someone in desperate need of rescue would ever bother to turn his radio off. The answer is that, like every other battery ever invented by humankind, the radio battery did not have an infinite life, and usually in survival situations there are no convenient places to recharge it. If rescue did not arrive soon—whatever "soon" felt like at the time, which was usually NOW, or shortly thereafter—there were procedures for turning off the radio to conserve battery life, then turning it back on for five minutes each hour or until the distinctive *whop-whop-whop* sound of Jolly Green helicopter blades could be heard.

A typical rescue attempt involved possibly four or five layers of aircraft, depending on availability, locality, fuel on board, and other factors. The highest aircraft would be an EC-130 or an EC-135 aircraft with command and control personnel and equipment aboard to coordinate the mission. The workhorse in Vietnam was the F-4 Phantom, which provided tactical cover as necessary for the mission aircraft below and for the downed airman/airmen on the ground (or close proximity thereof). If a versatile OV-10 Bronco was around, the pilot would assume Forward Air Controller duties, providing suppression against the enemy with machine gun fire, or air-to-air or air-to-ground missiles, depending on its external weapons configuration. By radio coordination with the downed airman and the F-4, the pilot of the Bronco could mark the precise location of the enemy by firing white phosphorous ("Willy Pete") smoke markers for the F-4 to guide its ordinance on. Flying not too far above the treetops was a heavily-armed A-1E Sandy, which would provide even closer cover (protection) for all the good guys below it, including those in the Jolly Green.

The Jolly Green flew just above the trees or rice paddies or whatever the terrain was in the area. It was equipped with a 7.62 mm mini-gun and the rescue team, which included the actual guys who were trained to extract the airman under less than optimal conditions, be it out of the water, a mountain jungle, a tree, or an open field under gunfire attack. Often the vulnerable airman, soldier, sailor, or marine was injured and incapacitated, requiring these men to leave the helicopter to effect the rescue, placing recovery of their fellow countryman-in-arms above their own safety. Every effort conceivable was expended to retrieve our personnel in trouble, regardless of branch of service. By that I mean not just downed airmen, but troops-in-contact on the ground, floating in the South China Sea, or whatever the situation. All of these recovery team personnel, and especially the guys that had to get right up close and personal to make the rescue, were willing to give their lives in order to save a fellow American. They were not trying to be heroes, although they most certainly were. Many were later awarded the Purple Heart, Silver Star, a (Specific Service) Cross, or even the Medal of Honor. And too many—meaning even one—of these were awarded posthumously.

I for one thank them while also being thankful that I personally never had to require their service.

Enough said about that.

Our Nation's highest military award—the Medal of Honor
(Shown: Army MOH medal, ribbon, and lapel pin)

Back to the story. As you may recall, the Captain was in a tree with NVA looking for him not far away. He could hear voices and AK-47 fire below. As anyone might imagine, he was in what was most likely the highest stress situation he had ever encountered—even more than when he had had to bail out of his flaming aircraft. You could get killed bailing out of an out-of-control jet; but if you were captured on the ground over enemy territory, it could be . . . unthinkable. There he was with bad guys closing in on his location, being stuck up some tree somewhere in the jungle (which in itself was probably a good thing, if he had had the inclination at the time to consider the good points of his misfortune), after having just survived a high-speed bailout, wondering what shape his body was in. . . . Stressful? You betcha.

However, when he was able to make radio contact—good ole radio!—with a rescue team, there was elation of the utmost primal kind. He knew he was going to get out of there alive and only a little worse for the wear. Once the guys in the Jolly Green had found his exact location based on his description of his surroundings, they verified that it was indeed the Captain. First security question (I'll make up some Q and A dialogue here):

"Who won the World Series last year?"

"What are you talking about? How do I know? Just get me the $%$#!! outta here!"

"What is your mother's home town?"

"Who? What? I don't remember! There're guys with guns real close!"

"Captain, what is your dog's name?"

Again, his mind was not on such mundane details. "Just get me outta here! Now!"

"I'm sorry Captain, we can't risk coming in without ID verification," and they started to leave the immediate area.

Hearing the Jolly Green departing, in desperation and anger the Captain hollered over the radio (something like): "HEY YOU #(&^*&^$@%^'ERSERS GET BACK HERE! WHERE THE %%#$$&*^ ARE YOU GOING? THERE'S SOME *%^$#^%^&%%^&%ERS DOWN THERE SHOOTING *%@$)*&^%% AT ME! DON'T LEAVE ME HERE IN THIS ##*^*&)$*@# PLACE!" . . . (More of the same.)

The Jolly Green turned back around and successfully extracted the Captain—obviously, since he was there in our class at Fairchild relating his story to us of his adventure. Later, when they were carrying him safely on the way back to a more friendly location and the captain had a moment to ponder his recent experience, he asked the crew what made them turn back around to get him.

The reply was, "Captain, no Vietnamese could ever cuss like that."

Our POW classroom instruction included an overview of what to expect when we began the actual field training. We would start after dark, duck walk and crawl for a mile while negotiating barbed wire and evading notice by instructors patrolling the area, before ultimately being captured. We would not be treated gently, but neither would anyone be physically hurt. We would be interrogated, most likely more than once. We would spend time in the prison camp and be expected to try to escape. I forget how the last day ended, whether we were "rescued" by good guys or whether we were gathered for a summary briefing, and then the training was over. Piece of cake (or in my case, fudge).

During the classroom instruction, besides being taught such things as different ways to cope with various situations we would definitely encounter in the training camp, we were also told certain words or phrases that might be used by the "NVA" instructors as a "time-out" from the role playing. These time-outs were used by the instructors to put the situation on freeze for a few moments while they gave us timely feedback whenever they thought it would be helpful or necessary—comments and critiques on our particular performance at the moment. There were also some words or phrases students could use in case of an actual emergency or other necessity. It was explained to us that if the procedure was abused, a student could be required to retake part or all of our two weeks of training at Survival School. Needless to say, that threat was certainly sufficient to dissuade anyone from attempting to circumvent the system.

I do not remember any of the certain words or phrases, but they were chosen to be entirely out of context with anything we might otherwise be experiencing while in the POW camp. For example, during a (student) prisoner interrogation, the interrogator might suddenly say, "Walt Disney. Do you understand what that means, lieutenant (or whatever your rank was)?" and that would be the cue that role playing was suspended for the moment while he went into instructor mode. The instructor would then comment and critique, giving immediate feedback, perhaps noting something the student was doing wrong that could be detrimental to maintaining any degree of safety in an actual POW situation. He might also comment positively on the efficacy just demonstrated by the student, if that were the case. When he was finished, he might say, "Donald Duck. Do you understand what that means, lieutenant (or whatever your rank was)?" and we were all immediately back into where we had been right up to the instructional pause.

The reasoning for these time outs had a sound basis, in my humble opinion. There would be no other time for a student to get that specific one-on-one immediate feedback. If, for example, the instructors made notes to be reviewed with the student in a debriefing after the camp was over, the recall factor would come into play to interfere. Instructor: "Do you remember when you were . . .?" Student: "I think so. Was that when…?" Multiply that by two hundred students in the two-week class, with another two hundred starting in another day or so, and one can see where it would create a huge bottleneck, not to mention being so much less effective for the student.

Another suggestion strongly made in class shortly before we were to begin the field training was for each one of us to buy two plastic baby bottles at the BX (Base Exchange), fill them with water, and take them with us while we did our E&E maneuvers. Before being captured—surrounding activity let us know when capture was imminent—we were to finish drinking the water and discard the empty bottles before we were captured. "In case you were wondering, you WILL get captured." This was decades before bottled water became the prevalent and ubiquitous staple that it is today. I don't know what happened to all those empty plastic baby bottles. Hopefully they were collected, sterilized, and distributed free to mothers in need in the community. I don't remember if my two bottles had pink tops, blue tops, or one of each. The blue would have been less noticeable in the dark, I would think, but it did not really matter—plastic baby bottles would not be part of our GI (Government Issue) survival accoutrements in Southeast Asia.

I wonder what the folks at Base Exchange headquarters thought about the continuing orders for thousands of plastic baby bottles. Someone must have been at least curious.

With POW academics completed, the start of the physical part of our POW training began on the evening of our last day of class. You might be wondering why we did not start until the next day or evening after we had gotten some rest, but that was the whole point—no rest. After the trauma of combat gone wrong, adrenalin spikes, and finding ourselves in an E&E situation, we would not realistically have been all rested up for a saunter through the enemy's real estate. The whole point of the POW training was to make it as realistic as possible without having to actually kill any students—which was a nice thing, I do not mind saying. We had been briefed in the classroom on the different phases we were now about to enter, so we could put into play all of the procedures and techniques we had hopefully been sufficiently attentive to.

Before heading out, we checked to see that each other's faces were properly camouflaged, and we were led to the E&E area. We were all spread out—we were each on our own at this point—and told where and when to get started. We were to stay low to the ground by either crawling or duck walking for about a mile, until we were captured. Either one of those methods of locomotion over uneven cold ground was not uncomfortable—for about a half-minute. Oh, did I mention that there was concertina wire we had to negotiate here and there along the way? And oh, did I also forget to mention there was shooting above where were doing our E&E? (They told us it was "above," anyway.) That is why we had to stay low—that and the fact that there were instructors roaming around—camouflaged, of course—and if you were caught too soon you would be sent back to the start. That last bit was enough to add some realism to the "exercise." And don't forget about the search lights and flares. Did I also mention we student prisoners-of-war-to-be did not have night vision goggles? The roaming instructors did.

The mile of E&Eing was tiring, to say the least; it was designed that way. By the time you heard a soft voice from somewhere tell you to finish any water you had left (Where did he come from? And where did he go already?), you knew that the jig, as they say, was about up. By that time, other than the anxiety of the unknown, you were ready for a "rest"—hopefully, anyway. That had been a tiring day. And it wasn't over yet. . . .

I will not try to reproduce any uninterpreted Vietnamese conversation here (you are welcome), but apparently there were actual Vietnamese "captors" lurking around just waiting for us. All of a sudden bright lights were shining in my face, and these little guys were yelling at me in a language I did not understand. They had AK-47s and were apparently not overly happy that I was not doing what they were yelling at me to do. They stood me up off of the ground and searched me. They took everything useful; they left our boots on. In real life in the jungles of Vietnam, most prisoners were stripped of their boots, socks, belts, and most of everything else. Then they roughly bound my hands behind my back, and put a black hood over my head, jostling me around all the while. I was led . . . somewhere . . . until I heard more voices yelling. I was tied in line with what were other newly-captured Yankee pigs, and we were marched . . . somewhere. Once in a while a phrase in broken English made it clear what was expected next. We clearly got the message that talking among ourselves was strictly verboten (oops—wrong war, wrong continent).

As best as I can recall, we were all separated and taken "inside" somewhere. I was smushed into a box-like wire cage barely large enough for me to scrunch into, my hands still behind my back, my feet on the floor, and my knees on either side of my head. There was not enough room for my head to be upright. When I had trouble finding a position and fitting myself in, I was given some "assistance" in a manner that encouraged me to get my ass in NOW. I started to get the distinct impression that this ordeal was not going to be all fun and games like I had thought it might be. I was far from being the largest GI in the class. I am not sure how they managed to get some of the bigger guys contorted into these cages. Either there were different size cages or some were adjustable. As tightly as I was packed into mine, I knew that one size definitely could not fit all. Remember poor Marvin from Water Survival Training at Homestead?

I also knew I could not stay in this position for any length of time. Talk about misery. As luck would have it, about the time I knew I would not be able to tolerate this scrunchiness any longer, my cage door opened and I managed to fall out—with a little help from my "friends." I did not know how long I had been boxed in—or even how long it had been since I had first been captured. I slowly—too slowly, apparently, based on them prodding and yelling at me—regained my footing in a standing position, and I was then led—a polite euphemism, under the circumstances—somewhere else.

I was put into a black four-by-four-by-four-foot box. This space was simply cavernous compared to the wire cage. While one guy stood guard outside the door, another guy removed my hood and untied my hands. I was told no sleeping and to stay on my feet— no sitting or lying down. If caught, I would be punished. Still, now I had breathing room—the Life of Riley. I had been moved into the "suburbs." But just when I thought things were getting better, time passed. (Did I happen to mention that most American GIs I have ever known were/are taller than four feet? Even me. Even the two-dimensional diagonal is only a fraction over five and a half feet, from the very corner to corner. I am pretty sure the NVA were aware of this little mathematical fact.) Now we were talking misery again. Some "rest" this had turned out to be. It was completely dark inside the box. I could hear bad guys around outside, banging on doors with the butts of their AK-47s (I assumed). Once in a while I could hear a door being suddenly opened and more yelling and banging around. I couldn't hear these little tormentors coming with all the other outside noise around. Abruptly my door opened and light from outside rushed in, revealing the outline of a guard in the doorway. Whew! I had been on my feet that time. It didn't matter; he yelled at me in Vietnamese anyway, pushed me to the back of the box, and closed and locked the door. Whatever the locking mechanism was—perhaps just a slide bolt—it could be unlocked very quickly.

From the outside.

Eventually I tried to find a relatively (EIR) more comfortable position, one which violated the commandments I had been given. Even though the Survival School personnel—Americans, Vietnamese, or others—were making this training as realistic as possible and I knew in the back of my mind that they would not really physically harm me, they could make things miserable while I was there. But I reached a point that I had to try to get a little nap sitting down. Not much of a nap, although how long it was I had no clue. Eventually the door opened again, and a metal container was slid into my box. "YOU EAT ALL!" and he closed and locked the door again. Apparently the Vietnamese are no different from Americans in one regard: When talking to someone who speaks a different language, the louder you say something, the easier it is for them to understand what you are saying. That goes for talking to blind people as well, so I have heard (unintended pun, but what the heck).

Dinner time. Or was it breakfast? Or lunch? Who knew? Who cared? The metal container was about four inches deep and contained what smelled like an onion broth. Not my first choice; a medium rare porterhouse steak was more what I had in mind, but so far the room service at this joint had not exactly been four star. But, prisoners cannot be choosers. As it turned out, the onion broth was not too bad, a judgement most likely influenced by the fact that I had had nothing to eat since dinner back at the Officers Club except a Hershey bar while E&Eing, however long ago that had been. There were even some little pieces of actual onion floating around. I could not see them in the dark, of course, but I could feel them as I drank of the potion. At least I had to assume they were pieces of onion. I did not even want to consider other possibilities. I have never been an adventurous eater anyway, as I mentioned when telling of the rabbit's eye.

Okay, things were getting more tolerable in this POW camp—until I discovered, after I had downed all the broth—all the onions that had settled to the bottom. My stomach was not really in the receptive mood for onions without au jus. The little guard guy said to eat it all, in similar words. His English was better than my Vietnamese. I made an effort, but I just could not finish all of them. The bottom was covered over an inch deep in onions. I was starting to get a bad taste in my mouth, not to mention bad breath in case I had to kiss somebody—like that was going to be an issue. I wondered what was going to happen when the guard came back and found all those onions in the bottom. To this day, over four decades later, I still refuse to eat French onion soup.

I did not have to wonder for long. The next time the door opened, there were two guards. They put the black hood back over my head and tied my hands again. I was led . . . somewhere else . . . which turned out to be one of the interrogation rooms. The interrogation room was really the place to have major concerns. Anything could happen in them. I was thrown inside—well, pushed. I was bigger than the guards, and they would have had trouble throwing me . . . I am just guessing here. Pretty much like one sees in the movies, there was an armed guard in a real uniform. Up to this point my captors wore makeshift uniforms, for the most part. The other guards removed my hood and dragged me to a standing position. After waiting a few moments, obviously designed to let one's imagination conjure unpleasant images in anticipation, a man with the air of accustomed authority entered—an officer, according to his uniform. He took a seat at the small table and metal chair. He put his wheel hat—what we in the US military call a garrison cap—on the table, emblem facing me.

He casually scanned through some papers in a file, supposedly about me, but I had no way of knowing for sure, of course. He could have been reading Vietnamese comics, if they had such things. But he wasn't smiling. He finally looked up as if confirming that I had just materialized in the room upon his mental command. He spoke fluent English. He commanded—I am pretty sure that whenever he said anything it was a command—the guards that had brought me there to untie my wrists. I have no memory of the nature of any of the conversations in this interrogation or the next one I had later. I do recall from class that one defensive ploy we could use would be to feign an illness or injury. At my second interrogation I had decided to feign a serious leg injury—broken or something. This time when the two guards brought me into the room and released me, I collapsed on the floor, both hands grasping at my "injured" leg, as I screamed and pleaded in pain. "MY LEG, MY LEG, I THINK IT'S BROKEN, I NEED MORPHINE. . . ." I have never been accused of being a thespian, and neither was I then, but I was "playing the game" as we had been instructed. When the guards tried to lift me back up, I was totally uncooperative. I was in agony and making sure everybody in the room and anywhere nearby knew it. More of the same. My face was twisted as much as I could make it to look like I was in agony. The interrogation officer ordered me to stand up and be quiet, but I took a chance, ignored him completely, and continued hollering and writhing on the floor.

"Walt Disney. Lieutenant, do you know what that means?"

I sure did. It meant "time out" and that I could be just me for a moment or two and catch a breather. "Yes, sir."

Then the interrogator, now in his role as instructor, proceeded to comment on scene and told me that I had done a realistic job of acting injured. It was a good distraction. But he warned me to be careful if I were ever in the real situation. A NVA interrogator might not give a dong about my injury and more than likely would use it to his advantage. (A dong is the Vietnamese unit of currency. At today's rate of exchange one US Dollar (USD) equals about 22,700 Vietnamese dong (VND). Viewed the other direction, one VND is about 44/100,000th of a USD). In other words, his level of concern for my well-being would be asymptotically close to zippety doo dah.

After too short of a discussion during which he critiqued my "performance" and then told me the situation to expect when we resumed—i.e., leg injury over—he sat back in his chair and said, "Donald Duck. Do you understand what that means, Lieutenant?"

"Yes, sir," and just like that, I was a simulated POW again.

Looking back, although I did not know it at the time, the worst was over, at least as far as I remember my experience.

I still had no idea what time it was, or even what day it was. I was pretty certain that it was still March 1972. But it was still dark, so I guessed it was the second night. We were put into groups of about twenty and "ushered" into dark, earthen underground bunkers. No door, but plenty of room to stretch out and take a nap; I can nap very easily, just about anywhere. I was all set for life as a retiree someday. A couple of guards managed to do what the lack of a door didn't—keep us in unless called for. It was while we were in these groups that several of us formulated an escape plan.

The bunkers were arrayed in a POW encampment bordered by high walls and/or fences. By high I mean perhaps twelve feet or more. There was a central headquarters building where the camp commander and his minions spent most of their time— I'm just guessing here—probably drinking beer and playing cards. There was also an open "kitchen," if I may call it that. Some of the POWs had been assigned KP (Kitchen Police) duty where they got a large pot of water to boil over a wood fire. They were given rice to add to the water and also some type of fish pieces. I have never liked seafood at all, and I really prefer my rice drowned in pot roast or fried chicken gravy. However, neither of these choices were on the menu that night, nor any other, I am sure. I took a little of the fishy rice because we were ordered to by the guards. Although I was hungry, especially after my previous meal of onion broth with sunken onions, whenever that had been, I managed to surreptitiously dump my fishy rice somewhere unseen behind the kitchen. The fishy rice concoction did get me to realize that if I did have the mighty misfortune of becoming a prisoner in Southeast Asia, I was going to get bone-skinny really fast. Either that or I would learn to tolerate seafood. Maybe both.

We were allowed to wander around the yard, with armed guards and search lights in towers on the corners watching over us, and other armed guards wandering around the grounds amongst us. I remember our little group planning a diversion during which a few of us could get out through or over a weakness we had found somewhere along the perimeter. It was probably designed that way so that we could employ some of the techniques we had been taught in class and have a chance to use them. I believe I was to be an escapee. The rules were that if any of us managed to escape, we would return to the camp and would be under a "relaxed" environment until the end of camp. Your guess is as good as mine what a "relaxed" environment meant.

One might wonder why, once we had escaped, we would even consider returning. Easy. Roll call. No shows, if any, would get to do it all over again, starting with the next class. And it would go on our military record. And it would not reflect favorable verbiage.

The POW camp was about over, as the commander called a gathering of all of us. I do not remember anything that was said; I was exhausted, hungry, and not of a mind to listen to any last words of farewell. Just open the gates!

When I got back to my VOQ room, I showered, ate a couple of pieces of fudge, and then fell asleep.

There was a final debriefing for the entire class at 15:00. I had not set an alarm. Oops . . . not good. I admit that I was not motivated to hear anything about a statistical analysis of the past two weeks. I had a plane ticket to San Francisco to meet my wife before finally heading across the Pond. Unfortunately for me, someone took names at the general debriefing and my name was absent from the list. They knew what room I was staying in—for not much longer, buckaroo—and I got a call. As instructed, I reported in uniform to a captain in his office. He asked why I had not attended the debriefing. I had a perfectly good excuse; however, apparently oversleeping is not considered an acceptable excuse in the Air Force. I had a hunch that would be the case, but I did not have any other excuses handy. And I had already played my broken ankle act in the interrogation room.

The captain fussed at me a little and told me he could have me stay and take the whole course again. I humbly advised him that I did indeed regret the negligence, admitted my error, mentioned that I had a plane ticket leaving later that afternoon to meet my wife, and asked what I could do. Apparently I was not the first person to be sitting in this chair in this situation, maybe not even the first that day. He realized how having me repeat the class would generate all kinds of paperwork forward and backward, and make a whole bunch of military clerks, sergeants, and commanding officers—uh, unhappy.

Orders putting me on a C-141 to Clark AB in the Philippines for Jungle Survival School would have to be rescinded and amended or new orders would have to be typed, starting with new orders sending me to the next available class there at Fairchild

AFB; new or amended orders to the jungle school, and ditto for transportation and new reporting date for my intended gunship unit in Thailand.

And that was just the Air Force side. Plans to meet Andrea in San Francisco would have to be changed, and I would possibly lose the money already paid for plane tickets. She had a teaching job, so it was not that easy for her to rearrange schedules again.

Happy ending, however. The captain just wanted to make sure I knew I had screwed up by not attending a mandatory briefing. Then he gave me a really brief synopsis of the debriefing and told me not to do it again. Properly chastised and immensely relieved, I departed his office.

- 34 -

PARTING IS SUCH SWEET SORROW; REALLY, THIS TIME

"Parting is such sweet sorrow." from Shakespeare's *Romeo and Juliet*; my wife taught English Lit in high schools for many years.

Upon completion of the Fairchild Experience, I caught a commercial flight to San Francisco to meet Andrea for a few short, happy, but tearfully-ending days. She rented a car and booked a hotel in the City (as it is referred to by locals). One can do a lot of sightseeing and enjoy many of the varied venues without using a car in San Francisco. When walking is not a particularly desirable option, such as at the end of a day of walking, the nation's only moving National Landmark, the famous Cable Cars, were handily available.

On our final day in San Francisco, Andrea drove me to Travis AFB for my departure. After checking in and saying our sweet goodbyes, I boarded a fully packed C-141 destined for an experience I could only imagine, and preferred not to. Andrea drove back alone to return the rental car at the San Francisco airport and board her flight back to Florida. The exact date that we parted was easy to remember: 1 April 1972 . . .

. . . April Fool's Day.

- 35 -

DEPARTING CONUS FOR JUNGLE SURVIVAL SCHOOL
(CONUS: Continental United States)

As I recall, to add to the already somber atmosphere of the day of my departure from my wife and from the US of A out of Travis AFB, located about fifty-four miles northeast of San Francisco, the day's weather condition was an appropriately gray overcast. My B4 bag (the green canvas Air Force equivalent of the Army and Navy duffle bag) and I boarded an Air Force C-141 Starlifter, along with just over another 150 passengers. Riding facing toward the rear of the plane, such as we were, is not as pleasant as one might imagine. That is, I imagine it might be what one would imagine if one were under the influence of so-called recreational mind-altering drugs. (Never having had any inclination to experiment with such phar-maceuticals myself, (I led a sheltered childhood which extended until—well, it's still extending) I can only imagine what one would imagine. Never mind. This is even confusing me, and I wrote this . . . stuff. It must be time to refill my wine glass.)

The C-141 was retired in 2006 after just over forty years of service. I do not know about current USAF passenger seat configuration on cargo planes, but back then we rode facing backwards. There was a theory that chances of survival would be greater for those of us in the passenger compartment in the event of a less-than-optimal landing after which the aircraft would in all likelihood never fly again, its various parts having been strewn about the impact—er, landing zone.

Adding to the "comfort" of the rear-facing seat orientation was the definite deficit of windows, most of which were in the cockpit. There we were, riding westward for about five and a half hours facing backwards inside a practically windowless tin can—actually, it was mostly aluminum—over millions of miles of water to Hawaii (thousands, millions—a seemingly negligible difference when one is flying over the Pacific; backwards; with no window seat). The fact that we were flying to Hawaii, the Land of Paradise, would at first thought seem to the casual observer to be a pleasant diversion for those of us riding "into the valley of Death" (Tennyson). However, we were on the ground only long enough to refuel, perhaps an hour or so. From there we continued for another semi-eternity to Yokota AB (Air Base) in Fussa, Japan, just west of Tokyo, for more fuel, a quart of oil, a check of the tires and battery and cleaning of the windshield (called a windscreen on an aircraft), and probably a flight crew change. It was my first (and only) visit to mainland Japan. That flight had taken ten or eleven hours from Hawaii. By that time I did not care if I ever saw the inside of another C-141. However, once again we were not there long enough to really go anywhere except for a short break into the air terminal.

Those of us travelling on had a final hop to make on the journey to Clark AB, home of the USAF Jungle Survival School. Clark was a rather large base on the island of Luzon, one of the largest of the 7,641 islands comprising the Philippines; even C-141s could land and take off from there and frequently did. My fellow travelers and I were there for more survival training. A person could get paranoid if he or she thought too much about all the survival training we went through just to get to a war zone: Water SURVIVAL School, Basic SURVIVAL School, which included Escape and Evasion SURVIVAL training and P.O.W. SURVIVAL and now Jungle SURVIVAL School. However, now we were on an urbanized part of a tropical island, about forty miles northwest of Manila, and scheduled to attend the three-day Jungle Survival School. But being concerned about surviving anything could wait until I actually got "in country," as it was called.

Although Jungle School was a three-day course, I spent ten days at Clark. I have no clue why there was the seven-day delay. I am just guessing here, but possibly the aircrew that was to take us on the last leg of our journey decided that their aircraft had some "issues" which needed attention. Okay, strange how these things seem to happen where there are sandy beaches and warm breezes. I never heard of anyone getting stranded for an extra week at Minot, North Dakota or Thule (too-lee), Greenland. That delay left those of us eager to get taken to the war zone with some tough decisions: Where do we go for dinner tonight? What to order at the impressive Sunday brunch at the O' Club? (I can heartily recommend the hot pastrami on pumpernickel—or would if the eruption of nearby Mount Pinatubo hadn't since changed the local geography.)

As in nearly all Air Force schools I have attended, whether it was for half a day or half a year, they all began with classroom instruction, and the Jungle School was no different in this regard. Without the information learned in the classroom, things could be dangerous later out in the field. There were always protocols to follow, sometimes life-saving protocols. Naturally we were told of some of the creatures whose existence, if encountered by unwary or untrained humans, could make one late for dinner . . . forever. Some of these said creatures would actually prefer that you stay for dinner—theirs.

For part of the Jungle School academics we were shown various fauna and flora to be found locally, many of which we might also have occasion to be introduced to, although probably not formally, should we happen to find ourselves roaming through some jungle environment into which we had been gently lowered by our parachute after departing a suddenly terminally inoperable aircraft.

Jackfruit Tree (Photo by Project Manhattan)

An idea of the size of a jackfruit
(Photo: Courtesy of Constantinos Petrinos)

For example, did you know that jackfruit is the largest tree-growing fruit in the world? I didn't until we were told about it. One jackfruit can weigh as much as 120 pounds. For comparison, imagine walking through an orchard or jungle under the over-hanging watermelon or pumpkin trees.

Some of the more dangerous critters were displayed in captivity at the school. To this day I still have a vivid visual recollection of feeding time at the Jungle School. We were in luck, if you are prone to call it that, when I went through the school. The school had in captivity a few of the local jungle denizens, the relatives of which might resent our intrusion into their native habitats. Some would merely be irritated, like the spider monkeys, although they can make quite a screechy fuss. A hungry fifty-foot-long python would have been a different tale altogether. Well, perhaps I exaggerate slightly, but if I ever come across one unleashed and staring at me and licking his lips, I can guarantee he would look every bit of fifty feet long. We were shown a caged python, or perhaps it was a boa constrictor or an anaconda except that anacondas are found in South America. Let us settle on python; the particular kind of large snake makes no difference here. Besides, python has fewer letters for me to type. All snakes look alike to me; what's more, I consider all snakes to be venomous, I don't care what the snake-ologists tell us. While doing a little research I read that ALL snakes are descended from a venomous ancestor; that is good enough for me and I rest my case.

A live chicken was put in the python cage. I do not know if chickens are intelligent enough to realize that, when trapped in a confined space with such a creature, the odds of it—the chicken—becoming dinner are pretty much 100 percent. Not that it (the chicken) can do anything to rectify its situation. It probably could not even do the math. Such was the scene we witnessed at this particular time of the sunny day in April. Based on a chicken-to-python size ratio, I would think that one measly little chicken would do for the appetizer. Maybe a whole cow would do for the snake's entrée. I remember watching in awe and with no small amount of disgust as the two-hundred-pound snake stalked the live chicken that was put into his cage (or her cage; snake gender didn't really matter to us, and I am sure it mattered even less to the chicken). I will not go into details here; if you want your own visual image, you are own your own. But to this day, even several decades later, I can still vividly recall the chicken's legs sticking out of the python's mouth waiting to follow the rest of the chicken in as it was swallowed. I did not bother to take a picture of it.

Not an image I relish (bad choice of words, I know).

We learned some other fascinating things about the jungle; specifically, that if a person survived most of the hazards prevalent in such an environment and did not get eaten by giant python snakes or other carnivorous creatures, he or she could live comfortably for extended periods of time. Two plants which are ubiquitous in Southeast Asian jungles, the banana tree and the bamboo tree, can provide all of the basic requisites a human would need: food, water, and shelter.

A machete would be very helpful. A machete was not part of our basic Air Force-issued survival gear, so I do not know where I would ordinarily have come across one. Let us just assume that I serendipitously located one in the aircraft before bailing out, or perhaps more credibly, I happen to come across some US Army or Marine troops who were more properly equipped for jungle living. The Jungle Survival School instructors issued us machetes when we went out into the jungle. We had to return them when the in-the-jungle part of our training was concluded.

The banana tree offers bananas (duh), which provide at least some nourishment, although I suppose a diet consisting only of bananas could get old pretty quickly. You can cut down a banana tree about three feet up the trunk from the ground, then hollow out a bowl shape a few inches in the top of the stump. Come back in about an hour, and the bowl will be full of water. Remove that first bowl of water; use it for cleaning or just splash it out, as it would not be particularly good for drinking. However, the bowl will keep refilling and yield a continuous supply of sweet-tasting drinking water.

Food and water are taken care of. The banana tree leaves can grow to about twenty feet long. Their use is limited only by one's imagination. They can be used in cooking, for clothing, or for shelter, to name three. They can provide a relatively (EIR) comfortable bed to sleep on and a roof and siding material for the shelter frame that one can build from bamboo. The banana leaf has a single vein down the middle. Make a longitudinal slit in it long enough to open and put it over your head. Voilà! Instant poncho.

The bamboo plant also has a variety of uses. The Reader may have used bamboo fishing poles as a kid. As I alluded to above, it can be cut into poles with your miraculously-acquired machete and used to construct a shelter and "out buildings"—dining room, pantry, latrine, store room, workshop and tool shed, et cetera. Other tools can be made: a shovel (to dig the latrine and a rain trench around the "bedroom"), weapons (spears, bows and arrows, knives, punji stakes (described below)), eating utensils (butter knife, steak knife, soup spoon, tea spoon, shrimp fork, salad fork, entrée fork), drinking straws, and any number of things.

We were cautioned to be careful when around cut bamboo—it is very sharp—and can slice through skin in a heartbeat. When we were out in the jungle, in spite of forewarnings, I still managed to get a small half-inch cut on the back of my hand; I still have the scar. In civilization it would not have been a concern; wipe off the blood, slap on a Band-Aid, and press on improvising with bamboo. However, in the jungle, even small cuts can get infected from a variety of bacteria my body had not been previously exposed to and developed an immunity to. The Philippino guide that accompanied us on our half-day jungle exploits found something that to me looked like dirt. He cleaned the cut using some water from our cut banana tree, mushed the "dirt" around on my "wound," strapped it on with a bamboo leaf, and it was pronounced that I should then be able to remain among the two-handed living.

There were displays at the school where the various nasty things the Vietnamese devised from bamboo were re-created for our viewing pleasure. These weapons were indigenous, ingenious, easily constructed at no cost, evil concoctions left for unwary victims, or even weary wary victims. They were concealed with natural ground vegetation, often with all but invisible trip wires. You may have heard of punji stakes. They are sharpened sticks of various lengths made from bamboo. The nature of the way bamboo grows makes the shaping of it into very sharp points with equally sharp edges easily done. Weapons systems acquisition in the US military and Congressional House Appropriations establishments is a lengthy and expensive process usually involving a number of years and billions of dollars in cost overruns alone. Bamboo is ubiquitous in all of Southeast Asia. From inception to completion and implementation, a "weapon system" over there was but a matter of hours or even minutes. Cost was zero. They obviously use the KISS method: Keep It Simple, Stupid.

The photo above exhibits the simple ingenuity of the Vietnamese. The center bamboo pole is about five feet long; the viciously sharp punji stakes protruding from it are about a foot or so long. Sometimes the stakes were coated with excrement on the ends to infect any wounds they inflicted. This booby trap would be located in narrow jungle paths and hidden by foliage blended with the environment. Someone unfortunate enough to step onto one end of the device could puncture a foot and/or lower leg while falling forward into the other end, which would be slammed into the upper body or face. Not a pretty sight. (Personal photo.)

In the above photo you can see a bamboo "bridge." The center support poles would be cut most of the way through so that they would break easily when walked across. The punji stakes would be concealed. Very creative. Very deadly. (Personal photo.)

Below is Bob Ray, a fellow aviator I befriended on my way across the Big Pond who was heading to a different unit at Nahkon Phanom Royal Thai AFB. He is carefully holding another jungle weapon—a version of "The Flying Mud Bomb"—a heavy ball of dried mud with punji stakes implanted in it. This unfriendly device was connected to a rope or vine and suspended along the narrow jungle path. When the concealed tripwire or rope was unwittingly activated, the mud ball would swing down along the path line, impaling some unfortunate bodies.

First Lieutenant Bob Ray examining—carefully—a mud ball embedded with punji spikes. (Personal photo.)

NVA automatic antiaircraft artillery; that's NOT an NVA in the photo. (Personal photo of me.)

The above photo shows "automatic anti-aircraft artillery," which resembled a large bow and arrow. The bow was a bamboo tree bent into shape. The arrow was another straight bamboo tree, trimmed and sharpened. The NVA could set these up just about anywhere and then leave. Cost: zero. Setup time: negligible. If a Super Jolly Green HH-53 rescue helicopter happened to hover over an area where one of these nearly invisible "automatic" weapons was located in an effort to extract a downed airman or other troops in trouble, the downdraft from the rotating helicopter blades would be sufficient to release the giant arrow.

If arrow trajectory happened to hit the rotating blades—on a helicopter they are called wings, thus the term "rotary-winged" aircraft—it could make for an unhappy day and the rescuers could find themselves needing rescue themselves and probably medical treatment. In the meantime, the NVA who had made the weapon at some point in the past might not be anywhere around. That would be desirable in an otherwise highly undesirable situation; however, in all likelihood, other nearby NVA would be drawn to all the commotion in the area.

Once they were made, all of these weapons and many more like them could simply be left in place and forgotten about. They could accomplish their purpose without further monitoring. Of course, I suppose it would have been possible for other NVA to unwittingly encounter these traps. I never heard if they had a system of surreptitiously marking the locations or otherwise communicating to their comrades where they were placed. Or if they even cared.

After seeing these weapons of individual destruction (as opposed to weapons of mass destruction—WMD, e.g., things like hydrogen bombs), I envied even less, if that were possible, our ground troops who marched through the dense jungles and rice paddies. Not my idea of a civilized way to fight a war. And yes, I am being completely facetious with that comment. (This has nothing to do with the current topic, but did you know this bit of trivia: "facetious" is a word that contains all the vowels in order? One better: "facetiously" also includes the y.)

Obviously as an aircrew member I was less likely to encounter any of these unpleasantries than our ground troops were; but if, through an un-serendipitous turn of events, I found myself traipsing along wondering if snakes really did "taste just like chicken," I had to at least be aware of some of the possible hazards that might make my already ruined night even worse. Fortunately for me, I had had a lot of survival training along the way, none of which I ever had to remember or use in an emergency situation. The closest thing to a punji stake I have ever come across in Marietta, Georgia, is perhaps an occasional wooden shish kabob.

Could be chicken—or python.

On the last day of Jungle School we boarded a Jolly Green and headed for the hills. We were going to get a chance to practice our skills hiding in a jungle. After exiting the helicopter, we got a briefing. There was a specified area we were to stay within, and we were to be given a certain amount of time—ten or fifteen minutes—in which to hide. We were each given two one-pound bags of rice. The rice was not for us to eat. As it happens, the Air

Force employed a number of Negritos—natives indigenous to the area—to find us when our time to get ourselves hidden was up. There might have been an aural signal, like a horn blast or whistle, to let us and the Negritos know it was time for hunting to begin. If we were found, we were to give the Negrito a bag of rice and then go hide again. I never did get found, and when I heard the signal ending the fun and games, I managed to find my way back to the group. Apparently the rice was the payment the Negritos received. Talk about cheap labor. But then, what use would they have for money? They lived in the jungle hills; they could not eat money. Rice they could eat. If I had known that beforehand, I might have made myself more findable after feeling sufficiently pleased about my hiding skills.

So much for Jungle Survival School. Not exactly a toughie; it was actually an enjoyable three days. I mentioned at the beginning of this chapter that I was at Clark AB for ten days. As it turned out, the airplane that was to be our transportation to Thailand supposedly really did have some mechanical issues; a likely story. With a cargo full of us troops there would not have been room for all of the aircrew's rattan and teak furniture and other local souvenirs. That delay extended my departure for a week (what a surprise). Darn; I so wanted to get to the war zone and experience being shot at for real. Too bad I had not thought to bring along my golf clubs . . . .

PART 3

- 36 -

ARRIVAL IN-COUNTRY

After a tortuous seven days of lying in the sun and suffering the travails of leisure on a tropical island (yes, I'll have another *mai tai*, please) awaiting my final flight to take me to Thailand to start fighting the war, the airplane, a C-130, was finally "repaired." That is to say, most likely the aircrew had decided that they had "milked" their TDY in the Philippines as long as they felt they could get away with; had bought all the wicker baskets, paintings, jewelry, and rattan furniture that they could manage; and were finally ready to take us onward.

The C-130 Hercules, a large USAF cargo plane, had four turboprop engines. Turboprop is a semi-self-explanatory hybrid word referring to the turbine (think: jet engine), each geared to drive large four-blade propellers.

While I was on active duty, the C-130 had the loudest cockpit noise level of any aircraft in the inventory, according to a study that was probably done by the ear plug industry. The aircrew members wore headsets which, besides allowing intercom and radio communication, also provided some sound muffling. Those of us sitting sideways in the cargo compartment in troop seats in the back of the plane—which were made of aluminum, canvas, and straps—were given small sound suppression thingies, a.k.a ear plugs, and told not to chew them. They were/are soft and spongy and could be mistaken for chewable sweet treats by children, none of which (children, that is) we were taking to a war zone, and by those of doubtful competency in English literacy and/or common sense. Most of us, however, were familiar with the ~~tasty~~ ear plugs, but there was always a first-time rider. That being said, you might want to be advised that they really are not particularly tasty. Maybe with a splash of Tabasco.

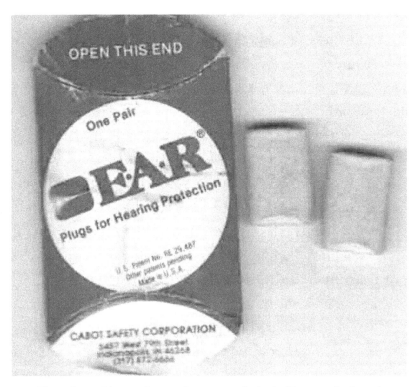

Ear plugs (shown largr than actual size) (Personal photo.)

I still have several pairs of these. They somewhat help decrease the decibels that reach one's eardrums. I have had the pair in the photo since sometime in the early 1970s. They are obviously not doing me much good going unused. During part of Undergraduate Pilot Training I was around the T-37 jet trainer, fondly known as The Tweet, a 6,000 pound machine that converts fuel into noise. After Southeast Asia I flew KC-135 tankers for seven years. It had the Air Force's second noisiest cockpit, according to the same study. Those ear plug guys really got around. But apparently they regarded any attempt to test the AC-119K as futile. There is a very good chance that the environments in the T-37, C-130, AC-119K, and KC-135 contributed to—i.e., definitely caused—my hearing loss and tinnitus. "Huh?" and "What?" and "Say again" are a predominant part of my vocabulary.

Nearly a year ago I finally capitulated to the complaints from the family about it, complaints such as "Hey, Chick, One Eight Hundred H-E-A-R-I-N-G." Fortunately for me, the Southeast Regional VA Hospital is down the road only about thirty miles. My wife had recently gotten hearing aids from a civilian audiologist for about $3,000 or so. The latest issue top-of-the-line hearing aids the VA gave me as a veteran benefit cost about $8,000; free for me, of course, other than the sixty-mile round trip a few times. Plus, they include free batteries.

On my first visit I was put in a mostly sound-proof booth and did the standard push-the-button-when-you-hear-a-sound routine. I have always had trouble with these tests. My tinnitus is a constant high-pitched noise that will be with me forever or longer, whichever comes first. I am never sure if the sound is inside my ears or from the earphones, so my button-pushing is rather erratic.

I told my son I was finally going there; he texted me a photo of an audiologist who worked there that he had dated. She was quite lovely in the photo and in person. I actually met her on my second visit and we exchanged a few brief comments.

The audiologist —not my son's acquaintance—confirmed that I certainly could use some help, and we scheduled my next appointment. While at that second appointment a technician packed some soft, gooey stuff into my right ear; it needed to take a few minutes to set. The procedure was very much like when the dentist puts gobs of soft, pink, or baby blue, or grey gooey stuff in your mouth. Next my left ear was treated with the same courtesy. When I went back on my third visit I was fitted with my form-fitting hearing aids. The VA audiologist told me he had already ordered a six-month supply of batteries to be sent to my home. Also free. And about every four years I can get new, latest, state-of-the-art devices. The VA is the largest purchaser of hearing aids in the country, or maybe he said in the world. I might not have heard him quite right.

If you veterans have not visited your local VA Hospital, I can definitely recommend that you do. But good luck trying to find a handicap parking place; there are several handicap-only parking *lots* at the Atlanta hospital. I occasionally have to make my own parking spot; I am very particular where I park my little car.

It seems I digressed somewhat again, but you should have come to expect that by now. I previously left us, which includes me the writer and you the Reader, leaving Clark AB on the C-130. I was on my last flight to conclude the seven-month odyssey that began with my graduation from UPT. At last I would be reporting to my new squadron at Nahkon Phanom (NKP) Royal Thai Air Force Base (RTAFB), Thailand, formerly known as Siam, where I would be able to start putting into practice some of the expensive extensive training I had received. I hoped I would not have to employ any of said training that had the words "Survival School" in the titles. My original orders after pilot training were to the 18th Special Operations Squadron (SOS) based at Phan Rang AB somewhere around Cam Rahn Bay in South Vietnam. Don't try looking up South Vietnam—or even North Vietnam, for that matter—on a map unless you have one that predates 1975. The old 1906 world geography book that is falling apart on our coffee table shows all of the area, except Siam, as being part of China.

Cam Rahn Bay is considered the jewel of Vietnam, but I would not know. During the interval between pilot training graduation and my arrival "in-country," the 18th SOS was relocated to NKP. Although it was not the jewel of Thailand, it was nevertheless a relatively (EIR) pleasant place to be assigned. More pleasant, in my humble opinion, during the hot dry season than the rainy season.

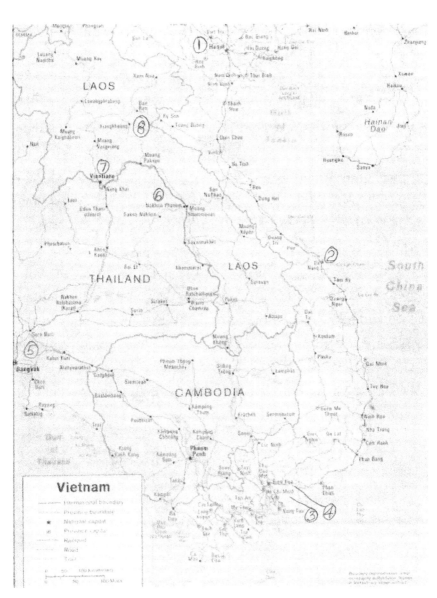

Southeast Asia, post 1975 (Personal photo.)

- 37 -

ARRIVAL AT NKP

The map may be a little hard to read, so put on your reading specs if you haven't already. I had to use mine plus an assist from a magnifying glass for some spots. (My electron microscope is in the shop for its hundred-hour inspection at the moment.) I could not find a date on this map, but it is obviously printed after 1975. Some telltale indications are that there is only Vietnam, not a North and a South Vietnam; there is no indication of the Demilitarized Zone (DMZ) about a hundred miles north of Da Nang; and the city formerly named Saigon is labeled Ho Chi Minh City. Some points that I mention in various anecdotes are, starting near the top and working generally approximately clockwise:1) Hanoi in former North Vietnam; 2) Da Nang in former South Vietnam; 3) Ho Chi Minh City, formerly Saigon in former South Vietnam; 4) Bien Hoa near Ho Chi Minh City; 5) Bangkok, Thailand (formerly Siam); 6) Nakhon Phanom, Thailand; 7) Vientiane, Laos; 8) Plain of Jars, Laos.

Compared to the flight across the vastness of the Pacific Ocean, the "hop" to Thailand was easily bearable. It was a pleasant sunny day (did I mention that the weather there was usually quite pleasant?) on 10 April 1972 when I arrived at NKP and reported to my 18th SOS squadron commander. After a pleasant greeting (pleasant weather tends to enhance general . . . pleasantness) and brief introduction to the squadron offices, I was told that the usual in-processing paperwork could wait until the next day. I was now officially "in-country," which was and would be important as far as the military was, and still is, concerned. Serving in a designated "war zone" had positive ramifications affecting future assignments, priority status, promotions, and a number of other military and civilian opportunities.

That's me serving my country from the chair in front of my hootch.
(Personal photo.)

I was assigned to a room in a VOQ, a.k.a. a hootch. I do not know where that particular name came from, and I never thought to ask. After I saw the building, it seemed like an appropriate name for it. Them, actually. Each combat, maintenance, and other unit on the base had its own hootch or hootches, depending on the number of personnel assigned to it. Officers were quartered (no, we were not cut into four pieces; that is a military term for "housed") together, two to a room, in separate hootches from the enlisted troops, but we were all assigned to areas where similar types were housed. That may sound a bit confusing, so to elucidate: aircrew members, whether officer or enlisted, were housed with others who shared similar working hours and schedules. Whenever we returned to our rooms, we would do so quietly in case the roommate was sleeping. My room was dark inside except for a lamp or two. There was one window, and the door had a glass pane, but they were both covered with metal foil, cardboard, and/or black cloth to keep the outside light outside where it belonged. We flew at night and mostly slept during the day, depending on our mission schedules.

When I hauled my A-3 bag and settled into my new "home," I met my roommate. Funny thing—when I had been in T-38s in pilot training back in Del Rio, Texas, 8,775 "great circle" (straight line over the surface of the earth) miles east of where I was standing, he had been the chief of T-38 Stan/Eval (Standardization and Evaluation). Talk about a small world. I do not remember ever having flown with him, but if I could remember his name I could check my pilot log book for it. I always recorded the name of the captain with whom I had flown a mission. I would have other similar encounters in the months to come. More similar meetings awaited during my visit to the Far East.

Do not let the compass directionality confuse you. Those of you who would like a brief explanation to clarify East-West travel, read on. Others may skip the next three paragraphs and miss out on nothing. Compass details were—detailed, earlier.

Although to go the shortest distance to Texas from Thailand one would travel eastward, there is the tiny matter of crossing an invisible, imaginary line designated as the International Date Line, the 180°meridian (the north-south lines on a chart or map), where west of it is tomorrow and east of it is yesterday. The line is straight, for the most part, but it zigs and zags through the Bering Strait and the Bering Sea, separating the Russian Kamchatka Peninsula (might sound familiar from the board game Risk) and the Alaskan Aleutian Islands. Beginning just south of the Equator, it does some more zigging and zagging to keep certain island groups together. West of the line is the East; East of it is the West. That is, until you cross the Prime Meridian, which runs through the Greenwich (or as the English pronounce it, Grenich) Observatory in Greenwich, England. Isn't it nice how that works? This is the 0° line of longitude (meridian) along which the perspective East of the line is actually East and West is West. Crossing the International Date Line reverses perspective and East becomes West and West becomes East.

There are actually two different circumstances being explained, and that may be why the Reader might find things confusing, at least as I have explained them. The *direction* one is travelling may be easterly or westerly. If I leave Atlanta, Georgia heading eastward, I could cross every meridian on the globe and arrive back at Atlanta, never having travelled westerly. However, at any giving location on the planet, I would either be at an East longitude if my position were East of the 0° meridian to half-way around the world to the International Date Line. Likewise, the reverse is true from West of 0° to the 180° line. If this is still confusing, now would be an excellent time to go get yourself a small globe or a world map and re-read my explanation of easterly and westerly. Then go have another glass of cabernet and watch a movie on TV.

There. I hope that disambiguated travelling across Planet Earth geography for you.

The base at NKP was a Special Operations Wing with a special variety of aircraft flying a special variety of missions. Now isn't that just special? Besides our AC-119K Stinger gunships, there were QU-22Bs that flew electronic ground monitoring missions along the supply trails; HH-53 Jolly Green Giant helicopters that flew supplies to outposts, recovered American military troops in trouble, and other missions; OV-10 Broncos which flew close air support and area coordinator for troops in contact—i.e., on the ground fighting the enemy—and rescue missions; A1E Sandys that flew close air support and aircrew recovery; and probably some others I don't remember.

The next day, my first full day at the 18th SOS, I got a ride to my squadron for in-processing paperwork and briefings. Some briefings were briefer than others. Some weren't (brief). I was also issued equipment, especially the nylon mesh flight vest that had lots of pockets to hold supplies I would need if I ever found myself no longer in the safety and comfort of an aircraft cockpit. I was also issued a pair of jungle combat boots that were leather around the foot and with an olive drab green canvass-like material around the ankle. They were a little cooler than full leather combat boots, and they had a knobbier tread. We were issued new jungle boots every six months, whether we needed them or not. My first pair showed very little wear, so when my new ones were issued, I found somewhere to store them until they eventually wound up in my hold baggage shipment to the States, still new and unused.

- 38 -

THAI CUSTOMS AND COURTESIES

I was scheduled by our admin types to go through all the training on base, such as the "you really don't want to get yourself in this condition" film shown by the medical staff on the hazards of getting careless with the local girls off base. There was a flight line safety briefing. If any air crewman didn't know about flight line safety at this point, he or she should never have been allowed to leave the States. (Although there were no female Air Force combat pilots at the time, there were female officers and enlisted personnel in other AFSCs (Air Force Specialty Codes, e.g., doctor.) We were shown a map of where everything was on base and the hours of operation of each facility. Another briefing item involved getting a license to drive on base. Our military driver's license was stamped on the back accordingly. Over the years mine collected a few other stamps of approval.

There was also a detailed briefing on Thai customs and courtesies, some of them peculiar to Thailand, as far as I know. One custom to be respected at all costs regarded the King of Thailand, Bhumibol Adulyadej. He and the Queen were highly revered by the Thai people; the King's picture was present in every business establishment and every household in the country. His likeness also appeared on all Thai currency (the baht) and coins. One baht was equal to five US cents then; it is around three cents now. One story told at the briefing was about a young and not so bright enlisted GI who, while visiting downtown and feeling arrogant, portrayed the personification of Eugene Burdick's and William Lederer's book *"The Ugly American,"* though it is highly unlikely that the airman ever heard of it, much less read it. He lit a cigar with a 100 baht note ($5 USD). The kid's blatant disregard, or perhaps forgetfulness, led to a serious incident requiring the attention of the US diplomat to Thailand. The airman was immediately accosted and put in jail. The diplomat had to intervene to keep him from a lengthy jail sentence or other severe punishment. Of course, the airman was expeditiously returned to the US and probably received further attention from the military.

An interesting Thai custom was their view of the hierarchy of the body. By this I mean that the higher the part of the body, the more respect was afforded. The head, and actually the top of the head, was therefore the most esteemed part of the body, and ipso facto the bottom of the feet were held in the lowest regard. One did not put one's hand on the head of a Thai, or even pat him/her on the back or shoulder. The fact that the hand could be raised higher than the head did not alter their relative (EIR) significance. It would seem to be a simple enough custom to respect.

However, consider: if you were sitting somewhere with a Thai person around and you crossed your ankle across your knee, and who among us has not done that as a matter of comfort and without forethought, you would be insulting the Thai person, perhaps unwittingly, but it certainly would be noticed by the Thai. You had just exposed the bottom of your foot, considered by the Thais to be unclean, to the eyes of the Thai. Most Thai, at least those more genteelly bred, may not say anything to The Ugly American, but the insult would have presented itself just the same. It would be highly unlikely of a Thai to allow you to date his or her son or daughter. That custom was one that we Americans had to be consciously aware of over there, or even outside their country. Over four and a half decades later I still notice it when I see someone sitting that way, and I am not even Thai. It does not insult me, but that little bit of custom still rests on the edges of my mind.

A number of religious congregations across the United States used to host international college students over the Christmas break. Most US students, faculty, and staff would head home for the holidays, leaving college campuses quiet and lonely. Many foreign students could not afford to go back home and return again, some because of the financial burden and some by virtue of their home country's bureaucratic restrictions, the Peoples Republic of China, for example. My wife and I used to host three or four such students each year for two or three days. Most of them were fairly fluent in English, or at least understood enough English that, perhaps with a bit of help from physical gestures, we could communicate and keep them fed and entertained. Occasionally we would get a Thai student or two, and remembering a couple of courtesies was not too foreign to us then. Also, it made the students feel somewhat more at ease when my wife would greet them with "*Sawadee ka,*" and as a male I would use the greeting" *Sawadee krup.*" These greetings are spelled with variations, depending on whose source you read, but the pronunciation differential is barely noticeable. Like "*Sayonara*" in Japan and "*Aloha*" in Hawaii, the terms are also used as farewell.

Another Thai custom strange to Americans is, or was at the time, the Thai view regarding the expression of affection in public. In this country, as well as in Europe and many other areas of the world, public affection, in moderation, of course, is a natural human trait, and so it is in Thailand, but with a twist. Co-sexual interdigitation—i.e., persons of the opposite sex holding hands in public—is frowned upon. If I were holding my wife's hand as we strolled along in Thailand to visit a Thai, the person we visited would be insulted because of their perception of the female that accompanied me—a woman of obvious low character, what we might sometimes refer to over here as "a working girl." It would not matter that she was my wife. And yes, the double standard was accepted. The female was considered to be the person of lower class. (The prevalence of the internet has caused the planet to effectively "shrink," and some customs may have changed.) I'll touch on this topic again when Andrea arrives in-country in a later chapter.

On the other hand (speaking of hands (he wrote offhandedly)), it was perfectly common and accepted for males to hold hands or walk arm in arm; likewise for females. There were no concerns of inappropriateness nor any connotations of sexuality. (Try that in this country . . . .) Of course, as anywhere else, there were limits to the constitution of acceptable public behavior, but we did not need to be briefed any further on the topic.

During our in-country briefings we were advised to adhere to Thai customs when among the Thai people. Sage advice anywhere, regardless of the country. I did not read the 1958 novel *The Ugly American* until after returning to the States.

There were no doubt other in-coming briefings about things we needed to know, but I believe I have covered the highlights.

While I was in pilot training, the Air Force transitioned from the old, easily-flammable but cooler cotton flight suits to the new Nomex nylon flame-retardant ones. Flame retardant meant that rather than burning easily, it would melt on your skin first. But apparently—and I am speculating now—the melting point of the nylon fabric is higher than the flash point of the cotton. Since it is hot in Thailand, even up in the northeast corner of the country where Nakhon Phenom is located, we wore the old cotton flight suits for non-flying duties. They were modified by having the sleeves shortened, various patches sewn on, and personal info— name, rank, wings—embroidered on by local tailors, seamstresses, or other such handy persons. Of course, the metal zippers got hot, just like coming fresh out of the dryer at home.

Finally on 19 April I had an orientation flight, which was an actual combat mission at 4500 feet over the Plain of Jars. (AHA!—I told you I would get us there eventually.) My second mission—the one that got my attention—was the next evening . . . .

- 39 -

TAKING THE "WAR" PERSONALLY

And now, to finally continue this tale of adventure, so to speak (really, this time).

There I was (still) at 4500 feet over the Plain of Jars (PDJ) in the Kingdom of Laos, sitting in the copilot's seat of an old AC-119K Stinger Gunship.

Plain of Jars, Laos (Photo courtesy of: Misadventures Magazine)

We had departed the relative (EIR) safety of our main base at Nakhon Phanom on a combat mission northward across the Mekong River to our target area in the PDJ in Laos. That was my very second combat mission since arrival in-country. The trip to our target area took about forty-five minutes or so, as I recall. Not surprisingly, it took about that much time to return to base (RTB), depending on which particular target area in the PDJ we were initially fragged (short for fragmented orders, i.e., assigned) and the area to which we had roamed looking for other targets of opportunity until departure time. RTB time was calculated based on where we were and the amount of fuel remaining; however, most of our missions were about 3.3 hours of logged flight time. Some simple mental calculations will quickly reveal that we had a little less than two hours "on station" in the target area.

On most flights we were loaded with approximately 12,000 rounds of 20 mm ammunition for the Vulcan cannons and 30,000 rounds of 7.62 mm for the mini-guns. That might sound like a bunch of firepower, and it was. However, as the Reader may recall, the two Vulcans were set to fire at a rate of 2,500 rounds per minute (rpm) each, and the four mini-guns were set at a rate of 6,000 rpm each. That was enough for just under two and a half minutes of total firing time for the Vulcans and only a minute and a quarter of total firing time for the mini-guns, assuming all guns were put on the line—i.e., switched on to activate when the pilot squeezed the trigger button.

Not all guns were on the line each time; the gun selection was determined by the composition of the target. For example, if trucks were spotted on the Ho Chi Minh Trail, the Vulcan cannons were used. If we spotted troops, usually just the mini-guns were put on line. We would get the attention of other mixed targets—i.e., troops, trucks, AAA gun emplacements—with all six of our guns ablazing. With the six mini-gun barrels each spitting out bullets at one hundred rounds per *second*, jams could and would occur in one or more guns at any given time. Ditto with the Vulcan cannons, even though they were set to rotate more slowly (EIR). As I mentioned in an earlier chapter, with the six barrels of each gun spinning so rapidly, if the pilot did not allow a few seconds between firing bursts, the spinning barrels would not have a chance to slow sufficiently before being energized to begin spinning again. The result often meant that the mechanics of the gun would cause it to jam, thus earning the gunners' appreciation for the opportunity to have to spend time correcting the (pilot's) error, thus relieving them from the opportunity to get bored. (Sarcastic? Who, me?)

The three gunners in the plane were trained in managing and correcting any such mishaps quickly and efficiently, so a gun would usually only be off the line momentarily, depending on the nature of the jam. Typically, depending on our target, all six guns would be put on the line if supply trucks were targeted. I would not even want to try to imagine being the driver of one of those trucks when the sudden torrential flood of lead came raining down literally all around. There would be no place to go; not that it would really matter. With that much screaming destruction everywhere, death would mercifully leave no time for fear.

Some nights were more productive than others for any particular mission. Usually the 18th SOS was tasked to fly about three or four sorties to the PDJ on any given night. As the first airplane was leaving the target area a second would be arriving—

at a different altitude and location. A mid-air collision would have made for a long night's trek back home for everyone concerned, not to mention having to explain to the commander and the commander's commander, et cetera, on up the chain of command, why we had left Laos with two perfectly good (EIR) aerospace combat vehicles all bent up and in pieces on the ground somewhere in hostile territory.

During the more productive sorties, we located enemy troops, supply trucks, and ammunition or fuel storage "facilities." These evenings passed more quickly, and we felt we had accomplished something useful on a successful mission. The supply trucks and fuel and ammunition storage dumps presented bright visual evidence on the ground below when the 20 mm rounds we had fired had indeed found their targets. We usually flew around to various known target areas. The table navigator plotted where these target areas were located for each sortie, based on our pre-flight intel briefings, and we looked for other targets of opportunity—i.e., NVA who just happened to be in the wrong (for them) places at the wrong (for them) times. If we managed to have a busy night, we would have expended all of our ammunition except for the forty .38 caliber rounds each of us carried in our survival vests. Every one of us would rather have traded in his .38 caliber six-shot government-issued pistol for a second survival radio and batteries, but the Air Force Powers That Be had decided otherwise.

On less productive nights the missions were more boring (EIR) and seemed longer, although they were much quieter since there was less shooting, and sometimes no shooting at all. More often than not, though, we at least found "something" to shoot at.

"Looks to me like it could be a truck; how 'bout you?"

"Yep, sure looks like it could definitely possibly be a truck to me, too, maybe. We oughtta' shoot it."

And so we did.

My very second combat mission . . .

. . . was not one of those slow nights. We were in the target area over the PDJ, doing our job of NVA supply line interdiction. When we did not need or want to use the flares or "flashlight" and when we were flying into areas of known or suspected anti-aircraft artillery (AAA: triple A), it was the job of the IO to strap himself in securely and hang part of the way out of the aircraft near the back. He would be on the lookout for "in-coming," which was AAA heading in our direction. With a little quickly-learned experience, he could distinguish between tracer rounds that were merely headed in our general vicinity and those rounds that were aimed accurately enough to get his attention.

For this next little segment of the story, those of you born after about 1990 might want to go into your dad's or mom's dresser drawer and find his or her watch—you know, that thing you have seen them wear on their wrists and look at occasionally when they want to know what time it is (but not the digital watches; they will not help you understand o'clock positions). It will have a strap or linked metal band that has a round (usually, although there are some fancier square-shaped ones) "face," or "dial," and on this face there are twelve numbers arranged in a circle around the edge. The twelve is at the top. The next number to your right as you are looking at it is the one. Next is the two, and so on all the way around to the eleven and back to the twelve, which should still be waiting there at the top. This direction is called "clockwise (cw)." Going backwards around the dial is called "counter-clockwise (ccw)," but we are not concerned with that here. Unless you are left-handed. If you are unlucky and your folks only have watches with marks where the twelve, three, six, and nine should be, you may have difficulty understanding when I refer to "o'clock" positions. Muddle through as best as you can. It isn't rocket surgery.

Getting back, the IO, for example, normally would call in a voice loud enough to be heard via the interphone to which we were all connected and listening, "Triple A seven o'clock no sweat," meant there was AAA being fired at us from the left rear of the aircraft, the nose being at twelve o'clock. I know that you geezers—er, you more chronologically advanced persons—understand o'clock. This overly-explained info herein is for the benefit of those (what's the opposite of geezers? Whippersnappers?) Future Rocket Surgeons of America (FRSoA). In movies like *Top Gun*, some police movies, and other action films and TV shows, you may have heard the expression "Check six" or "I've got your six." These mean, "Watch out behind you" and "I've got your back covered," respectively.

"No sweat" meant exactly what you think it meant—that the AAA was inaccurate, of no immediate concern, and ergo, not creating body chemistry that results in sweat. The IO was able to assess fairly quickly—out of necessity, in a second or less—the accuracy of the tracers coming at us. Remember, the tracers were only one out of every several rounds, and in our case nine; I do not know the ratio in the case of those coming against gravity in our direction. The more accurate the AAA, the higher, faster, and louder the IO's voice was over the interphone.

To visualize the technique used, hold a pencil between your thumb and index finger about an arm's length from your face (that's probably about as far as you could reach anyway). Notice that you can observe some length of the pencil, depending on the pencil's angle to your eyes. Slowly turn the pencil in your fingers so that it aims to point straight at your eyes. Now notice how the pencil's image seems to shorten as the pencil straightens toward you. Its cross-sectional area diminishes until it is at a minimum when the pencil is pointed right at you. The IO could identify the accuracy of the incoming tracers by their visual presentation. If he could see short lines streaking through the night sky, they were not coming directly at him—meaning all of us, which included me. The shorter the tracer lines he saw, the more head-on they were coming. If all he could see was a point . . . .

On the night of my very second combat mission in Southeast Asia, we were taking some in-coming AAA here and there. At that time I was too inexperienced—did I mention that this was only my very second combat mission?—to have a proper frame of reference about the inherent dangers of hunks of 23 mm lead flying in one's direction at about Mach 2. I remember well those words echoing in my headset and in all nine others:

"TRIPLEANINEO'CLOCK BREAKRIGHT**BREAKRIGHT** **BREAKRIGHT!!!**"

With the index finger of my Nomex-gloved left hand I bent the two jet engine throttle toggle switches fully forward, running the rapidly-spooling engines up to 100% rpm; the flight engineer probably shoved the recips faster. I'm not sure; I was busy grabbing the copilot yoke to help the captain get the aircraft turning to the right and away from the dead-on accurate AAA, and . . .

. . . I looked out my window on the *right* side of the cockpit.

I could see the 23 mm tracer rounds just outside my window! Outside MY window!! And we were turning right towards them!!!

On the night of 21 April 1972, in the right seat of the cockpit of Stinger AC-119K gunship tail number 830, at 4,500 feet over the Plain of Jars in Laos . . . that was the moment I started taking the war in Vietnam personally. . . . .

A mini-epilogue of what went on in those few seconds might clarify things in case you are not familiar with the terminology.

"Break right!" could be translated to mean: "Pilot, if you are not otherwise engaged in activities requiring your full attention at the moment, we have very accurate triple A heading in our direction that should reach us in a minimal amount of time with potentially disastrous and possibly deadly results unless you choose to bank this aircraft to the right in an expeditious manner. **NOW** would be a good time. Sir." Of course, all ten crewmembers were connected to the intercom via the headsets we wore, and everybody heard the "Break right!" warning at the same time. Even though the triple A coming at us was doing so at a rate of Mach whatever and the AC-119K could turn away at a rate of a turtle in January, it is amazing that we did not lose more airplanes and crew than we did.

Banking to the right—toward the side that my window was on—was the evasive maneuver to be taken when the AAA was coming from nine o'clock (the left side, for you FRSoA Readers). In a fighter or acrobatic-type airplane, the aircraft response would be immediate. In the old converted cargo-to-combat AC-119K, even with the two jet-engine augmentation, turning right, or left, or any which way, would take about a week and a half. That is probably why the tracers outside my window just flew harmlessly on past us—and me. We couldn't turn into them fast enough to get hit. And from my perspective, that was a good thing.

You might be wondering, if the AAA was coming from the left, why I was seeing it to the right. Lo and behold! The NVA were firing more than one round at a time at us, and the IO was hanging (partially) outside the left side of the airplane. Most of the important stuff was on the left side—the four mini-guns, the two Vulcan cannons, the NOS, and the Illuminator. I suppose I should also include the captain, also on the left side, and the gunners; that leaves only the FE, the FLIR, the table nav, and me. When the IO saw points of AAA coming at him, he was not too concerned about the rounds heading away toward the other side of the plane, especially when he only had fractions of seconds to make decisions.

- 40 -

THE BITCH

This chapter will be a bit of a departure from my customarily-adopted lighter style found in the rest of this collection of memoirs. It has little or no humor in it, because the topic is not in the least bit humorous. It is about a person who is, in my opinion, a traitor to our country. However, it is not just *my* opinion; thousands of other patriotic Americans share it with me. It is no coincidence that I was inspired to begin the writing of this particular memory on 9-11-2016. There are several reasons why I will not mention her name, the primary reason being, as you will discern upon reading further, is that I hold her in such contempt—the same contempt she has shown to her country and its service men and women—that I would dishonor them by mentioning her name.

According to definitions presented on Wikipedia and other sources, *treason* is specifically defined in the United States Constitution, the only crime so defined. Article III, section 3 reads:

"Treason against the United States, shall consist only in levying War against them, *or in adhering to their Enemies, giving them Aid and Comfort.*" (Italics mine.)

The United States Code at 18 U.S.C. § 2381 states that "whoever, owing allegiance to the United States, levies war against them or adheres to their enemies, giving them aid and comfort within the United States or elsewhere, is guilty of treason and shall suffer death. . . ."

Over fifty-eight thousand Americans died in combat in Vietnam. Thousands more died directly from combat-related wounds, but their deaths were undoubtedly classified otherwise by the government for purposes of attempting to ameliorate the dismal public relations situation extant at the time. Over two million more were injured. More subjectively, no one knows how many more lives and families were cataclysmically disrupted or ruined because of the psychological effects of combat. I was among the more fortunate of the men and women who survived serving our country in Vietnam. However, to this day I still harbor an undaunted ill will for her. Some memories are not easily forgotten, and some reprehensible deeds are not easily forgiven.

For personal reasons, I prefer to not say or use the name of person who is the subject of this chapter. She and her companions so blatantly "gave them [the North Vietnamese government] aid and comfort" that it defies logic, the law, and the US Constitution that they were not tried, convicted, and severely punished according to law for their actions.

An American woman aiding and abetting the enemy

The above photo appeared on the top half of the front page of the *"Pacific Stars and Stripes* (PS&S)," a newspaper published for the benefit of the US military personnel serving in the Pacific Theater of operations, which included Southeast Asia. My research so far has been unsuccessful in tracking down the exact date of the publication in which this photo was displayed with the accompanying front page headline and story. The exact date is not critical at this juncture in time, it being several decades after the fact. However, the photo, headline, and article were in a PS&S issue in approximately June 1972.

I was stationed at Nakhon Phanom (NKP) RTAFB at the time. I was assigned as a copilot on the AC-119K "Stinger" Gunship. There are many details about any number of subjects that I do not remember from that long ago, but to this day I still vividly remember where I was when I first saw the photo in my morning copy of the PS&S. I was relaxing outside my hootch on a pleasant, sunny day, pretty much like I am in the photo below. Yes, the guy in the middle of the photo is me, back when I was slightly more studly (he said modestly).

Look familiar? It is the same one as earlier.

The Caucasian woman in the middle of the black and white newspaper photo, wearing a helmet, is looking into the gunsight of a quad-23 mm (four barrels) anti-aircraft artillery gun somewhere in the vicinity of Hanoi, the capitol of North Vietnam. These guns were used heavily in defense of Hanoi and throughout North and South Vietnam. Many of them, especially in the Hanoi area, were radar-guided. They could put a lot of multi-supersonic lead in the sky in the vicinity of our military aircraft.

23 mm

The black circle above is the cross-sectional size of the 23 mm bullets, thousands of mini-missiles filling the skies over Vietnam. It only took one of them hitting any of the many right places on an aircraft to convert it from a speeding aerodynamic vehicle to a collection of materials that, within a moment or so, would become junk scattered and burning somewhere in a Vietnamese jungle below. It also changed the lives of the aircrew men forever; for many, it ended their lives.

All too often those bullets managed to find their targets, frequently resulting in the necessity for the aircrew to bail out over very unfriendly territory. Many were subsequently captured, beaten, and force-marched barefooted to the real unpleasantness awaiting them in the infamous Hanoi Hilton prison. The so-called Hanoi Hilton was not in the Michelin registry of four-star hotels.

The hand holding a cylindrical barrel-shaped object pointing at her from behind is not holding a weapon (unfortunately), at least not a physical weapon. It was indeed part of her (the villain of this story) arsenal of psychological weapons, however. It was a microphone being held by a member of her publicity entourage. The young girl to her left is holding what appears to be a handheld recorder. The Reader may or may not recognize the woman, especially if you happen to be a bit more on the youthful side (i.e., anyone younger than me (EIR)). If I saw an out-of-context cropped photo today showing just the woman, I probably would no longer recognize her, although the helmet might be a significant telltale clue.

The subject female was born into the privileged Hollywood elite (yes, I am aware that may be redundant). As a misinformed adult with pie-in-the-sky ideals, she used her family status and affluence to travel into the heart of the enemy territory, where she decried the US involvement in Vietnamese affairs of state. Millions of US citizens disagreed with the executive branch of our government when the Powers That Be decided that sending our troops over there was a good idea. For that matter, it has yet to be disambiguated for me exactly why it was a good idea for us to be there. Many US military personnel felt the same way, but they went when ordered to do so. The American casualty numbers from the Vietnam "War" are the fourth largest of any war the United States participated in, exceeded only by the Civil War (or War of Northern Aggression, as it was and is known in the South), WWII, and WWI. Those soldiers, sailors, marines, and airmen who were sufficiently unfortunate to be captured and taken to Hanoi were not treated as honored guests like the traitor and her accomplices were.

There were at the time, and still are, numerous legal methods of expressing one's opinions of dissension apropos government actions. Written and verbal comments to the media, protest rallies, marches, letters to those holding public office, etc. None of these include "giving aid and comfort to the enemy."

After a number of years I finally decided in my mind to attribute her misconstrued and misplaced ideologies to her youth at the time (even though she is chronologically nine years my senior) and contented myself to accept her right to her own philosophies, since by that time it was evident that she was never going to be tried, convicted, and executed as a traitor. However, just about the time I was rationalizing in my mind her egregious activities, she publicly apologized for them all, admitting that she had been wrong.

My interpretation of her apology has always been this: She held her convictions and acted upon them, not realizing that her manifestations were criminal and deplorable. Okay, what was done was done. But her subsequent apology was an admission of guilt, denying the righteousness of her little Hanoi visit years before. In one stroke she brought me back to my senses; she (finally) realized the error of her ways and wanted forgiveness. I had nearly forgiven her (not that she had ever been concerned a whit about my or anyone else's standards of rectitude), but her apology said to me that she no longer held to her earlier convictions (not the best choice of words here) and thus undermined any hints of my reconciling her activities with justice. There is no statute of limitations for treason she publically admitted to."

I cannot adequately express my utter disdain for this woman. Fortunately for me, I do not have to expose myself to anything having to do with her. She and I do not move in the same social circles; I am not likely to be exposed to her presence anywhere. I would not have even bothered to write this bit of ranting, as it were, except that nearly every military person of my generation that I have had occasion to reminisce with has felt as I do. This is for all of us. Sorry I could not find humor in it.

- 41 -

DUTY OFFICER AT NKP

Getting back on track (Track? What track? Did any of you see a track?), part of my in-processing to the squadron involved the mandatory choosing of which additional duties I would prefer. "None" was not one of my options. In UPT we had had enough to keep us busy just studying and learning to fly, and all of my time in the interim since graduation had been in a Temporary Duty status. At last I was at a Permanent Change of Station (PCS) location where many of the various non-full-time jobs were assigned to squadron personnel, commensurate with rank. "Commensurate with rank" means, for example, that officers and NCOs would not be assigned to emptying the trash cans. All of us FNGs (friendly new guys (just go with that one)) were put on the schedule to pull duty officer after normal business hours. Well, after normal daylight office business hours. As a gunship unit, our normal "business" hours were when it was dark over the Ho Chi Minh Trail and the Plain of Jars.

Short of any kind of emergency, these nights spent as duty officer were typically very slow and quiet. Times spent as duty officer were mostly spent catching up on reading or going through the Pacific Exchange (PACEX) Catalogue to select stereo gear, jewelry, porcelain figurines, or other items of interest to send to folks back home. Naturally there was a checklist of items to be done. However, it was nothing like checklists for getting an aircraft ready to become airborne. The military thrives very well on checklists; it would be easier for all concerned if the civilian world did also. While otherwise engaged passing the time, an occasional phone call, usually about something of a trivial nature, would interrupt a duty officer's reverie.

Also, while on the eight-hour or four-hour or however-many-hour duty, we were not allowed to leave the phones unmanned. One could get hungry, and even at NKP most places were closed at oh dark thirty. Fortunately, we could call a little Thai restaurant that would deliver. However, as one might reasonably expect, there was not an extensive delivery menu during those hours. Hamburger, cheeseburger, French fries, and Coke just about covered it. And you did not want to ask what the hamburgers were made from. The French fries were not all that great either, but when one is hungry and has limited choices, one does not complain. Nobody would care anyway. There was a war going on, or so we were told. The most memorable item, however, was the Coca-Cola. Imagine my surprise the first time I received my fresh cuisine and the beverage du nuit. The Coke did not come in a bottle. It did not come in a can. It was not brought by a woman. It was brought by a man. (My apologies to Dr. Seuss, R.I.P.) It did, however, come in a plastic sandwich bag, a.k.a. a baggie, with a straw sticking out and held in place by a rubber band wrapped around a few times. A baggie of Coca-Cola. Go figure.

It is odd the small experiences in life one remembers.

- 42 -

FANCY MEETING YOU HERE

With a net growth rate currently at about 20,000 people per hour and increasing at an increasing rate, the world's population is over seven and a half billion people. The number written in numerical form when I started this small chapter is more impressive: 7,652,589,000. I have to round off somewhat because it is already 7,652,590,000 after writing one sentence. The net growth rate, i.e., births minus deaths, is not increasing seemingly as fast as you have just read, because I assume just about anyone literate in English can read much more quickly than I can compose and type, with constant oops's, corrections, and revisions, and that is when I am using BOTH typing fingers.

While searching the web for world population data, I found a chart showing estimates of each billion people and the approximate year that number was attained. The first billion since the human population was assumed to have begun was reached close to the year 1800. It took nearly 125 years for the population to double. A third of a century later, yet another billion folks had joined the crowd. It only took fourteen years to add another billion (we were up to four billion). Since the mid-1970s, the *rate* of increase has leveled off somewhat, but whereas it is estimated that it took 200,000 years to reach the first billion and 125 years to reach the second billion, it has taken only eleven years to add the most recent billion. But please don't look askance at me; I did not do it. Andrea and I claim responsibility for only one; our second child was twelve hours old already when we met him, although it took seven months for his adoption to become "official."

As the astute Reader has by now noticed, I tend to write seemingly copious amounts of extraneous information that, upon first reading, creates curiosity as to where I might be going with it and as to just how it relates to the story line, such as it is. The Reader will also notice that I eventually tie everything, or at least most things, in with the story. Often when I am doing a little research for factual details I get carried away, especially on topics that interest me. When in doubt, glance again at the Stephan Pastis comic strip at the beginning of this manuscript.

Now that the world population is understood, the reason I delved into it in the first place is to frame a reference for this chapter. In our travels, even if it is only to the grocery store, all of us at one time or the other have run into (hopefully not literally) a long-lost friend, or acquaintance, or relative. When it happens at the local grocery store—better make that The Home Depot . . . the majority of my Readers are most likely of the male persuasion—smiles usually manifest themselves and witty greetings like, "Hi, haven't seen you in a while," may begin a conversation. Sometimes it is the other person who says it to you, activating the synapses of your mind into high gear as you try to remember who this person is, where you know him or her from, and especially his or her name. The farther from home we find ourselves—in another city or state—the greater the surprise. Being across a continent or an ocean, or both, adds an order of magnitude to the equation. Having it happening more than once in the same area adds another order of magnitude.

In an earlier chapter I mentioned that my first roommate at NKP had been a T-38 Standardization and Evaluation pilot where I had gone to pilot training in Texas. I did not really know him, but I knew who he was. He was one person out of almost four billion possible people I could have been roomed with.

An even more incredible event occurred not long afterward. I was with our crew one night in base operations at NKP preparing for a mission. Lo and behold, Doug Malloy came strolling in wearing his flight suit. He and I had been in AFROTC together at Miami University. I had last seen him two years prior and 8,452 miles away from where we stood. Doug was flying or navigating an RB-66 or an RB-57—one of those, as I recall, but I am not sure which. He was not stationed at NKP, but he just so happened to have landed there to refuel and had come into base operations right at the same date and time that I was there. NKP was not on his usual route, which made the coincidental meeting even less likely. And—here is where I bring in the world population statistics you have been waiting for—at that particular moment in the time-space continuum, there were still just under four billion people on our planet. Furthermore, he was the *second* guy I had known previously when we crossed paths in Thailand. What are the odds? I do not know, but if Isaac Asimov were still alive, I am sure I could email him the data and he could run the permutation calculations for me.

But we are not finished yet. In early July, Andrea came to Bangkok, and I hopped on the C-130 Klong shuttle from NKP to meet her. Why the route is called the Klong shuttle escapes me; perhaps it has to do with the klongs—small canals and waterways—in Bangkok. The details are covered at length (oh, goody) in a later chapter. One morning I sat on the civilian side of Don Muang Airport in Bangkok trying for the third day in a row to get back to Nakhon Phanom on the C-130, and I was told for the third time in a row that the plane was full and there was no seat available for me. As I sat there, along came the C-130 aircrew walking in front of me to the plane. I recognized one of the guys—"Gualt" Gualtieri. I cannot imagine where he got that nickname, but moving right along, Gualt had been in my pilot training class back in Del Rio, Texas. And there he was, right there in Don Muang Airport, at the same four-dimensional time/date spatial coordinates as I was, allowing for a two or three foot separation. *Now* what odds do the bookmakers in Las Vegas give it? First the Stan/Eval pilot, then Doug Malloy, and now Gualtieri. And just to make the coincidences even less likely, Gualt was the copilot on that very same C-130 shuttle I was trying to get on. When he asked me what I was doing there, I told him of my plight. Gualt said, "You are in your flight suit; you can ride in the cockpit jump seat." There is a jump seat in many airplanes that is reserved for other crew members. He told me he would get the okay from the captain, but that it would be an inconsequential formality. He didn't actually say "inconsequential formality," but it translates the same even if the Reader prefers other verbiage.

Let us figure now—that makes three different guys from the States on three different dates in three different locations. The chances of all three happening have to be getting pretty slim. (Stop here for a moment as I digress briefly: Why do "slim chance" and "fat chance" refer to the same odds?)

But wait! There's more, K-mart shoppers!

A few chapters later I briefly mention yet another guy from my pilot training class, Terry Tabor, who was flying OV-10s out of NKP. That makes four guys now. Out of nearly four billion people. That's billion with a B. It would seem totally improbable to me, except that I was there for all four.

Now that we all know that the odds are apparently impossible and could never have happened and that I must drinking some of that el cheapo 59 cents a gallon Wednesday afternoon vintage of Ripple (I can assure you that the odds of that are even less likely), it occurs to me that there are certain factors which mitigate the odds against. One, all four of us were active duty USAF. I cannot find a website that has the information I need, so let us make a WAG (Wild . . . Guess) of about 300,000. Next, we were all officers. How does 100,000 sound? Continuing, we were all rated, meaning that we were all pilots (or navigators—not sure about Malloy, although I think he was a pilot also). That brings us down to perhaps 70,000. Next, we were all male, and since there were no female USAF aviators in combat at the time, divide by two, giving us 35,000. Next, we were all company grade officers, meaning rank below major (though I think the Stan/Eval guy might have just made major). Call it 25,000 now. We were all flying in Southeast Asia at the time, so perhaps 12,000, okay? All in Thailand. 6,000? Remember, these numbers are all complete guesses on my part, but this method of deduction is approximately the method Isaac Asimov would have used.

No further data points come to mind to continue reducing the odds, so we are now at one in 6,000, which is just a tad fewer than nearly 4,000,000,000. Statistically, we start with odds of one in 6,000; however, we must calculate the combinations three more times, which drives the odds of four chance encounters back up a bit, a "bit" being something in the gazillion range; either that or I have done the math incorrectly. (The odds of that happening are perhaps one in two. I don't think Asimov had these issues.)

Hmmmm. The Reader might want to disregard this chapter.

P.S. The world population is now about 7,652,606,000, which is 17,000 more than when I started this bit of scientific investigation. I type rather slowly, even using both fingers.

- 43 -

MARS CALL

No, this chapter has nothing to do with the planet Mars or E.T. calling home. To quench your thirst for science fiction or knowledge of astronomy, I recommend that you refer to numerous other sources. Isaac Asimov is an excellent source for both of the above, especially for disambiguating science.

The Military Affiliate Radio System, as it was known in 1972 when I had a few occasions to use it, is now known as the Military Auxiliary Radio System. "A rose by any other name. . . ." The system is a program run by the Department of Defense incorporating the services of military and volunteer private amateur ham radio operators to provide auxiliary and emergency communications. Its function for most of us overseas was to provide "phone patches"—i.e., relays—to our families back home. This system was in place many years before the advent of the ubiquitous use of cell phones. Even so, the MARS system is still in use today, providing a reserve of personnel trained in military radio communications, techniques, and procedures.

Such procedures may have changed some over the years; I have not had reason to keep up with its evolution. My experience stems from the few MARS calls I made while I was in Southeast Asia in 1972 or, more specifically, NKP RTAFB, Thailand.

There were several means of communicating back home allowing loved ones to know we were still alive and doing well—or at least doing okay . . . or at least still alive—and letting us hear news from home. Letters were the mainstay. For those of you born after about the mid-1980s, letters were things written on actual paper by hand using a pencil or pen or by using a typewriter. Naturally, the process of physically transporting a piece of paper in an envelope nine thousand miles across an ocean and a continent (or portions thereof) was not the most efficient means of communication, and, depending on how often one wrote, letters could and occasionally did get temporally crossed.

My wife, Andrea, and I wrote to each other nearly every day. In order to keep some semblance of "Who's On First?" we learned early on to number our letters to each other. It was not uncommon for two or more letters to arrive on the same day, or even for letter number twenty-eight to arrive before letter number twenty-seven.

Another medium of communicating back home was via cassette voice tapes. Again, for those of you who are relatively late-comers to the planet . . . oh, never mind; go ask your grandparents. This process involved sending the occasional personal-recorded rambling message back home on a magnetic tape in a plastic dual-spool thingy about the size of the palm of your hand. The recipient would listen to the tape a time or few before recording a reply over the tape or sending a new cassette back across the Big Pond. Unfortunately, a lot of personal first-hand histories of the goings on in the war zone were lost by having been recorded over. Probably many forward-thinking or perhaps sentimental recipients would keep the received voice cassettes and then record return messages on new tapes. These cassettes travelled the same way as paper letters and took about as much time to make the journey. The typical length of time for what is referred to today as snail mail to cross the Pacific was about a week. In 1972 that seemed like a long time. On the other hand, whenever I order wine from California to be shipped to me in Marietta, Georgia, it takes seven days. I could pay really expensive (EIR) shipping fees to have the wine shipped by air-conditioned air and ground, but I would rather spend the money on wine I can buy here than on humongous shipping charges.

My family and I were not so prescient as to save the cassettes for posterity. While recently (EIR) cleaning out a drawer, as I am wont to do every couple of decades, I came across a 1972 voice tape labeled "Chick to stateside folks" (from Thailand). As far as I know, that is the only surviving sixty minutes of my voice droning on about "much ado about nothing." We no longer have a cassette tape player, but our 2000 Dodge minivan had one. Amazingly, Andrea and I were able to listen to the entire tape during a road trip. The amazing part was not that both of us were able to listen to my not-so-fascinating commentary in my unremarkably droll voice (my recorded voice sounds to me to be distinctly from the back-woods of the South). The amazing part was that this 44-year-old cassette tape had not deteriorated and was still intact.

However, we have since sold the Dodge minivan after our son Ian gave Andrea his BMW SUV. (There is a nice story about that, which I have written and will put in another book someday. It does not have a cassette player. Go figure.) Since then, a friend who has the knowledge and right equipment was able to transfer the cassette tape onto a CD for me, presumably a more durable medium, one would think. Time will tell. However, chances are not optimal that I will live to age 113 to find out.

A fourth means of communicating with persons of interest stateside (no, you do not have to backtrack in your reading; I did indeed skip the *third* method, but I promise I will circumnavigate us back to it momentarily) and certainly by far the most desirable of any, was to actually visit with them in person. This method was facilitated via that magic phrase, R & R (Rest and Recuperation, or Recreation, or Relaxation, or . . . (different roses, same pleasure). During the Vietnam conflict, R & R usually involved meeting someone in Hawaii or some other Pacific island paradise. When aforesaid meeting was between a military person and a very dear-to-the-heart stateside person with whom there was a romantic attachment, any actual "rest and recuperation" most likely did not occur until the GI returned to the war zone.

As promised, the third and final method of across-the-Pond communication I will discuss was not at all the most desirable method. In fact, it was definitely the most awkward, but at least it was among the arsenal of methods available to us under the normal circumstances of everyday-type chit chat. At last we get to the MARS calls.

At the outset I described the nature of the MARS system. (Yes, I know that Military Affiliate Radio System system is redundant, but such is the lexicon of our language. As a prime example, nothing is perhaps more commonly pervasive today than the redundant PIN number. Along those lines, and because when I really get warmed up on the keyboard I use *both* fingers, rather than type a request for an "email address," I simply ask for an eddress. Seems only logical to me.) Getting back (unfortunately for you, perhaps, a Reader cannot control an author's wanderings), I can only speak from my own experience with MARS at NKP and do not imply that it was the same everywhere in Southeast Asia, although I suspect the protocol was pretty similar.

One did not merely find a phone and dial home through some mysterious MARS station located somewhere on the planet—Earth, that is. A little coordination between Andrea and me was involved. We would schedule a time period when she would be home to receive a call and when I would be available to try to initiate it. On the night—it always worked out to be night on my end of our call—I had to go to the MARS station on base and place my request. I would leave the local radio operator the name and stateside telephone number of my wife, and he would give me an approximate time for me to return for the call to be patched through.

The mechanics of the way MARS calls worked were a little similar to how the old Mayberry RFD switchboard worked. Sheriff Andy Taylor would pick up the phone and say, "Sarah (pronounced Say ruh), would you please connect me with Aunt (aint) Bea?" We were given instructions on the correct use of the system, on subjects to avoid, and on adherence to security. Like Sarah, the MARS operator, or possibly even an operator at each end, had to listen in to monitor the conversation. The reason was more mechanical than anything else, as a mechanical to/from switch had to be switched, depending on who was speaking. The person on each end of the conversation had to say "Over" after speaking to let the operator or operators know to switch from transmit to receive and vice versa on the other end. When the radio operator on my end had the call ready, my first MARS call to Andrea since I had left her in San Francisco a month or two prior went something like:

Me: "Hello . . .

. . . uh, over." (This saying "over" business took some getting used to. Plus there was a slight time lag between speakers speaking and hearing.)

Andrea: "Hello . . .

. . . over." (It wasn't just me.)

"Can you hear me okay? . . . Uh . . . over?"

"Pretty well. Can you hear me okay? . . . over?"

"Pretty well. How have you been? . . . over?"

"Fine. How are you doing? . . . over?"

"I'm doing fine. I got your letter number twelve, over." (Starting to get the rhythm of saying "over.")

"I got two of yours yesterday—Saturday, over."

Operator: "Sir, you have one minute left." (We only had five minutes to talk, maybe ten. I do not remember for certain; others were waiting to make their calls.)

"Okay, I guess we have to go. I love you. Over" (Although it was necessary under the conditions, I never liked saying "over" after "I love you." Even whenever I wrote/write it in a letter or note, I did/do not add any ending punctuation.)

"I love you, too. over."

"Bye. over."

"Bye. over."

That may not be an exact transcript of the conversation, but it is close enough for you to get an idea of the initial awkwardness. Conversation did not flow smoothly. Even in subsequent calls, the awkwardness was present, though we got used to saying "over."

Fortunately, after her school year of teaching in Florida was finished, Andrea moved to Bangkok for the duration. No more "over."

Be glad you have cell phones, or cranial implants, or whatever you Readers in my future may enjoy.

Over.

- 44 -

GOOD NEWS/BAD NEWS

MG Badge

The good news is about Charlie's 1953 MG TD . . . .

While we were going through training together at Hurlburt Field, Florida, one of the guys—Charlie; I do not remember his last name—had a really nice classic car, a yellow 1953 MG TD. He had spent several years rebuilding and restoring it, getting authentic replacement parts, getting pieces re-chromed or re-painted, leather replaced, the whole nine yards. It was truly a labor of love. The car was an absolute beauty; running boards, chromed radiator grill and bumpers, "bug eye" headlights, low slung body. Everything about the car that you could see was pristine. I had to be careful not to drool on it. I got to ride in it with him a couple of times, smiling all the way. *Popular Mechanics* magazine tested one like Charlie's and reported an acceleration from zero to sixty miles per hour in just over 18 seconds, which was better than the previous models' time of just over 22 seconds.

1953 MG TD, listed for sale for $35,000

Andrea and I had planned for me to extend my stay in Southeast Asia until June of 1973, when her school year teaching at International School Bangkok was over. (She had come to live in Bangkok and had gotten a high school teaching position. More about all of that a little later.) We had planned on ordering an MG Midget, which we would pick up in England after spending a few days in Singapore. We were in no hurry to get back to the US and thought we would take advantage of an opportunity to take about a month's leave touring Europe in our new little car. We would then have it shipped to wherever my next assignment would be, unless, of course, I was lucky enough to get an assignment anywhere in Europe. In that case we would just drive it there.

None of that happened. ("The best laid plans. . . .") At the Paris peace talks, Dr. Henry Kissinger finally managed to negotiate a cessation of hostilities in Vietnam, which meant no more shooting at people and things. Since doing just that was the Stinger job description, our Stinger unit was out of a job, so to speak. My two-month extension turned into a three-month curtailment. So much for our grandiose plans. And so much for a European assignment. Wright-Patterson AFB in Dayton, Ohio, was not a bad assignment, but it wasn't Europe.

When Andrea and I got settled at Wright-Patt AFB in the summer of 1973, we bought a blue 1972 MGB for $2,200. It was a fun little car. It was my first—and eventually last—experience with British Leyland. Those Readers familiar with British Leyland are most likely smiling at this very moment. They know what is coming. Or perhaps they are frowning because I have just reminded them of unpleasant memories.

1972 MGB Roadster

British Leyland was a British automotive engineering and manufacturing conglomerate. Its chief notoriety was in the field of automotive electrical systems. The MG series of cars is one; Triumph is another. And let us not forget Jaguar, Austin, Land Rover, and several others.

My introduction to the troublesome British Leyland electrical system occurred only a month or two after we bought the MGB. It was a dead battery, which I finally found not under the hood (American English for bonnet) as in most American cars, nor in the trunk (boot), which I found out eight years later is where the Germans prefer, but in the small space behind the driver and passenger seats, under the fabric thingy and metal plate covering it. Not enough room for a child seat, but my flight manual bag would fit okay. Alas, I had found not one but two batteries. Two six-volt batteries wired in series to yield twelve volts for the electrical system. After determining which battery was the dead one—the one that did not generate sparks to the jumper cables—my next job was to locate a place that sold six-volt car batteries of the size I needed to fit into one side of the battery compartment. Amazon.com had not yet been invented. About one month later, the battery on the other side died. At least by that time I did not have to reinvent the wheel, although someone should have reinvented British Leyland (actually, that did eventually happen).

There were also three windscreen wipers. Naturally, they are sold in pairs. Americans have a mismatch very much like that. There are ten hot dogs in a regular size package. There are only eight buns. To get them to come out evenly, one would have to buy five bags of buns and four packages of hot dogs. Just another engineering marvel of the twentieth century. Back to the MGB, it had two carburetors (remember those?), which is not unusual, but they had to be balanced using something like a tuning fork. (Sounds like a B-flat; better bring the front one up another half-tone.) About the time our first kidlet was born eight years later, it was time to sell both the MGB, a two-seat roadster, and our Pontiac Lemans, a sporty two-door sedan. Other than being a two-door, the Pontiac would have been okay, but the MG got so that it would not hold a charge. If I charged it overnight, it would last long enough to crank the engine once. Then pffffft. We bought our first Honda wagon (minivans would not come out in the American market for another six years) and first BMW sedan, both family-friendly cars.

About now the Reader may be wondering, and justly so, what all this MG and British Leyland business has to do with the go-ings on in Vietnam. I began this chapter describing Charlie's 1953 MG TD, the one he had worked on for five years.

The bad news is also about Charlie's 1953 MG TD. Not long after we had settled down at NKP, Charlie got a call (or it could have been a letter) from his wife back home. His yellow pride and joy had burned up from a fire caused by the electrical system.

All in all, he took it rather stoically. There was not much he could do about it from 9,000 miles away.

- 45 -

P1D1 AND MICKEY MOUSE

At the NKP O' Club the P1D1 was not quite this fancy,
but the pineapple was freshly sliced

Nakhon Phanom RTAFB was a relatively (EIR) quiet base, as far as Air Force bases go, even with aircraft taking off and landing all the time and it being in a war zone (sort of). Even though the actual fighting was being done mostly in Vietnam and Laos – and Cambodia, but only those who were actually there and the

Powers-That-Be who ordered them there were supposed to know anything about the clandestine American involvement in hostilities in that particular country (the Secretary disavows any knowledge of…) – there were at least a half dozen USAF installations in Thailand, bunches of US Army inhabitations, and probably some Navy and Marine facilities as well, from which the "war effort" – and it certainly was indeed an effort – was supported. NKP was in an out-of-the way location out in the boonies in northeast Thailand, just across the Mekong River from Laos. Although quite a variety of "war birds" were based there, the noises and other vestiges of war were not evident in the otherwise peaceful serenity of the countryside atmosphere.

Around dinner time each evening, it was not a matter of having to decide *where* to eat; choices were rather limited. There were the clubs: Officers' Club (O' Club) for officers (duh), the NCO Club for NCOs, and I believe there was an Airmen's Club for the airmen. Clever how that works. There may also have been a grill at the bowling alley, but I really do not remember if NKP even actually had a bowling alley, and if it did, I do not remember ever eating there. The big decisions each night were *what* to have for dinner. And even those decisions were made from very finite menu choices. As is (or was) typical in Southeast Asia at the time, menu items were frequently numbered. My favorite dessert in the land of heat and humidity was P1D1. P1 was the first pineapple choice: one slice of freshly-cut pineapple. D1 was the first dessert item: a scoop of vanilla ice cream. P1D1 was a slice of pineapple with a scoop of vanilla ice cream on top. Quite refreshing.

Of course, for those of us not scheduled to fly within eight hours, there was a reasonable assortment of alcoholic beverages to choose from—to accompany and supplement dinner, of course. Having led a relatively (need I say it? EIR) sheltered life, I was introduced to various drinking games designed to determine who would buy the next round of drinks.

One game I remember in particular was a dollar bill game. I don't remember now how to actually play it, although it was not rocket surgery; it was about four and a half decades ago. The bottom line was that whoever lost the game bought the round of drinks. I distinctly remember playing during one happy hour at the O' Club. There were seven of us sitting around the table, enjoying the company and revelry. This was before I had "discovered" the pleasures of the vine—there may not even have been any wine behind the bar anyway. Most of us were consuming mixed drinks. You know the kind—appletinis, pink ladies, mimosas—the kind of frufru stuff that hardcore veteran USAF-trained killer pilots drink when we are 10,000 plus or minus miles away from home.

I finally lost a round and had to buy for everyone, on my meager 1st lieutenant's salary. I still remember having to shell out the $1.40 to cover the bill for that round of drinks.

Most of us just kept a tab at the club; it was easier all around for both us and the club. Whenever we incurred charges there, we simply signed our name and O' Club number to the ticket and settled up each month. A famous (at NKP) story that went around was about one particularly clever lieutenant, probably a business major in college, who thought of an intriguing idea—probably inspired after a couple of hours of happy hour drinking. He and his buddies started signing Mickey Mouse on their tickets. Others heard about it and started doing it also. After a couple or three weeks went by, someone working at the club noticed what was happening and had a brilliant idea. The waiters/waitresses were instructed that the next time they saw someone signing Mickey Mouse, they were to immediately get the club manager. The manager brought the ticket to the lieutenant and verified that it was his ticket, which the unsuspecting lieutenant confirmed. The manager then presented the culprit with *ALL* of the Mickey Mouse tickets for immediate payment.

That was supposedly a true story. Obviously, the lieutenant's career was at an end, to say the least, and I believe he may have even been court-martialed. Fraud is conduct unbecoming an officer.

- 46 -

JELLO REEVER

During the mid- to late 1960s and early 1970s, political commentary and disenchantment weaved its way through pop culture and, naturally enough, into popular music. Some songs were such obvious protests against the US involvement in Vietnam that even I figured it out. However, last year (2017) a friend loaned me a book written recently by a B-52 pilot of the era. Although he was never stationed PCS in Vietnam, he did fly bombing runs over Southeast Asia. He was a bachelor, so his book, although not particularly offensive, in my opinion, did have some content not to be read to or by elementary school-age children. He also had done something I had not before come across; he listed popular music of the Vietnam era to accompany the reading. He may have included CDs with the book; I don't remember, but I thought he had done his homework well.

And although I never thought of it at the time, he explained how the words of some of the pop songs back then, rather than having on-the-surface innocence, were actually about war. Not being one for "deep secret hidden meanings" (if the Reader will remember back to an earlier chapter), the one I remember the author mentioning was by CCR (Creedence Clearwater Revival): *Who'll Stop the Rain?* I never really listened too deeply to the lyrics of songs. In my naiveté I always thought the song was about rain. But in his book the B-52 pilot said the meaning behind the words referred to the "rain" of bombs over Vietnam. "Have you ever seen the rain?" was a question posed in the lyrics. According to Wikipedia, the title "Who'll Stop the Rain?" is a reflection on the failure of past generations, flower children, and politicians in Washington to end war. I suppose the song could have that meaning; I think of the rain of bombs now whenever I hear or think of the song, even though I have never seen the iron rain that the words might refer to. On the other hand, we Stingers created enough of our own "lead" rain.

On a slightly lighter side, the 'Clubs—the Officers Club, Top-Three Club (referring to the top three NCO ranks), NCO Club, and Airmen's Club (I think that covers all of them)—hired bands to play for the entertainment of us troops. Depending on the base, on what clubs any particular base had, and how many nights per week the various clubs had entertainment, said entertainment was mostly small bands. Not the Guy Lombardo or Tommy Dorsey type Big Bands, but the typical three- to six-person band like those in the United States and England. The Reader might unwittingly think that the government was frivolously spending their tax dollars to send bands all the way across the Pacific Ocean from the States and from Europe to Southeast Asia. And although an excellent point could be made to support this disgruntlement, it would, however, be misplaced. Yes, bands were hired, but no fortune was spent to bring The Beatles to Saigon. I was told that all of the bands we GIs had entertaining us in Vietnam and Thailand were not from Great Britain, nor were they from America, nor were they even from Vietnam and Thailand. Apparently the Philippines cornered the market on bands playing in SEA. It may or may not have been true, but that was as I understood it to be, and it made not one whit of difference anyway.

There were, of course, some culturally different phonetics affecting pronunciation of some words, but that was to be expected. Many of us can remember Filipino bands (why Filipino instead of Philipino?) playing music that was popular back home. "Jello Reever" was always a hit. Some songs were obviously anti-war. From 1965 was *Eve of Destruction* by Barry McGuire, and of course the Beatles' *Revolution* and John Lennon's *Imagine*. Most of the bands had similar repertoires of some of the popular 1960s hits like *Hang On Sloopy* by the McCoys, and *Yellow Submarine* by the Beatles, which I heard was about getting high from smoking banana peel. Never having been in the "get high on drugs and other stuff" scene myself, I have to wonder where some of this stuff comes from. Like I mentioned earlier, I had a sheltered childhood.

Andrea's and my favorite at the time was Neil Diamond's *I am . . . I Said*. Go ahead, smirk all you want. A lot of us "old fogies" like Neil Diamond. Although I had not yet begun my appreciation for wine, his song *Red Red Wine* was quite apropos. Some other biggies back then that the bands played and I especially liked were *Proud Mary* by CCR and *Light My Fire* by Jose Feliciano. Always a big request to be played again was John Denver's *Take Me Home, Country Roads*.

We always joined in whenever a band played what was no doubt the biggest and loudest song played in Vietnam, a song by The Animals, a song which said it all: *We Gotta Get Out a This Place*.

- 47 -

RICE BUGS

Lethocerus indicus, a.k.a. Rice bug

FAIR WARNING! Although I will try to make this story as un-disgusting as I reasonably can, the Reader who tends toward a weak stomach or who is otherwise easily appalled by subjects an eight-year-old farm boy would find fascinating may choose to skip this short discussion without missing out on any other excitement contained herein.

The hootch maids at NKP and the Vietnamese maids that cleaned our rooms at Da Nang Air Base suffered from a health issue common to many of the indigent inhabitants of that area of the world, namely, periodontal disease. Professional dental care was pretty much non-existent, and personal dental hygiene was all but unknown. A full set of clean, healthy teeth was a rarity. As a result, and as you can well imagine, what teeth these people did have were ravaged by cavities, and their gums were no better off. Their mouths apparently were uncomfortable much of the time, especially when eating.

The source of one local remedy that provided transitory relief from the discomfort is the topic of this short monologue: rice bugs.

Apparently there was a chemical compound in these creatures that acted much like a mild anesthetic in that it created a numbing effect. When our maids had their lunch break, they would eat the Southeast Asian equivalent of a bag lunch, which included a variety of local fare and a plastic baggie (when available to them) of the rice bugs du jour. After eating their lunch, they would attend to their version of dental hygiene. (Here comes the disgusting part to most of us not accustomed to such things.) To relieve the pain in their gums and teeth, they would bite off the head of a rice bug or two and literally suck out the insides to get the numbing juices.

After observing the locals in action, this practice was not something most of us "rich" American servicemen and women would want to witness a second time, believe me.

That is about all I have to write about rice bugs, which is probably more than you wanted to read anyway. No excuses! I warned you. . . .

- 48 -

THERE WAS A WAR GOING ON...

Each of the military services has its own dress codes and grooming guidelines. They are perhaps not so much guidelines as they are commandments, as in "Thou shalt . . ." or "Thou shalt not . . . ."

For example, while I was a freshman in AFROTC at Miami University (the real one in Ohio; the other one is the University of Miami), I was once informed of my transgression by a senior, much to my chagrin and astonishment, that umbrellas were not permitted to be carried open while in uniform. This bit of nonsense was sprung upon me just about the time I was walking between classes on a uniform day. Tuesdays were the days that we AFROTC-types were to wear our uniforms, at least at Miami. Not coincidentally, the heavens were at that time springing a proverbial downpour upon me and, I suppose, everyone else in southwestern Ohio. Naturally, as common sense would suggest, I was using a black umbrella. He told me that I should go to supply and request a rain cover for my wheel hat—the round one with the visor. He was serious. As if one of those would actually keep a person dry and pneumonia-free. Gimme a break. It was not as if I was carrying a pink umbrella with yellow daisies or cute little kittens on it. Mine was a very somber, military-like solid black umbrella. But that did not matter. Regulations were regulations, regardless of the total and complete lack of any semblance of cognizance of their effect in the real world. Maybe someone thought carrying an umbrella would hinder rapid deployment of an M-16 during a live-fire skirmish with the enemy. That must be the (non)reason.

In defense of Air Force regulations, at least I was issued my USAF coat... initial issue. Translation into civilian-ese: raincoat. Supply-type personnel have their own descriptive language and order of expressing such. However, it did little to keep the rain from entering one's uniform via the neck opening—even with a plastic waterproof wheel hat cover. I do not know if this regulation still exists or not, nor do I care. It no longer affects me, although I still feel no need to carry a pink umbrella with yellow daisies. Or kittens.

Puppies maybe.

Have you ever considered expressing, in writing, regulation style grooming and facial hair standards? Me neither. I admit it might be a bit tricky, but the military specifications go to extremely great lengths to leave no room for doubt about any aspect of potential nonconformity. While doing a little research, I just read that the Army specifications for a general use writing implement, namely, a pen, are squeezed into sixteen pages. If described in nicely general terms - general as in common, not general as in senior officer—it is easy to imagine a myriad of interpretations being applied. If the regulations pertaining to head and facial hair stated, "cut and styled to look nice and appropriate," the Commandant of the US Marine Corps might have a slightly different idea on what constitutes "nice and appropriate" than, say, the ZZ Top guys.

For those of you who may be unfamiliar with ZZ Top, you might want to google them. They were a rock band formed in 1969; they had scraggly hair and beards longer than most women's hair. They would probably not meet even the Navy's beard criteria. As a reminder to the Reader, I am using as my frame of reference the military as it was during my early military days in the late 1960s and 1970s. Some things may have changed in the interim, but any such changes do not have any effect on anything written on any of these pages anyway.

ZZ Top grooming standards

Of course, as seems to be my style herein, the preceding paragraphs in this section really are leading, albeit circumventually (I just made that word up, as far as I can determine. Circumvent slammed into eventually; it seems logical.), to a brief experience I had during one of my TDYs to Bien Hoa Air Base. But first, a little more background information is needed about speaking and grooming.

First, Air Force training films and manuals and all else were always very dry and devoid of any humor or original thought at all. Speeches were to have an introduction, three (not two, not four) main points, and a conclusion. Paragraphs were to be structured the same way: introductory sentence, three supporting points, and appropriate segues between each paragraph, although I do not remember "segue" being a term in vogue at the time. They were called transitions back then. Even a semi-astute observer may have noticed that I myself have avoided at all costs any semblance whatsoever to this writing style. Call me a rebel if you will. The Air Force attitude was always inside the precisely defined box. We Air Force pilots enjoyed seeing an occasional Navy training film; the Navy seemed to have a sense of humor.

"What the Captain meant to say . . ."

Second, a further note on speaking and grooming. There was one film circulating around back then about a news media guy interviewing a USAF fighter pilot in Vietnam. This was definitely NOT a film produced by the Air Force. Some of you may remember it. It was called, *What the Captain Meant to Say*.

The gist of the short movie is the interviewer asking the pilot a series of questions about what he (the pilot) thought about various topics, such as the war in Vietnam, the NVA, Hanoi, politicians in Washington, etc. The pilot then answered in, shall I say, very colorful language not printable here. "Those blankity blank politicians don't know blankity blank blank about blankity blank . . ." You get the point. The interviewer was wearing the typical coat and tie. The unshaven pilot, sporting a long Pancho Gonzalez mustache and obviously needing a haircut, wore his flight suit unzipped down to about his navel. After each question and answer, the interviewer switched the microphone to an "official Air Force spokesman" (yes, spokes*man* back then, not the currently politically correct spokes*person*), who appeared crisply clean cut and wearing his Air Force blues. The official spokesman would then always begin his interpretation of what the pilot had just said with, "What the Captain meant to say...."

I was always a clean-cut kinda guy, even before the military. Of course, we all were until the Beatles arrived on the world scene, except Elvis perhaps. He was a little before his time, but his time came soon enough. A quick perusal through any high school yearbook from the early 1960s will easily verify the plethora of short hair styles we guys wore. Even today, over a half century later, my personal hair style has changed relatively (EIR) little, although I am sporting more of a forehead these days—probably from all those years of accumulated knowledge pushing my hair farther back. I haven't yet reached the comb-over stage; if I ever do, it will be time to start sporting the currently popular shaved head hairdo.

A clean-cut kinda guy (1965)

After pilot training, or maybe during, I grew a mustache. The Air Force, as I have already alluded to, had very definitive grooming guidelines apropos facial hair, among other things. Take the mustache, for instance, since it is already the current topic hereby under review. A mustache could not extend below the vermillion of the upper lip, could not extend past a vertical line at the corners of the mouth, and must be kept trim at all times. Nothing "outside the box." Really. I do not have the imagination to make up something like that. So, being a young, clean-cut, impressionable first lieutenant, I usually kept my mustache within the limits, both horizontally and vertically. However…

…there was a war going on, and I had seen *What the Captain Meant to Say* at least a couple of times. Finally being in Southeast Asia where the war actually was going on, I decided to let my mustache push the limits just a little bit. There is a natural underlying musculature curvature to most faces for a mustache, especially if one happens to be a male of the human persuasion. My natural mustache growth line, shall we say, extends about a quarter of an inch, or maybe three-eighths of an inch, a half an inch at the most - past the arbitrary, in my humble opinion (as Dave Brown, a long-time friend and fellow Air Force retiree, is fond of saying), horizontal limit imposed by Air Force regulations. It was not really that much out of official limits, and I did keep it neat and trimmed—just a little wide, to accommodate my smile. That sounds enough like sufficient plausible deniability to me. I thought it was looking more natural on me that way.

Lieutenant Colonel Dick Ring did not think so, however. Or maybe he really did, but he was the Detachment Commander for our unit at Bien Hoa Air Base in southern South Vietnam, and he was responsible for us "kids" while we were there. He was also responsible for making sure we carried ourselves responsibly, in accordance with Air Force guidelines (they're everywhere, they're everywhere). Doing his duty, one day Col. Ring "suggested" that I, a first lieutenant, trim my mustache. Col. Ring was a good-natured officer and "one of the guys." I smiled and said, "Yes, sir," thinking he was just kidding. I assumed he had seen the movie also. I hoped that he had seen the movie also. We all had. After all, in case you had not heard, there was a war going on. About a week later, he told me again to trim my mustache. He was not quite as friendly about it that time. I replied, "Yes, sir. I thought you were just kidding before. There's a war going on." Fortunately for me, he had indeed seen the movie also.

He smiled, but I trimmed my mustache and kept it trimmed, even after I left Bien Hoa. I hope Lt. Col. Ring made at least full colonel; he was a decent guy.

(I could have written this anecdote in about three sentences, but what fun would that have been?)

- 49 -

THE BICYCLE

Nakhon Phanom was a relatively (EIR) small base. Even though it was the closest USAF base to communist North Vietnam, 75 miles from the border, and only about five miles from the communist-infested Laotian border just across the Mekong River, it was quieter than one would think. The Air Force viewed NKP as being in an area of significant communist presence and activity. The biggest threat was from sappers, but because of the degree of security established, by triple-layered concertina razor wire and barbed wire and dog patrols to all of the special operations units—including various air attack units such as Stingers, Broncos, and Sandys—the base was relatively quiet. I had heard of sapper attempts on occasion and certainly not on a regular basis, although there were times when personnel not on base security patrols were advised to remain clear of the base perimeter.

In case you are wondering, US Army sappers are combat engineers or soldiers who support the front-line infantry in a variety of ways. They build bridges, clear mine fields, breach fortifications, do demolition, et cetera. Sapper is also the informal term used by the US military to apply to enemy soldiers who attempt to sneak inside our lines and lay time-delayed explosive charges. They had varying degrees of success or failure, like just about any other military venture.

So, tucked away in that cozy northeast corner of Thailand, the on-base threat at NKP was usually fairly low, unlike that of Da Nang, which was too frequently on the receiving end of NVA rocket attacks. One could walk to most places on base at NKP, such as the base gym, BX, theater, squadron admin offices, and such. However, it was either quite hot and very humid during the dry season or raining and raining and raining during the monsoon season.

Nahkon Phanom during Monsoon season

Either circumstance made it much more convenient to have covered motorized transportation, ~~air conditioned~~ (disregard;

let us not get too ridiculous), motorized transportation, which was not available just to putter around the base in; or perhaps to have a bicycle, which actually made the short (EIR) trips more agreeable, except during the Incessant Downpour Season during which time nothing was agreeable; or to walk, which, out of necessity, was the usual mode of transportation.

Adequately inspired, I decided I needed a three-speed bicycle. Ergo, I headed to the BX, expecting to ride my new bicycle back to the hootch. There was just a slight fly in the ointment—the NKP BX did not have any three-speed bikes and would not be expecting any to arrive in the foreseeable future—or even in the seeable future, which was still outside my personal limits of patience. I knew how to ride a three-speed; I had never ridden a five-speed or ten-speed and did not care to learn. NKP was fairly flat. Also, five-speed and ten-speed bikes were more expensive, and I was but a poor (EIR for sure) first lieutenant. However, a helpful BX employee checked around and found that the BX over at Udorn RTAFB did have three-speed bikes on hand. I asked the NKP BX person to ask the Udorn BX person to put one on hold for me, which he or she did.

As fortune would have it, I had a friend who had been in my Jungle School class and who was assigned to fly the Jolly Green helicopters out of NKP. I asked him if they ever went to Udorn, and he said that they did, regularly. He invited me to hop on for a ride the next morning, wearing my flight suit since it was a military aircraft. The day of the flight was nice and sunny; monsoon season had not yet started. We, meaning the Jolly Green crew, had an enroute stop to make at the Channel 99 TACAN (TACtical Air Navigation) site, which was a small place (EIR), meaning possibly as much as an acre, on the side of a mountain, to rotate the crew that manned and guarded the facility. By using the term "facility," I may perhaps be exaggerating too much about the comforts and décor, of which there were pretty close to none. The Jolly Green stop there was also for resupplying food, water, and other necessities, like perhaps toilet paper and toothpaste.

The site had literally been cleared out of the jungle and had no visible access by ground transportation that I could see. I do not think Agent Orange was used to clear the area; at least the Veterans Administration seems inclined that way. A lawn mower or weed whacker was not necessary; the ground had been saturated with what appeared to be and smelled like used oil. I walked around and stayed out of the way while whatever was needed to be done was, well, done. I think there were three guys manning the nav aid (navigation aid), and I also seem to remember that they rotated in/out only one or two guys at a time so as to maintain continuity. The TACAN station provided azimuth and distance information to aircraft navigation equipment, which were in range and which were tuned into that frequency, in this case, channel 99. The small patrol maintained the TACAN station and guarded it from any ill intentions of ne'er-do-wells.

We were on the ground for about twenty minutes while the supplies were offloaded and the TACAN crew exchange was made. Then we were off again to Udorn. Come to think of it, I really don't know the reason for the Jolly Green trip to Udorn, if it was a specifically tasked mission, or if the crew were free to borrow a large USAF helicopter whenever they wanted to make such trips to accommodate friends who needed bicycles. Regardless, we got a ride from the Udorn flight line to the BX, where I was dropped off while the crew took care of their business, whatever that may have been. I was to meet them back at the helicopter at a designated time, which was in about an hour. I found the customer service desk to get my three-speed bicycle order and paid the $30 for it while waiting for someone to retrieve the bike from wherever it had been kept somewhere in the back.

Naturally, it was in a box. Since I did not happen to have an adjustable wrench in any of my flight suit pockets, the sergeant who had brought my bike to me just happened to have one handy, plus a utility knife to cut open the straps and cardboard. It only took a few minutes to get the bike out of the box and into a fully-assembled, air-in-the-tires, ready-to-ride condition. I had a hunch that perhaps he had done this before. I was grateful for his help, but he would not accept a small remuneration for his kindness. I should have written down his name and sent a letter to the BX manager commending his going "beyond the call of duty" on my behalf. These days I generally find a way to put in a good word to someone's boss for exceptional assistance or service. For exceptionally crappy service I simply avoid any further business with the person's company, if it is possible to do so. If not, I start asking for supervisors up the chain of command if it is a large company. I may not always get satisfaction, but I have no qualms about ruffling a few feathers.

Time to try out my shiny new orange-ish bicycle. After inquiring for directions back to the flight line, I took it on its initial test ride. Nothing exciting or adventurous happened on my way to the Jolly Green. I had my flight line badge on and was able to ride all the way up the rear cargo door, which had been lowered;

it was a lot easier to ride into the helicopter that way. If you are not familiar with a Jolly Green, there is a very good reason for the name. It isn't like the much smaller six o'clock news traffic helicopters. In fact, if you folded its propeller blades back, one could probably fit inside a Jolly Green. Maybe not, but now you should have a better perspective.

Perspective of Jolly Green size (Photo: historynet.com)

The flight back to NKP was uneventful; no intermediate stops. Upon arrival back at NKP, I thanked my friend and the other crewmen and rode my bike out of the big chopper and back to my hootch. For any Reader who may be curious, my bicycle is shown in the photo below. Surprise! It looks just like what you would expect a bicycle to look like.

From left to right: my orange-ish bicycle, someone a little too heavy
for the hammock but obviously unconcerned, and me
hoping not to get the same color as my bike.
(This photo should be looking a little familiar by now.)

That particular bicycle-purchasing experience was much more fun and enjoyable than ordering something out of a catalogue or going to a store for one. And memorable. That event took place over four and a half decades ago. Do you remember going to buy your first bicycle?

- 50 -

WAR IS HELL ..., PART 1—NOT SO MUCH

... or so I had heard. This is definitely a topic in which EIR really comes into consideration. My father (deceased), step-father (recently deceased), and father-in-law (deceased) were all in WWII, the second "war to end all wars." My step-father was Charles A. Maupin. Family called him Charlie; friends called him Charles (pronounced Chaahlz in Columbus, Georgia, where he had lived all his life except for the European vacation gratis from the US Army seventy-plus years ago; the kids, grand-kids, and great-grand-kidlets called him Gramps). Until he died sixteen days before his hundredth birthday, he was one of the rapidly dwindling number of remaining D-Day survivors still living, and he was acutely articulate when telling of his experiences as he remembered them. Whenever there was an occasion such as an anniversary of D-Day, Veterans Day, Memorial Day, or some other media event inspiring recognition of the military, the local newspaper and/or TV stations and/or radio stations came to him for another interview. He must have been the last known, or at least best known, D-Day survivor in Columbus, since he was always the one the media went to. Or maybe it was his photogenic smile and wavy silver hair. When the movie *Saving Private Ryan* came out in 1998, he and his long time army buddy, Jim Scott, who had made a career in the Army and is now deceased; and my mother and Mrs. Scott were invited to a private pre-release showing of the movie at the theater at Fort Benning. The media interviewed both of them afterwards, asking them if the movie reflected reality as they remembered it and what memories it brought back. Jim was quoted some, but Charlie was quoted quite a bit. It was not the best of times; it was no doubt the worst of times for those who experienced the horror and mayhem of those days of war. (Thank you, Mr. Dickens, for your contribution to the English fountain of cultural knowledge.) Charlie was quite humble about it all and managed to credit the fallen that did not return from Omaha Beach.

In fact, after one particular interview with him, someone wrote a song about his experiences during the first two days of the invasion of the northern coast of France on 6 and 7 June 1944. The song was recorded, a video was added, and it is now available on YouTube. Google: "D-Day Plus One - YouTube." It is the listing dated April 15, 2015.

You have no doubt seen and read about the horrors of the United States military involvement in Vietnam and the atrocities our POWs and MIAs had to endure at the hands of the NVA in the Hanoi Hilton and elsewhere. Rest assured that at this point I have absolutely no intention of regurgitating more of the same for your reading displeasure. Some of us have a different perspective entirely. Don't get me wrong—in 1972 I was indeed in Thailand and Vietnam and flew over Laos. I survived flying 106 combat missions, which is a lot fewer than many aviators who flew the UNfriendly skies. But the way serendipity was working for me at the time, that "war" afforded me mostly pleasant experiences and memories, as contradictory as that may seem.

However, it was not all a cakewalk over there. Earlier I mentioned the phrase RTB—Return To Base. That is what we did after completing a combat mission—RTB (except once, which I will discuss later). Usually when we were fragged (fragmented orders) to fly a mission, we departed our base of operations and headed to variously-assigned target areas as determined from the latest available intel (no, not the same as Intel Corp.). In the case of my unit, the 18th Special Operations Squadron, we flew missions over the Plain of Jars in Laos out of Nakhon Phanom, our main base. We also had a detachment of planes and aircrews and all associated support units in Da Nang in northern South Vietnam, which was about a hundred miles south of the Demilitarized (yeah, right) Zone (DMZ) separating North and South Vietnam. We usually flew perimeter defense south of Da Nang, which was a major base and a major city in Vietnam, especially after all the refugees significantly swelled the population after having fled to the outskirts from the North. The third base of operations we flew out of was Bien Hoa Air Base, about twelve miles from Saigon, then the capitol of South Vietnam. It was located in southern South Vietnam. After the "fall," Saigon has since been renamed Ho Chi Minh City, which you will find on current maps. Out of

Bien Hoa we flew to a number of outlying target areas, most notably An Loc.

Except for the perimeter defense missions around Da Nang (our target area was only about seven miles from the base), whenever we headed back "home" from a mission and we had entered relatively (EIR) safe airspace, someone on board would break out a bag of RTB candy and pass it around. There were at least ten aircrew members on board—more if there happened to be an instructor for some reason. As you can imagine, after spending over three hours cramped in a less-than-comfortable, semi-open-air, hot and humid aerospace vehicle (with deference here to our astronauts), the RTB candy was a definite morale booster, signaling that we had yet again flown into the face of death, sometimes closer than other times, and had lived to tell about it. Of course, we were not safely back on the concrete yet, but that was never a concern, except possibly when a crusty old colonel or a relatively inexperienced copilot facing a crosswind was going to make the landing. As is the nature of all Air Force pilots, I greased all my landings on the runway; that's MY story and I'm stickin' to it. My personal favorite RTB candy was—and this will come as no surprise to those of you who know me—a large bag of M&Ms. I do not even remember what other choices we had back then, but I do remember M&Ms. RTB candy—all was right with the world again . . . for the moment anyway.

At this point you may well be wondering what all this rambling about RTB candy, of all things, has to do with the "War is hell" topic du jour. I felt it was necessary for me to provide you with some background of the whys and wherefores so I could build up to this upcoming exciting explanation:

Occasionally the BX (base exchange, or PX, post exchange on the Army side), would actually commit what was, from my personal perspective, the egregious and unforgiveable snafu of . . .

. . .RUNNING OUT OF M&Ms!

The outrage of it all! What were we supposed to do? There was a war going on, as we were on occasion reminded, and we were going out night after dreary night into the trenches, metaphorically speaking, of course, putting our lives on the line for God and Country, and all we asked in return was to have a morsel of chocolate, with peanuts (nobody was allergic to peanuts back then) available after surviving the shootout. Maybe tomorrow night. . . .

BUT WAIT! THERE'S MORE!

Running out of RTB candy was not the only hardship we faced in Southeast Asia. Some of you will find this next bit of historical news to be a real stretch of credulity, but it is absolutely true. Ask anybody else that was there at the time.

In 1972, Bien Hoa Air Base was the busiest airport in the world, even including Atlanta Hartsfield and Chicago O'Hare and all the other major airports in the world, as measured by the number of takeoffs and landings, which makes you really wonder how such a busy and popular place could possibly run out of M&Ms. I don't think Vietnam was marketed very well by the Mars Company. I'll bet the sergeant in charge of the BX did not even have an MBA. But like I just foreshadowed, having no M&Ms was not the only tribulation we faced.

Yeah, sure, so the Army guys at Bien Hoa slept in foxholes and tents on the other side of the runway. I found out about that bit of wartime trivia from Donnie Johnson, a friend of mine going back to junior high days in the very late 1950s—after we were both back home from Vietnam at the same time. He had been an Army platoon leader, and it turned out that he and his platoon—his "troopies," as he referred to them; must have been a technical Army term—called those foxholes and tents "home" part of the time while I was stationed there TDY for a week or two at a time. I didn't know he was there when I was, and he also had no way of knowing that I was there. Otherwise I would have invited him to come over to my VOQ and shoot some pool.

Of course, as a US Air Force aircrew member, I was quartered in the air-conditioned Visiting Officer Quarters on the "good" side of the runway with my fellow Stinger pilots and navs and those from other units. The enlisted troops stayed in Visiting Airman Quarters which, I believe, but am not positive, were also air conditioned, at least for our aircrew men.

Once again, you may be wondering what my Army friend, sleeping in a tent on the other side of the runway while I was in an air-conditioned building, has to do with me experiencing the depravities of war. Hold on—you are absolutely not going to believe this . . .

. . .We ran out of chalk for the pool table in the VOQ lounge!

As anyone knows who has ever tried to give an iron-clad leave to him/herself from a three-rail billiard shot (thank you Meredith Wilson and Robert Preston), you just cannot shoot pool without chalk for your pool cue. Without chalk, you will wind up shooting like Ed Norton in an episode of *The Honeymooners*. I guess it is just as well that Donnie didn't come over to shoot some pool. He would have been disappointed.

Times were particularly difficult when we were already crabby from having no RTB candy, only to get back to the Q, take a refreshing shower, plan to snatch a few relaxing moments or spend a few hours honing our skills around the pool table, perhaps lightening the load in someone else's wallet for him if we were lucky—and then discovering there was no chalk. That was a disaster in the making. We certainly were not being pampered into maintaining that steely calm that all pilots possess as we take to the skies to do battle once again.

I wonder what Donnie Johnson (now Colonel, US Army, Ret.) would have thought about that?

BUT WAIT! THERE'S STILL MORE!

By now you may have ascertained that this next bit of Vietnam war history as espoused by yours truly may not be quite as excruciatingly painful as you were at first lead to believe, and if you have so concluded, you would be correct. Regardless, or, if you insufferably prefer, irregardless (I shudder!), the truth must be told, as any newspaper reporter or TV newscaster or White House spokesperson will have you believe.

Moving back up north to Da Nang. In the 1970s Vietnam, dental hygiene was not uppermost on the minds of the poor and homeless refugees, none of whom actually lived on base. Even the adults who managed to still have teeth usually experienced constant dental discomfort. (No need to skip over anything here; no more rice bug stories though.) Many native residents worked on base. However, our maids—did I forget to mention that we had maids in our air-conditioned aircrew quarters? I mean, who else was going to clean the rooms and wash the sheets and make the beds? After all, there was a war going on. Must have slipped my mind.

As I was saying, our maids were among those approved to work in on-base housing areas. I imagine they went through some sort of initial background checks and security clearances, as well as daily security checks before entering or leaving the base. At least I hope they did, not that it really matters at this late date, forty-five-plus years after the fact. I do not know if they were paid anything by our military or the Vietnamese military, but each of us paid them a bit of money to take care of our rooms. The going rate at the time was five US dollars per week—or was that five US dollars per month? I do not know what the currency conversion rate was then, but I just checked today (29 August 2018) and it is just over 23,301 Vietnamese dong to one USD (US dollar).

We were supposed to pay them with military payment certificates (MPC) instead of with US greenbacks; actual greenbacks apparently commanded considerable premium in the black market off base. In an effort to control the outflow of US currency and MPC off base and into Vietnamese hands, and possibly eventually into North Vietnamese hands, the finance office or some other authority would "change" the MPC every now and then, perhaps every month or two. When this happened, a notice would be distributed on base explaining that in twenty-four hours or whatever cutoff time/date was determined, all currently-issued MPC would no longer be accepted. If you had any, you needed to exchange your "old" MPC for "new" MPC at certain designated facilities. All MPC that had found its way off base where word of the currency expiration was not generally known subsequently became worthless, as did all expired MPC currency, even if carried by US personnel.

Obverse and reverse (or vice versa; I'm not sure which)
of an MPC nickel

Once in a while, especially if I was low on MPC, I would give my maids five dollars in US currency. A grandmotherly type Vietnamese woman and her granddaughter cared for the rooms on my floor. They spoke very little English, and about the only Vietnamese I spoke was for "thank you," which I no longer recall, but somehow we GIs managed to communicate the basics, mostly with hand gestures.

There was a decent BX on base at Da Nang which we could usually get to and from without being shot at. Not all of the refugees were "good guys." Go figure. I remember the time I went to BX to buy some basics, like M&Ms and toothpaste. (You know it's coming . . .) No toothpaste.

No Crest, no Colgate, no Pepsodent, no toothpaste at all. Once again I suffered the slings and arrows of outrageous consumer product deficiencies. (My apologies to Shakespeare and Hamlet.) However, there were boxes and boxes of Polygrip. Really. Polygrip. Boxes and boxes of it. It does not require an orthodontist to determine what's wrong with that picture. Who needed Polygrip, for crying out loud? I certainly did not know anyone who did, and I had never even seen anyone who used it, especially in Southeast Asia. Not on any base where I was stationed. All the guys I knew used toothpaste. I do not know if there was even a military dentist on base, although I suppose there must have been at least one. Anyone could have come up with a toothache or have chipped a tooth while showing off how to open a beer bottle with his teeth. Who in his right mind—and I realize I just made a certain assumption there—would have ordered boxes and boxes of, or even any, Polygrip? Probably the non-MBA sergeant that ran out of M&Ms at Bien Hoa got himself transferred to Da Nang.

The thing about Polygrip in Da Nang is this: There were not many military types stationed there old enough to need it. Hmm—perhaps that is the operative phrase—I should have said US military types. The Vietnamese military personnel may have very well needed it and perhaps had access to our BX. I don't know for sure. This is just speculation on my part as I actually give the memory words on paper. Okay, so it's on a computer screen. That's what paper is these days—computer screens and cell phone screens.

I managed to borrow a spare tube of toothpaste from my roommate, a major—a person more experienced in the occasional inconveniences of military TDY living than I.

The war Charlie was involved in on D-Day really was hell. So was the day Donnie was injured in Vietnam. My complaints fall into the category of super-silly-ousness.

Charlie had a relatively (EIR) minor injury in WWII; Donnie received multiple life-threatening injuries in Vietnam. A couple of months ago as I was driving in the parking lot of a local Home Depot, I noticed a new sign where you would usually find a handicap parking sign. This particular parking space was reserved specifically for those awarded the Purple Heart. . . .

Parking space sign at a Home Depot

- 51 -

WAR IS HELL, PART 2—PURPLE HEART

The Purple Heart Medal is awarded to US military personnel for "being wounded or killed in any action against an enemy of the United States or as a result of an act of any such enemy or opposing armed forces." It is the oldest United States military award still being given to military members. It was first awarded 22 February 1932.

Charlie's Story

Charlie Maupin, my step-father and D-Day Plus One veteran, had his Purple Heart framed and hanging on the wall in the living room of his independent living apartment. As Charlie told it:

"Somewhere in Germany, in early 1945, my unit, HQ Co 3 Bn 175th Regt 29th Infantry Division, had set up headquarters in an old German mining building. I walked outside one day, just looking around, when suddenly an incoming German artillery shell exploded in a nearby tree. A small piece of shrapnel hit my left hand causing it to bleed and lose feeling. It was only a superficial wound, but when a lieutenant saw it, he told me to go to the aid station about a hundred yards or so behind the building and get it taken care of. I was a bit hesitant to go because the Germans had been shelling that area, intermittently, but I went. For that small incident I received a Purple Heart. Of course, I could have been killed if a larger piece of shrapnel had hit me in a lethal spot. Fortunately, it didn't."

Charlie had always been a modest, soft-spoken man all the time I had known him the past sixty-plus years. Though his injury was serendipitously not life threatening, as he said, it very easily could have been.

Donnie's Story

Donnie Johnson had been my friend since junior high days. "Junior high" is merely a phrase to give you a frame of reference;

in Columbus, Georgia, in the late 1950s and early 1960s, there were no actual junior high schools per se. We went to elementary school through the eighth grade and from there into high school. Donnie and I were in the same class in seventh and eighth grades (it was a small elementary school) and in some of the same classes in high school before I moved to Cincinnati after my sophomore year.

Before I met Donnie he had lived in Germany when his father, an Army sergeant, had been stationed there. One impact that assignment had on Donnie manifested itself one day in Spanish class in high school. And no, I do not have my geography confused. He and I were in Ms. Thompson's Spanish II class together. (Technically speaking, that was before "Ms." had been invented as a female title classification, but since I do not remember if Ms. Thompson was a Miss or a Mrs., I choose to err on the side of neutrality. Besides, since it is our custom to not differentiate the marital status in the masculine title, Mr. (no Missster), it is my contention that, accordingly, we have no need to make the distinction with the female members of our species. That is my opinion, and you are entitled to it free of charge.)

As it happened one day in Ms. Thompson's class, each of us was instructed to stand in the front of the class and speak for a full minute without using any English. Rising to the challenge, when it came Donnie's turn, he got up, walked to the front, and when Ms. Thompson nodded and started her stop-watch, Donnie began, "Eins, zwei, drei, vier, fünf. . . ." That got a great laugh from the rest of us, but Ms. Thompson was not amused. (I would wager that in her mind she actually might have been, but that was not something a teacher could outwardly display and still maintain credibility.)

As I mentioned a bit earlier, after high school graduation I went to Miami University and into Air Force Reserve Officers Training Corps, and subsequently I became an Air Force pilot. Donnie went to The Citadel (formally known as The Military College of South Carolina, The Citadel, but only a Citadel graduate would know that you were referring to The Citadel if you should use the formal name; besides, the full name would take seemingly forever to scroll across the college scores banner at the bottom of the ESPN screen). He received his Second Lieutenant commission into the US Army; his father had been a retired Army sergeant. That made Donnie an "Army brat," as the vernacular would have it.

In school Donnie used to draw detailed pencil pictures on ruled notebook paper of his idea of what he described as a ballistic missile with an anti-ballistic missile heading toward it and an anti-anti-ballistic missile missile heading toward *it* and an anti-anti-anti-ballistic missile missile missile heading toward *it* . . . and so on, depending on how bored he was in the class. Later, as a 2nd lieutenant, Donnie was a gung-ho career officer. Thus, it should be no surprise that his goal in the Army was, and I quote from the prevailing attitude at the time (1969) "to go to Vietnam and kill gooks."

And that he did. After graduation and further training in the Army, he got his assignment as a platoon leader in a combat unit that shipped to Vietnam. A US Army platoon is the smallest unit led by a commissioned officer, typically a 2nd or 1st lieutenant, and he is assisted by a platoon sergeant. A platoon consists of approximately fifteen to thirty soldiers, depending on the nature of the unit (infantry, artillery, etc.). My recounting of the following bit of history is based on my memory of what I was told at the time.

Somewhere in the jungles of Vietnam Lieutenant Johnson (Donnie) and his platoon were ambushed by a larger force of NVA. There was a severe firefight and every man in his outfit was killed except for him and his platoon sergeant. I cannot help having visions of *Forrest Gump* come to mind. I do not know the details, but Donnie and his sergeant were rescued; Donnie was medically evacuated all the way to Walter Reed National Military Medical Center in Bethesda, Maryland. He had taken about half a dozen hits in his shoulder. He spent several months in and out of the hospital recovering from his injuries.

Donnie's Vietnam career had lasted twelve days. Not months—days. When he was told he would not be going back into combat, he was disappointed, and just a bit angry. To his mind, he was not finished over there. I believe he got his father to contact some army buddies still on active duty, and he managed to pull some strings with Georgia Senator Talmadge's office to get Donnie another Vietnam assignment. I do not know what his father thought about his son going into combat again, but he must have been supportive, proud, and understanding, not knowing if his son would return safely after another tour over there. I imagine most parents of military offspring heading to the Far East felt the same way.

Colonel Donald Robertson Johnson, Jr. is retired from the military now. I don't know how many oak leaf clusters he has on his Purple Heart. . . .

- 52 -

WAR IS HELL, PART 3—MY STORY

War Injury but No Purple Heart

As may be expected, since I have been out of uniform for some time now, often I would get asked if I had been injured while I was participating in the activities going on in Southeast Asia. I truthfully and accurately answer "Yes." When I was wearing my dress blue uniform with the rows of ribbons on it, the absence of the Purple Heart ribbon, itself recognizable by all US military and by many civilians, was a sufficient and self-evident statement. However, my answer would be deceptively simple and therefore misconstrued without further explanation. Ergo, here is my story and I am sticking to it:

As military installations go, Nakhon Phanom RTAFB was a relatively (EIR) small and quiet base. The atmosphere there was almost like what I would sometimes describe as country club-ish. Any US Marine thinks that *all* Air Force bases are country club-ish, and relative to (EIR) the Marine environment, maybe they are. Yes, NKP was a Special Operations base, and yes, there were many different special operations aircraft flying out of and (hopefully) back to the base from a variety of special operations missions, but the effects of the hostilities of war were not otherwise intuitively evident on the base itself. Located as it was in a northeast corner of Thailand across the Mekong River from Laos, it was rather isolated from all the actual blow 'em up boom bang rat-a-tat-tat stuff going on in Vietnam, parts of Laos, and (you did not read it here; the Secretary still disavows any knowledge of our presence . . .) in Cambodia. It was quiet, even for a place where military aircraft were taking off and landing at all hours of the day and night. This was because none of the noisier (EIR) aircraft in the Air Force's inventory—meaning jets—were based there. Fighters like the F-4 Phantom, the ubiquitous workhorse during the Vietnam Conflict, were quite loud when the afterburners were lit for takeoff. And also like those of the F-15, when lit, afterburners make their presence known for miles around when they begin to convert a fuel/air mixture into a tremendous roar.

Most people, including the engineers that design them, believe that the rapid expulsion of hot gasses reacting against the exhaust end of the aircraft engines, in compliance with Sir Isaac Newton's Three Laws of Motion, is what actually starts the aircraft in motion and accelerates it down the runway. Let me dispel this myth here and now: The truth is that it is the frightful roar itself which actually makes the aircraft try to flee in its vain attempt to escape. Thus, "fleeing" became easily transposed into "flying." I was an Aeronautics major in undergrad school; you will have to trust me on this. You will not find this explanation in any physics, aerodynamics, thermodynamics, or aviation books, or any other books on the subject. Except this one, of course. (I may have had one glass of wine too many when I wrote the above technical explanation.)

There were also the F-5, F-102, F104, F105, and F-111 fighters with afterburners. The F-5 was a fighter version of the T-38A supersonic trainer we flew in undergraduate pilot training. There were also a number of not quite as noisy but noisy nonetheless non-afterburner-equipped jet-engine powered planes. Among them were combat jets such as the RB-57 and RB-66 (RB: Reconnaissance Bomber), the A-10, and the A-37, which was a close-air-support attack version of the little T-37B that we also flew in pilot training. On occasion one of these planes would land at NKP to refuel; usually for some minor maintenance, or to rearm, if the appropriate armament was available on base. These would be the only times those of us on base were subjected the aural assaults of jet engines. One slight exception, which some really sharp Readers might have been asking themselves about, were our own AC-119K Gunships which, in addition to the two large—and noisy—reciprocating engines, also had two small, not quite as noisy (EIR), jet engines. Because of the noise from the recips and the large propellers slashing their way through the air, you really did not notice the jets so much.

I did not even mention the Strategic Air Command's (SAC) B-52s with eight jet engines and KC-135s with four jet engines, both planes of which were based at U-Tapao (Oo-ta-pow) RTAFB, a much larger base with a much wider and longer runway to accommodate these airplanes. A joke about the B-52's size is that its wingspan is longer than the Wright Brothers' first flight. Although at 185 feet the B-52's wingspan is impressive enough, especially if you are standing under it looking up, it falls a bit short of the 852-foot-length of the first flight of the Wright Flyer. I never saw either of these two SAC aircraft at NPK, for a very good reason: The runway was neither wide enough nor long enough for either to successfully land on or take off from.

So, NKP was quiet and secluded (EIR). There were the usual dining facilities, including the Officers Club, which I will mention again elsewhere in another chapter, a swimming pool, a small hospital, and other amenities. Unlike most country clubs and many bases, there was no golf course. There may have been tennis courts, but since I have never been much of a tennis player, I do not remember for sure. There was, however, a gymnasium which had, among other things, a basketball court, a weight room, and two racquetball courts. This is where our story actually begins; the previous several pages up to this point have been what one might refer to as "setting." My wife, Andrea, taught English Literature in high schools for a bunch of years; the exposure brushed off on me a little.

Since there were only the two racquetball courts for the whole base, even though it was a small base, reservations were required for one-hour blocks of playing time. The gym was open only certain hours extending into the night. At some time not too long after my arrival at NKP, some fellow Stingers asked me if I wanted to play racquetball. They needed a fourth player. I had never heard of racquetball, but after someone briefly explained it to me I decided I would like to learn to play. If you are not familiar with the sport, think of it as something like a faster version of tennis played with short-handled racquets in a twenty-foot by twenty-foot by forty-foot enclosed room and no net. There are several reasons I prefer racquetball to tennis; one reason is that it is a faster game. Another is that you never have to chase the ball very far, except in some of those courts designed with the upper half of the rear wall open for spectators. But since the courts at the NKP gym were fully enclosed, that was not an issue. There are pros and cons to each sport, and we each have our personal preferences. You know mine.

The base gym had loaner racquetballs and racquets, which was fortunate, since I do not remember knowing anyone to whom it occurred, before departing their homes in the United States, to haul such recreational equipment nine thousand miles into a war zone. It did not take long for me to learn the fundamentals of playing doubles. There were four of us guys, Air Force trained killers, as it were, all running around in a rel- atively small (EIR) court, each armed with a heavy wooden rac- quet—no modern graphite, aluminum, or composite rackets available back then—each of us chasing the hollow rubber ball, which is a little smaller than a tennis ball and with no fuzz on it, and trying to slam it against the front wall. There were some rules, of course, which were easy to learn, and also playing techniques—especially while playing doubles—which one ac- quired with experience.

A thought: Isn't experience rather like inverse entropy? No, I suppose not, but it is something to cogitate about.

As in tennis, teams alternated hitting the ball toward the front wall. Two basic strategies that could be employed by a team were for the players to either cover side to side, or one player up closer to the front and the other back, similar to tennis. Player positioning could and would change very quickly, depending on the where the opponent players were or were headed at any given moment and ditto for the ball. It was necessary to know where the other players were, including your partner, either by actually seeing or intuitively anticipating movement. The latter is one of those skills one acquires with experience. For example, if the ball had gone behind you for someone else to hit, it would behoove you to ensure that your body would not be in the path of said projectile on its way forward again. Think of Serena Williams with an overhand drive slamming a tennis ball 120 miles per hour, then add about 40 miles per hour. If you were not sufficiently adept at avoiding hindering the path of the ball—your fault if you got hit!—even a glancing blow could sting and leave an angry red welt.

I was still pretty new at the game. One night I forgot a basic rule—never look backward. There is a very good reason for that: It could be dangerous. Unfortunately, I momentarily forgot that very basic rule once, as it was not yet ingrained in me as a player, and I looked back …

… about 0.13 of a second before the ball very abruptly ended its trajectory with a direct hit square against my eye.

Pain! Agony! Those cartoons about stars and fireworks flashing? I can personally testify that they are too true. I don't remember seeing anything out of that eye for some time; I kept it closed and my hand over it—as if that was going to help. But that is what we humans do when we are physically hurt—we put a hand over the wound to . . . do what? I don't know; that is just what we reflexively do. Maybe it is to prevent any more pain from getting in.

I dropped my racquet and crumbled onto the floor, tears in my eyes. At least I guess they were also in the injured eye; believe it or not, I no longer remember which eye got hurt. Game over, at least for my roommate partner and me. After I recovered sufficiently to get up, he escorted me back to my room. I managed to get undressed, take a shower, and get into bed. All I could do at that point was to try to get to sleep. Did you ever try to sleep when your eye was on fire? It doesn't happen. And it didn't then. Finally I got my roommate to take me to the emergency room (ER) at the base hospital. Being a pilot, I naturally had concern for my vision and subsequent flight status.

At the hospital I told the medical personnel on duty what had happened. Someone looked at my eye and somehow managed to see it through my squinting, which also did nothing to relieve the pain. They put some drops in my eye—some drops to dilate it, some other drops to ease the pain, and some to dye the cornea. Then they gave me something to put me to sleep— not like you would an old, ailing dog, of course, but at the time I would not have cared. They kept me asleep in the hospital for three days, waking me up just long enough to eat, hit the potty, and take another sleeping pill. In Scotland the potty is called the loo; in the Army it's called the latrine; in the Navy it's called the head; since to my knowledge the Air Force does not have a specific nomenclatural reference for that receptacle for receiving human waste, then, as far as I am concerned, in the Air Force it's the potty. I am sure my Marine friends would agree, considering that they consider the USAF as the country club service anyway. I will admit that that regimen of keeping me asleep suited me just fine, as there were no comfortable situations for which my eye did not hurt as long as I was conscious. After the three days the doctor decided I could be released on DNIF (duh Niff) status—Duty Not Involving Flying—for a week. (Really, DNIF is an actual USAF acronym; I didn't make it up.) That meant pretty much what it says. I could be back on duty and could do "regular" activities, except no flying as a pilot. However, since my job was being a pilot, I was not overwhelmed with excessive extraneous activity. My eye was feeling a lot better by then. It was basically undamaged after having suffered the traumatic impact, except for a resultant corneal abrasion, which the doctor said would heal quickly. The major issue remaining concerned my vision (duh). Remember, I mentioned that the medical types in the ER had dilated my eyes when I first arrived. However, no one had thought to ask if I was on flying status before they selected the types of dilating solutions to use on me. As it turned out, it took ten—count 'em, ten—days before I could hold one hand up before my eyes and see only five fingers clearly. Finally the doctor returned me to flying status, and I went about my merry way.

And that was my only war injury. It was not one that inspired heroic novels with Paul Newman starring as me in the Hollywood version. Charlie's non-lethal but genuine wound was received from the actions of an enemy of the United States. Donnie Johnson's nearly fatal injuries were also received from the actions of an enemy of the United States. My injury did indeed occur during a time of armed conflict, in a war zone, so to speak, and while I was on active duty. However, the nature of my injury did not justify the award of the Purple Heart. Even if that type of injury had qualified, I still would not have gotten a Purple Heart. . . . The guy who had hit me with the racquetball had been my doubles partner.

- 53 -

BATTLE OF AN LOC—STINGER MISSIONS

An Loc, South Vietnam, 1972 (Photo: Wikipedia)

An Loc (an lock) was a strategic target area in the effort to interdict the North Vietnamese supply lines through Cambodia. As you will no doubt remember from the Preface, I mentioned that this writing is not a recount or summation of the many dissertations on the "War" in Vietnam, including the Battle of An Loc. Below is a map to give the Reader a geographical frame of reference for the next few anecdotes. Although there is no date annotated on the map, you may notice that it pre-dates 1975, the obvious feature being that the capitol city is Saigon and not its renamed designation of Ho Chi Minh City.

An Loc is about 64 miles almost due north of Saigon,
about twelve plus or minus air miles from the Cambodian border

Most of the missions I flew on out of Bien Hoa were in the An Loc area. An Loc is about 61 "highway" miles from Bien Hoa, and about 40 +/- air miles. As was our operations procedure, the first Stinger sortie of the night would remain on station—i.e., in the target area—until the second sortie reported at an entry point, whereupon the first Stinger would depart the area via an exit point. And so it would go throughout the night, and mid-air collisions were avoided.

At any given time anywhere over the Southeast Asia Theater of Operations there were all types of military aircraft flying around, each aircraft or aircraft cell going about its own particular mission. An "aircraft cell" typically refers to two to four aircraft flying on the same mission and in somewhat of a formation, depending on the type of aircraft and operating procedures being followed. In the case of B-52s, they usually flew in three-ship cells, maintaining one mile in trail and 500' vertical and 500' lateral separation. As each plane reached the target area, 500-pound or 750-pound bombs would be released. This bombing pattern resulted in what is known as saturation bombing. (*Who'll Stop the Rain?*)

There were always command and control (C&C) aircraft flying around, typically a KC- or EC-135 or a C-130. When a fighter or bomber air strike was nearing somewhere, there would be an announcement over the military guard (emergency) channel to all US aircraft (because all US military aircraft monitor the guard channel at all times). The announcement would be, "This is Pawnee Target (the C&C call sign) on guard. Avoid by ten nautical miles . . ."; the information that followed would be latitude/longitude coordinates defining an area and a time window given in Zulu (Z for the zero° Prime Meridian, you may recall). Aircrews, usually the navigator if there was one, which, in our case, meant the table nav, would plot the coordinates of the area to be avoided. Usually when we heard the advisory it meant the B-52s were on their way.

B-52 Stratofortess on bomb run (Photo: Wikipedia)

The bombers flew relatively (EIR) high, perhaps FL350 (35,000'), whereas we were practically (again, EIR) in the trees at 4,500' AGL (Above Ground Level).

One night as we were on our RTB route, having finished our excitement for the evening—or so we thought, and as we had every reasonable expectation to believe while remembering we were still in a war zone —when suddenly there were multiple large WHOOMP! explosion impacts on the ground below us. It only took a brief moment for someone in the cockpit to determine that we were in danger of being bombed by B-52s above. The table nav quickly gave the captain a heading to get us (hopefully) out of harm's way. The situation was a bit hairy for a few minutes until it got quiet below us again.

Somebody somewhere had goofed—I believe that is the technical term. We never heard the Pawnee Target on guard call; considering that there were ten of us on that -119, we could not *all* have missed the call. I'm just sayin'. As any sharp Reader would have surmised by now, the fact that I am now writing about this little incident post mortem (perhaps not the best choice of phrases) is an excellent clue that we all survived.

"Who's got the RTB candy tonight?"

A short primer is due for those Readers unfamiliar with aviation time terminology. Zulu is the phonetic for Z. If you are in doubt, see Appendix 4, which, by the way, I included but did not invent. Zulu is the time in the zero-longitude time zone. The 0° longitude Prime Meridian was established by international accord. This time zone is also known as GMT, or Greenwich Mean Time. It is also also known as UTC, or Coordinated Universal Time. One might reasonably wonder why it is not CUT or, viewed another way, Universal Time Coordinated. I do not know why; I was not consulted about these matters, although perhaps I should have been.

There is a difference between GMT and UTC even though they both describe the same time. According to worldtimeserver.com, "GMT is an actual time zone, whereas UTC is a time standard that is used to keep time synchronized across the world." Regardless how one spells it, Zulu or GMT or UTC, it is always happy hour somewhere in the world. I will take a break here and refill my glass of Margaux.

- 54 -

BATTLE OF AN LOC—LOST A STINGER

As I mentioned previously, the Stinger missions were about 3.3 hours long chock to chock. Higher Headquarters (HHQ) tasking for the An Loc area increased significantly in 1972 in efforts to interdict NVA supply lines to their troops through Cambodia. Activity on both sides of the confrontation had intensified. In order to enhance our mission results, the 18th Special Operations Squadron got orders to fly more and more flights per night. After all, the Stinger mission was designed to fly at night. During daylight hours we would be an easily visible target and too low and slow to avoid any incoming artillery.

HHQ tasking eventually had us flying seven sorties per night. A little ~~math~~ arithmetic—will show that 3.3 hours per sortie times seven sorties per night adds up to 23.1 hours. If we figure about a 40 minute overlap (I like to use round numbers whenever extreme accuracy is neither critical nor data available) per mission for when one aircraft takes off, travels to the target area, engages in the wartime activity our mission is tasked to do, then returns to base while another aircraft replaces the first one or is replaced by the next one, that still only shortens the diurnal mission schedule by four hours. Since there were not 19 hours (23 hours, minus the four hours of overlap) of darkness available, the first sortie took off sometime before sunset, and the last sortie landed sometime after sunrise. At least that became the ill-advised plan.

We as a unit were lucky for a while, but eventually one aircraft and crew would come to an unfortunate and fatal end. With a crew of ten to exit in an emergency, and exit portals on the aircraft totaling one, there was a designated bailout order if such ever became necessary. For one flight, bailout indeed became necessary.

There are three basic steps in any aircraft emergency: 1) Maintain aircraft control. 2) Analyze the situation. 3) Take proper action. That was drilled into us from day one of pilot training.

1) I was not a crewmember on that ill-fated flight, but I can explain what *may* have happened. The pilot and copilot attempted to maintain control of the aircraft, but they were losing to adverse dynamics. The aircraft took some serious damage from ground fire, most likely from AAA. I do not know what the damage was or if anyone was injured at that point. I also do not know the details, but the pilots and flight engineer maintained aircraft control as best as they could under the circumstances. At the low altitudes the aircraft flew, about 3,500 to 4,500 feet above the ground, losing an engine was serious, as were severed flight control cables, or as were a fire inside or outside the plane—these are all speculations on my part of some possibilities of what may have happened.

2) Analyzing the situation, it was determined that the aircraft was no longer flyable. The Aircraft Commander (A/C) is the final authority in a USAF aircraft, even if there are crewmembers or passengers on board who outrank him (or her, as females were eventually accepted into the USAF pilot genre. Likewise, the captain on commercial airliners is the decision-making authority.). He is the person who "signs for" the plane, thereby taking ultimate responsibility for the aircraft, aircrew, passengers, equipment, and all else on board, as well as compliance with all rules, regulations, procedures, and mission objectives. He does not make arbitrary decisions; he uses input from all available information sources, especially including any other crewmembers. In single-seat aircraft such as those found in many fighter planes, the pilot is the only crewmember around, and he has to incorporate all information himself. In some emergencies there is no time to think about things; the pilot must immediately react, having been trained to react as necessary.

Even in a single-seat plane the pilot often has outside options before making a decision to attempt some sort of non-standard landing safely or to abruptly depart what had been up until recently an airworthy machine. For example, in a combat situation there are usually two to four other fighters tasked for a mission. When one plane is in trouble, outside visual confirmation of any visible damage from the pilot of another plane may be radioed between planes. A Navy or Marine fighter may be sufficiently controllable to do a "fly-by" of the aircraft carrier's control tower for visual observation. Anyone who has seen *Top Gun* or other air combat or aircraft emergency movies has at least a Hollywood version of situations. Sometimes there is time to think about things, sometimes there isn't.

3) In taking proper action, the decision was made to abandon the -119. The back-end crew—the three gunners, the IO, and the Nos—were to jump out in their designated order while the cockpit crew continued their effort to maintain aircraft control as it descended. Someone in the cockpit, either the nav or copilot, called a mayday over the guard channel and, if time permitted, gave location.

The mayday call would have generated immediate rescue operations from any aircraft around that could provide any assistance. Considering the intensity of the battle around An Loc, air rescue was primed and ready. At least one HH-3 or CH-53 Jolly Green helicopter would be on its way, as well as a heavily-armed A1E Sandy and/or OV-10 Bronco to provide some serious low-level fire power . . .

Jolly Green and two Sandys on a downed airmen rescue mission
(Photo: Ken Combs)

. . . possibly an Army Bell AH-1 Huey Cobra helicopter gunship to provide really up close and personal low-level cover for the guys on the ground . . .

Really up close and personal protection (Photo: The Guardian)

. . . an O-2 Skymaster spotter plane coordinating with downed airmen to direct incoming rescue birds in very close by radio and by marking ground positions with "Willy Pete" (White Phosphorous) rockets . . .

O-2 Skymaster (Cessna 337) spotter

. . . an armed OV-10 Bronco spotter that could do the same thing as the O-2 plus add fire suppression as well (one of the guys in my pilot training class flew OV-10s out of NKP) . . .

OV-10 Bronco—a spotter with an attitude!

. . . higher up, possibly an AC-130 Spectre Gunship with 40 mm guns and a 105 mm Howitzer...

AC-130 Spectre gunship firing its 105 mm Howitzer
(Photo: Fichier)

. . . maybe even an F-4 Phantom or two if any were available.

F-4 Phantom—the "workhorse" throughout the Vietnam conflict

There is a reason I have included all the photos. That reason is to leave the Reader with a visual reinforcement of rescue operations that occurred in Southeast Asia. When US military airmen were downed over land or sea, or when troops on the ground were in jeopardy, no expense was spared to retrieve them. Not surprisingly, sometimes rescuers needed rescuing themselves as a result of enemy activity.

One thing was certain—after a successful mission, no rescue crews ever had to buy any drinks at the 'Club. . . .

Since writing the above speculation about the Stinger that was shot down, I have read an account written by one of the seven survivors, CMSgt (Ret.) Craig Corbett, who had been an A1C (two-striper) *gunner when he was on the crew. Accordingly, what follows is my brief retelling of highlights from the story as it was written by CMSgt Corbett. ("Highlights" is perhaps not the best word choice.) My commentary will be in* non-italicized brackets: [ ].

349

The date: 2 May 1972

The location: Bien Hoa Air Base, South Vietnam

Target area: An Loc, about 45 miles north

The aircraft tail number: #826 [I never flew in that aircraft.]

Call sign: Stinger 41

Crew number: 13 . . . perhaps an omen, but the crew did not think so

On 2 May Crew 13 was tasked to fly one of the dreaded daylight missions. The preflight intel briefing mentioned possible AAA around An Loc and the best immediate bailout area was west of the city. The crewmen were a little nervous, as the previous mission flown over the city had returned to base with battle damage from AAA hits.

When Stinger 41 was cleared into the target area, they joined up with an O-2 to help spotting targets. The Stinger started drawing 37 mm AAA fire. As the plane circled the target area climbing up from 3,500 feet, the plane was hit. The right wing was on fire and both the right recip and right jet engines lost all power. With both engines out on the same side, maintaining aircraft control was difficult at best. The nav called mayday and gave the pilots a safe bailout heading. The captain gave the order to abandon aircraft. The IO acted as jumpmaster and ensured that everyone's parachute was tightly secured just before they jumped. Some of the crew were shot at on their way down.

The O-2, call sign Sundog, was talking to the guys when they had landed. He said to relax, Sandy [A1E rescue plane] *was on the way. A helicopter flew overhead firing guns and rockets at enemy on the ground. An AC-130 Spectre was also flying overhead. When Sandy arrived, Sundog laid down some smoke (Willy Pete). Sundog told the copilot, who was the last one out of the crippled Stinger aircraft, to "pop smoke"* [meaning the smoke end of the flare in the survival vest] *to identify his position. His chute had opened as he had entered the trees. One of the first guys down was picked up by an Army helicopter and flown to Bien Hoa.*

The two Jolly Greens flew the survivors of Crew 13 to a hospital at Tan Son Nhut Air Base in Saigon. The captain managed to control the plane enough for the others to bail out. He did not make it. Neither did two others.

[Years later CMSgt Craig visited the Vietnam Wall. As he so poignantly wrote:]

> **"I'll never know why the rest of Stinger 41 was not on that wall. I'll never know why there was a wall at all."**

[That is powerful. . . .]

[To read CMSgt's account of the ordeal, go to the Gunship Association's website.]

[I just edited (7 December 2018) a Wikipedia article apropos list of aircraft losses in the Vietnam War; I credited CMSgt Corbett as my reference.]

[The copilot and NOS from Crew 13 were friends of mine. In fact, the wife of the NOS shared an apartment in Bangkok with my wife.]

- 55 -

BATTLE OF AN LOC—CLEARING UP MATTERS

The Air Force Mortuary Affairs Office is responsible for handling and settling the affairs of those who have fallen while on active duty anywhere in the world. The office at NKP appointed a Summary Courts Officer (SCO) for each of the three fallen members of Stinger Crew 13. The official description is: "A SCO is a commissioned officer appointed by the installation commander to handle the personal property and effects of deceased active duty personnel and other eligible individuals as specified in AFI 34-244." As the Reader can already determine, this short chapter will essentially be void of attempts at levity.

I was appointed as the Summary Courts Officer for one of the individuals from Stinger 41 who served his country by paying the ultimate price. I was given a briefing of the duties expected of me, a checklist of tasks that needed to be done, and a copy of military regulations authorizing me to perform those duties. It sounds more daunting than it actually was, at least for the Sergeant I represented. (Out of respect for and to honor him, I will capitalize Sergeant and not use his name.)

My first step was to interview the Sergeant's roommates and friends to form a picture of the Sergeant's lifestyle, which in turn would help guide me in subsequent duties. I then asked one of the roommates to be present while I took inventory of the Sergeant's personal property and military-issued equipment in his room and anywhere else he might have had occasion to visit. There was a checklist and inventory sheet I had to complete. This part of my investigation involved "sanitizing" any inappropriate material I found, as the Sergeant's property would be shipped to the next of kin. Exactly what constituted "inappropriate material" was left to my judgement, although I did have some official guidelines. Any such items as girly magazines, compromising photos, certain categories of personal letters, et cetera—any such material that could cause unnecessary embarrassment, sadness, or suffering for those concerned "back home"—were to be disposed of.

My Sergeant had no such material. Also, he had not yet accumulated many of the things military personnel typically purchased overseas—stereo gear, jewelry, clothes, furniture, and whatever the PACEX catalogue offered or that which could be purchased locally. Of course, I had to determine and record the name, relationship, and address of the person to whom the shipment of the Sergeant's goods would be forwarded. This information was available from offices on base, including the 18th SOS. I also contacted the Stinger Detachment admin office in Da Nang to inquire if the Sergeant had left any personal items or had any known outstanding bills to pay. I did the same with our Forward Operating Location in Bien Hoa to arrange for the shipping of the Sergeant's goods to NKP to add to his other items. I also checked on base at NKP if the Sergeant had any unpaid bills, such as cleaners, tailors, a 'Club tab, et cetera.

Another important checklist item for me was finance. I checked and coordinated with the Finance Office to have any earned but not yet disbursed military pay issued to his designated beneficiary/ies. Also included was a notification to the Veterans Administration to pay his beneficiary the $255 death benefit. When I was first in AFROTC in college in 1965, the VA death benefit was $255. When the Sergeant was killed in action (KIA) in 1972, that benefit was still $255. As of September 2018 that death benefit is STILL $255. I suppose Congress does not believe in cost-of-living increases for the masses. At this rate it will always be $255.

For the most part, I did not find much of anything to complicate arrangements, which made checklist items easy to accomplish. I believe our squadron commander was the one who had to write "The Letter" to the next of kin. I think the Sergeant may have had a wife back in the States, but I am not positive. I had to write a report of actions and complete a form to accompany the checklist and other paperwork that I turned in to the appropriate office stating that to the best of my knowledge all outstanding affairs had been settled.

The Reader may be wondering about the recovery and disposition of the Sergeant's body. I had no involvement with that side of settling matters. There was another office that would oversee any arrangements necessary.

When the Mortuary Affairs Office, or it might have possibly been my squadron commander, or both, was/were satisfied that my task had been completed, I was relieved from Summary Courts Officer duty.

Only God could relieve the Sergeant. . . .

- 56 -

LIFE AT DA NANG

Da Nang was, and still is, a coastal city located between the South China Sea to the east and the Bà Nà hills to the west. It is a popular vacation spot now; not so much in 1972, although it was the locale du jour for all of the 50,000 refugees from North Vietnam, when there actually was a North Vietnam to be from. The geography remains pretty much the same—there have been no destructive typhoons or earthquakes. However, the political delineations have changed, as they frequently have over much of the planet.

Other than the frequent nocturnal rocket and sapper attacks, an Air Force aircrew member's life at Da Nang was bearable. There were tennis courts right behind my VOQ. Correction: As I will discuss momentarily, we 18th SOS aircrew members were not there on a "just visiting" basis. A rose by any other name. . . .

I managed to play at tennis some of the afternoons that I was at Da Nang. Rather than just play, I intentionally said "play at," as anyone who has had occasion to be entertained by my lack of prowess on a tennis court would corroborate. Besides, racquetball is a more logical sport; rarely does anyone have to chase a racquetball over a twelve-foot-high fence, hoping to not be shot at. Also, racquetball points are scored in integral intervals. Tennis scoring must have some significant historical value to compensate for the lack of linearity. However, as there were no racquetball courts on base that I knew of, I managed to abuse the tennis courts.

The base swimming pool was close by—at least it was for one whole day after I arrived. It did not really go anywhere itself, but a rocket attack soon rendered it unusable for water festivities. We were quartered in the area known as Gunfighter Village, although I never witnessed two guys facing each other while waiting to see who would draw first and who would be left standing.

- 57 -

DUST BUNNIES

Really. Dust bunnies. In a war zone. Okay, bear with me, and I will disambiguate. (I have heard that if you use a new word at least three times, it will be yours, so to speak. Perhaps by reading this one several times in my epic tome it may, if you so choose, become yours also.)

My unit in Southeast Asia, the 18th SOS (only coincidentally related to the international mayday distress call) was headquartered in Nakhon Phanom, but we had a detachment in Da Nang, which was located about a hundred miles south of the demilitarized zone in northern South Vietnam. (It may have been demilitarized. We took the politician's word for it. (Sure we did). Well, maybe some of the Army or Marine or other units did, but no one in our unit that I knew of ever had occasion to test the theory.)

We also had a Forward Operating Location (FOL) at Bien Hoa Air Base, a tiny bit over five hundred miles to the south of Da Nang and about twelve miles from the city then known as Saigon. However, Bien Hoa has nothing to do with any dust bunnies, or at least any dust bunnies of my acquaintance, so I will steer the Reader back up north to Da Nang.

Although NKP was our PCS location, i.e., our main base of operations, the way the 18th SOS Stingers managed personnel assignments was apparently designed to keep us individuals from becoming bored, complacent, or perhaps both. Most likely there were other immaterial and more mundane criteria involved, such as the needs of the Air Force, but I believe that these two factors were dominant. When some newly assigned troop such as me, for example, would arrive as a Friendly New Guy (FNG) at NKP, we would expect to spend most of our tour there performing our various duties, be they in maintenance, intelligence, admin, flying combat missions, or whatever our particular job was. My job, of course, was being a gallant Stinger Gunship copilot. I included the "gallant" part to add a little color and flavor to the story. Da Nang now is a city with a population of over one million and is a popular vacation destination. About two or three months after initially arriving at NKP we would be "rotated" over to Da Nang for 130 days.

There was some significance to that 130 days number —it was not arbitrary—but I do not remember what it was. This rotation formula was via a neat little smoke and mirror trick discovered by an Air Force accountant who was probably holed up in a Pentagon dungeon somewhere nine thousand miles away, plus or minus a couple of miles. To wit, we were sent over PCS without a PCA (Permanent Change of Assignment). When we rotated to Da Nang and later back to NKP, we ferried one of our own gunships over. The aircraft rotated back to NKP for inspections and required maintenance. Most of us, at least those of us junior officers and junior enlisted troops, had never heard of such an animal —I am trying to be polite here —as a *PCS without a PCA*. The way this magic phenomenon was explained to me was that it was all a matter of economics. If we were merely sent to Da Nang on a Temporary Duty status, we would have to have been paid an additional five dollars a day per diem pay (that is what officers got paid (correction—would have gotten paid). It may have been the same for enlisted troops also, but I do not know). That would have come to an additional $650 ($5 x 130 days) of non-taxable pay per person over and above our regular pay. One would think. But one would be incorrect in thinking so. There were only two problems with this line of reasoning: 1) One would be using non-government logic, and 2) Don't forget about the accountant in the Pentagon dungeon. Somehow that got translated to mean, "Although we are moving you somewhere else, you are still assigned here and have the same job assignment, and since you therefore are not TDY, you are not entitled to TDY pay."

TDY pay is designed to partially offset the extra cost of incurring expenses in two locations at the same time. The $650 is not a whole lot of money, especially when spread out just a little over a third of a year, but when multiplied by however many personnel we had there at any one time on a continuous basis, it apparently totaled a sum of sufficient quantity to get an accountant's attention. In 1972 dollars, it was even more noticeable. He or she—the sharp-eyed, ever-diligent Air Force accountant-type person—probably eventually got a job as a chief financial officer in a major corporation making enough money in one year to have paid all of the five dollars per day for everyone and not have even noticed it. Capitalism works.

When we were sent to our Forward Operating Location at Bien Hoa for a week, or sometimes two, it was on a TDY basis, and we got paid the five dollars per day. We were sent there TDY from either NKP or Da Nang—from whichever base we happened to be PCS at the time. There were not as many of us at Bien Hoa as there were at Da Nang. The difference between a detachment and an FOL is primarily size and purpose. A detachment such as the 18th SOS unit at Da Nang had a significant and permanent presence, as far as "permanent presence" may mean in military terms, of personnel and equipment at its location. An FOL such as the 18th SOS unit at Bien Hoa Air Base, on the other hand, is supported by a minimal number of permanent party personnel and minimal amount of equipment and may host rotational forces and equipment as needed. An FOL is usually established to address regional threats.

Bien Hoa was a relatively (EIR) major military facility in southern South Vietnam, but we Stingers were limited as to where we could wander around the base, even if we could scrounge ground transportation; round trip was highly preferable. Accordingly, there was not a lot to spend money on, at least for me, so I managed to live on less than that five dollars a day.

Of course, large quantities of money could be and were spent on things ordered from the ubiquitous glossy one-inch-thick, color PACEX catalogue. There were 200-plus glossy pages of furniture, clothing, beaucoup jewelry items, and especially stereo gear. Before leaving my little "vacation" in SEA, I was no different from every other person ever stationed anywhere west of

California. Before leaving Southeast Asia I ordered a "standard" stereo system to supplement—i.e., replace—my $30 portable cassette recorder that I used to make "voice tapes." (The Reader may recall that voice tapes were vocal letters on cassettes to send and receive from home.) Four-channel quadra-sonic systems were the latest in vogue for stereo systems at the time. I decided that I "needed" an Akai 7-inch reel-to-reel 4-channel tape deck; a Sansui 6500 4-channel tuner/amplifier (it had output terminals for ten speakers; I used them all at home); a Garrard Zero-100 4-channel turn table, and four Pioneer CS-99 speakers—the big ones. At home we had lamps on top of a couple of them. Such stereo gear was encased in wood and was attractive to view and touch.

Many guys chose to receive their stereo gear and set it up in their rooms at NKP. Since we were assigned two to a room, which were about the size of college dorm rooms, it got a bit tricky when both guys set up their stereo gear. Careful where you walk. Ergo I was able to check out the various pieces of equipment first-hand before deciding on exactly what I wanted—the Garrard or the Dual? The Akai or the TEAC? The Sansui or the Pioneer? Decisions, decisions. Some guys also had reverberation units, cassette decks, 8-track decks (something of nostalgia now, like more recent VCRs), pre-amps, and I don't know what all else. I remember seeing in a catalogue a Bose tuner—it was a tuner only, meaning a radio which needed an amplifier to operate and speakers to hear anything for—$2,000, just for the tuner. That was considerably more than I paid for my entire stereo system. After all, I was still on a lowly 1st Lieutenant's pay.

I had my stereo components all sent to my stateside training location at Castle AFB, Merced, CA (pronounced Mer-SAID, not merced as in rhyming with nursed). Andrea and I stayed in an efficiency room in a Motel 6—back when it really did cost only $6 a night—for about three or four months while I and a number of fellow former Stingers trained on the KC-135A. The boxes holding all my stereo gear were stacked in a corner in the motel room; somehow we still managed to have barely enough room to get around them. It was a sad day for me about forty years later when I finally parted with my lovely stereo gear. I say lovely because back then the electronics were encased in teak and other woods. I had paid about $400 (maybe $403) for my tape deck in January 1973. When it needed some repair work a number of years later, I was told that parts and labor would cost about $1,000. Needless to say, I could not find it in myself to spend that kind of money on my poor, well-aged tape deck. Those of you who were "over there" are probably fondly remembering your own stereo systems right about now.

At this point the Reader may well be wondering what all this has to do with dust bunnies. Sorry, I got a little carried away on the stereo bit. I have heard that patience is a virtue, but I have never had the patience to indulge in it myself. Eventually my turn came to rotate to Da Nang from NKP. The flight only took about two hours. It was a hot Saturday afternoon when we arrived. I was given a newcomer's briefing, was able to convert my "greenbacks" to Military Payment Certificates (in Thailand we used baht or US Dollars), and was issued a flack vest and a helmet. Needless to say, these last two items got my attention and aroused my curiosity. I had heard reports that Da Nang Air Base was the target of NVA rocket attacks. The Stinger operation at Da Nang was to fly perimeter defense missions south of the base where the

NVA operated. I was told to put vest and helmet someplace in my room out of the way but readily available, like under the bed.

The next day was a sunny Sunday. That evening I was sitting at my military-issue desk—you know the type: non-descript gray vinyl writing surface, dull steel legs—writing a letter to Andrea to tell her about my new environs. Above the desk was the room air conditioner. I remember being distracted by strange sounds unfamiliar to me. They sounded muffled and a little distant. *Whoompf. Whoompf.* Then suddenly I heard a *WHOOMPF!* and the plastic cover to my air conditioning unit fell off onto the desk in front of me. Being the ever-alert, quick-witted, combat-experienced pilot that I was, I immediately surmised, after a moment or two of contemplation, that this was a rocket attack. I remembered the flack vest and helmet under my bed. I reached under and retrieved and donned both; they smelled musty and army-ish, but I put them on anyway. Then I started to take cover under the bed—that is, until I saw lurking there in the shadow . . .

Dust bunnies (Photo: Shutterstock)

. . . Dust Bunnies.

Big, hairy dust bunnies. Just waiting for a victim for dinner. I didn't think that anyone had cleaned under there since. . . ever, probably. And I, for one, was certainly not going to share a space already occupied by these creatures. Sooo, quick-thinking and college-educated officer that I was, I employed the second two parts of the three-procedure plan common for all aircraft emergencies (here is a reminder for you non-aviators): 1) Maintain aircraft control (obviously, since I was not flying an aircraft at that particular moment, this first step did not apply. 2) Analyze the situation. 3) Take proper action.

1) N/A.

2) Probable rocket attack, about which I had heard.

3) I noticed my white laundry bag against the wall. I decided to lie on the floor up against the wall, wearing my flack vest and helmet, and I put my laundry bag over my head for further protection. We all know the axiom: What you can't see won't hurt you.

I found the sounds and vibrations from the impacts of the rockets to be disquieting. Being in the target zone of enemy rockets was a totally new—and unenjoyable—experience for me. When I heard and felt a very loud *WOOMPF*, which must have been very close, it really got my attention. For the second time since arriving in this "war," I felt fear. I knew I was in imminent danger and there was absolutely nothing I could do about it. I knew the next rocket would be a direct hit on my room. The feeling of helplessness quickly consumed me. The feeling of being scared was like nothing in my realm of experience; it was even greater than what I felt during "my very second combat mission" over the PDJ. Back then when we were flying in a sky nearly full of triple A, we could and did fly away somewhere to safety.

Fortunately, the cause of my fear was not long-lived. Seemingly as soon as they had started, the whoompfs stopped. All was quiet except for the pulsating sound of blood being pumped through my ears. The whoompf that I thought was the harbinger of my last experience on Earth, which made me think I was never again to see Andi, the love of my life, was not followed by any further explosions. However, as I crouched by the wall under the protection of my nearly empty laundry bag, I had no way of knowing at that time that the danger was over. After waiting for two or three more minutes for more whoompfs, my fear subsided sufficiently that I bravely stood up and assessed the situation. It is not an experience one can just imagine; it needs to actually be experienced to understand the thoughts and emotions that invade your mind.

Not long after they had started, the whoompfs had stopped. I was pretty sure that I had just survived my first rocket attack. And to my credit, my underwear was still clean. Time to reconnoiter and get some information from some of the guys that had been there longer than I. My Visiting Officers Quarters building had not been hit directly by any rockets—just a few small pieces of shrapnel had hit the building but had done no harmful damage.

The VOQ building next to and south of mine—the direction from which had cometh the rockets—had not been quite so lucky. Neither had the Stinger captain who had just been leaving to go fly a mission. I had not met him, but I saw him lying in his flight suit just outside his building's main entrance. A shoulder had been destroyed by a hunk of shrapnel. Another piece had pierced the inch-thick vinyl-encased pages of his checklist, which was still in a lower leg pocket of his flight suit, or what was left of it— and had unkindly ripped off a large portion of his leg. Those were his injuries that I remember seeing. He may have had others that I did not see or do not remember. Medical and spiritual efforts to save his life were unsuccessful.

Compared to that dismal scene, the report that the base swimming pool had been damaged and was closed until it could be repaired was rather nugatory.

When the activity settled down a bit and my curiosity was sufficiently satisfied, I went back to my room and finished the letter to my wife. I put my flack vest and helmet back under the bed so the dust bunnies could safeguard them until I needed them again. . . .

To this day, over four decades later, if I am anywhere and hear a sound similar to the whoompf—somewhat like the sound made by swinging restaurant doors between the kitchen and the dining area swooshing open and closed—it will instantly attract my attention. I feel a brief adrenalin rush as arm and leg muscles twitch, ready for movement to take cover. If I am with Andrea, I ask her, "Did you hear that?"

"Heard what?"

The Dust Bunnies know. . . .

- 58 -

A BRIDGE TOO FAR?

A few of my relatives and a lot of my friends and acquaintances used to play bridge, and I really enjoyed the game. A typical social evening would consist of dinner, wine (red, white or rosé?), and a few rubbers of bridge afterward. That was pretty much the way it was at Da Nang, except for the part about dinner and the part about wine. In my building we usually had an all-night bridge game going at a table in a common area on the second floor. There was a risqué (EIR) poster decorating one wall; some of you might remember the one, "The American Dream." If you remember it, you are already smiling. If not, disregard that I even mentioned it.

The way Bridge beginners are taught to arrange their cards

We flew night missions and did a bit of sleeping during the day. At some point after dinner a few of us who did not have to fly the first frag would get a bridge game going. (A frag was a sortie—i.e., a mission.) Four of us would play, and there were usually others around who managed to kibitz. We only had one table and four chairs available; otherwise, we could have had more games going at the same time, thereby potentially eliminating the kibitzers. However, kibitzers were not disruptive, since we all played that position at one time or another. When a guy needed a break or had to leave to go fly the next frag, a kibitzer would sit in and take his place. It was quite common for a player to start playing, later leave to fly a mission, return about five or six hours later still, and rejoin the game when another player had to leave. Those who did not have to fly that night or who had already completed their mission occasionally brought a six-pack to the table. If you did have a mission to fly, alcohol was, of course, strictly verboten, and no one considered violating that regulation. Federal Aviation Regulations and even more stringent USAF Regulations strictly prohibit any alcohol consumption within eight hours of flying as an aircrew member, period. No Ifs, Ands, or Buts. And no slack.

Speaking of butts, for practical safety reasons, smoking was/is not allowed within fifty feet of an aircraft. Only an idiot or a terrorist would think to light up around thousands of gallons of potential instant cremation. There is an old joke about not drinking within fifty feet of an airplane and not smoking within eight hours of flying. However, both regs are eminently serious.

Besides the minor ramifications of court martial, possible imprisonment, and losing your wings, it was just plain dangerous and not tolerated. It was not as if you were in a single-seat fighter or Forward Air Controller (FAC) aircraft and only had yourself to kill. Also, the Air Force Powers That Be would most likely be disappointed in having lost an expensive combat aerospace vehicle. There were nine other guys on the -119 crew whose lives depended on you to do your job competently. "Illegal" drinking over there was never an issue that I was aware of.

- 59 -

NO HAB KITCHEN

The Reader may think I am just making this story up. However, I assure you that all of it is completely true. Although they may not have been eye-witnesses to this actual event, there are thousands of military types still around who have been to the No Hab Kitchen and can verify the likelihood of the veracity of what I am about to relate to you. As I have said elsewhere, I am neither a creative nor an imaginative person. That is why I am writing about factual things I know and remember (maybe) rather than about fictionalized portrayals of Earth being overcome by a highly advanced (compared to any Earth-type inhabitants (EIR)) sentient, almost lavender, ethereal essence from the incredibly enormous black hole at the center of our next door (EIR) neighbor, the Andromeda galaxy, which is about 2.2 million light years away. One light year is about 5.879 *trillion* miles, with a T. Those people living far enough south—like in the southern hemisphere—who can find the Andromeda galaxy in the night sky, are looking at the farthest object visible to the unaided human eye.

If you are interested in reading some "out there" sci-fi, Fred Hudgin has written some quite imaginative and interesting books, including *The School of the Gods*. In his effort to present some accuracy in a part that was fiction but not science fiction, he had asked me some aviation questions. From there I was one of his proofreaders for the book. This link is to the Kindle version: https://www.amazon.ca/The-School-Gods-Fredrick-Hudgin-ebook/dp/B00M5EHTC6

This is the link to the paperback version: https://www.amazon.com/School-Gods-Fredrick-Hudgin/dp/1539728447

In northeastern South Vietnam there was an area on Da Nang Air Base called Gunfighter Village, mentioned earlier. It was basically the residential and commercial area of the base for us military types. When I was a resident in 1972, it was a relatively safe place to be during the day—at least on the inside of the base perimeter fence. After dark it was a different matter since that was when the NVA would set up and launch their six-foot-long rockets onto the base. The swimming pool had been damaged by a rocket in an attack the night after I first arrived. It was not my fault, in case you are trying to mentally associate time/effect causal relationships.

For dinner the Officers Club and NCO Club had limited menus offering fares not really worth traveling nine thousand miles over the Earth's surface, or just above it, in anticipation of epicurean pleasures. However, since I was already there, for dinner my fellow Stingers and I would wander on over to whichever club we had decided on for the evening. One could eat a well-done steak—not *done well* as in medium rare, but *well done* as in nearly charcoal—and instant mashed potatoes only so many nights in a week. At least the price of the meal was only a couple of dollars or so.

Fortunately, as it just so happened, for our gastronomic pleasure there was at least one other option for enjoyment nearby, a tiny Vietnamese food emporium ("tiny" and "emporium" are, I admit, slightly oxymoronic when used conjunctionally) called the No Hab Kitchen. Literally. That's what the sign said. I do not believe there was any eat-in seating available; I think there might have been a couple of outdoor tables and chairs.

I did not use it that much, but there were enough people on base to keep it in business. I suppose it was run under the auspices of the US military; it may even have been a military facility run by the local Vietnamese. It mattered not when one was in the mood for plain old junk food. It was not a restaurant. It was a tiny place with a counter in front and the "kitchen" plainly visible just behind it. The little Vietnamese man behind the counter would take your order, fry the burger or other culinary delights, and wrap the food so that you could walk away and take it back to your room or enjoy on a bench in the tennis courts or on the table out front. Pretentious would never be an adjective anyone would use to describe the No Hab Kitchen, but there still existed an unmistakable aura of fondness for the little place.

As it happened one pleasant evening—almost as if to provide me an anecdote for the future—I strolled down to the No Hab Kitchen, deciding what I might be in the mood for to satisfy my gastronomic desires. A hamburger or a hot dog? French fries or onion rings? The usual "bachelor" fare.

As I approached the open counter, the little Vietnamese fellow working as the short order cook du jour asked in his broken English, which was mucho bettero than my Vietnamese (or Spanish), "Herroh, GI, Wha you hab?" in whatever dialect he used and which I will not attempt to reconstruct at this time. We were all GIs to him and, technically, he was correct; GI just means Government Issue.

I said, "Hi, Tran," or whatever his name was. I stood there reading the posted menu on the large sign behind the counter. Hamburger, cheeseburger, hot dog . . . I had already decided while walking on my way there what I was going to have as my evening repast.

"I'll hab a hamburger, fries, and a Coke," (an all-American meal if there ever was one).

Tran said, "Sorry, GI, no hab hamburger." (And now you know why it was called the No Hab Kitchen.)

I looked over his head and re-read the large white menu board with the large black letters, which clearly included hamburgers, cheeseburgers, hot dogs, fries, et cetera. I really do not like cheese (yes, I'm the one). That was not my first time at the No Hab Kitchen, so I figured out a strategy to get around the problem.

I asked, in my broken English, "You hab cheeseburger, papasan?"

"Sure, GI, hab cheeseburger."

"You make me cheeseburger, no cheese."

"Okay, GI"

And that's the way I got my hamburger from the No Hab Kitchen. I left with the meal as I had pre-planned it, which included a hamburger, a.k.a. cheeseburger with no cheese.

True story.

- 60 -

THERE IS A COROLLARY TO THE STORY

The Eiffel Tower
The blue-ish twinkle lights come on
every hour after dark for five minutes

Just about forty years later Andrea and I were walking along the Seine River in Paris one lovely April evening—yes, "April in Paris"—and around dinner-time we came upon an outdoor restaurant beside the river. The Eiffel Tower was just across the street, so we were between it and the river. What a setting! It was a restaurant and not just a café; it was too large for a café, even though most of the seating was outside not far from the river. By "not far" I mean the distance would be measured in feet—or more likely meters, since France was among most of the rest of the world which uses the civilized metric system. We found a table for two, which worked out rather well since there were only the two of us. After waiting for what I considered a more than reasonable amount of time for the attention of a waiter or waitress—I do not think that they had upgraded to "servers" there yet—I got up and got a couple of menus myself.

There was not an extensive menu, but we were not interested in a big dinner that night anyway. We were mostly out strolling around enjoying the evening; we were only a little hungry, as we had just arrived the day before and were still experiencing a little jet lag. (I have never had it explained to me why jet lag is a little worse when flying from west to east than from vice versa. Perhaps it has something to do with Coriolis, entropy, and creamy peanut butter, but I cannot say for sure.)

I perused the menu for something non-cheesy and non-fishy. Okay, I do not like seafood either. I am a meat and potatoes kinda guy, and yes, I am fully aware of the severe menu restrictions this persnicketiness imposes on me at restaurants; just keep pouring the Bordeaux. I was left with my choice of . . . a cheeseburger. There were no hamburgers listed on the café menu. But! They did have cheeseburgers. Okay, been there, done that. I was in a situation with which I had previous wartime experience.

There was an attractive young (EIR) couple sitting close by at another table for two who happened to overhear my comment to Andrea about this being the No Hab Kitchen all over again. The couple at the other table apparently were fluent in English (who isn't these days, except for perhaps a large quantity of Americans?), and we saw them smile. Since the couple apparently understood English, I then related the No Hab Kitchen story to them. My wife had heard it many times, of course, and she politely listened to it once again.

After about a half hour, a waitress noticed me standing by our empty table looking around. I suppose I could have picked her up and physically carried her to the table, but in a prior decade I had read *The Ugly American*. Besides, I did not think my wife would have fully appreciated any such effort I may have suffered on her behalf. The waitress finally came over, reluctantly, it seemed to me, to take our order. Andrea ordered a salad. And the perspicacious Reader knows what is coming next.

After taking Andrea's order the waitress turned to me, pad and pencil in hand. "I would like a cheeseburger with *noooo* (emphasized) cheese, s'il vous plait," I said, showing off my copious multi-lingualness. I should have said "noooo fromage," but I did not remember the French word for cheese at the time. In college, two years of French and I had not gotten along particularly well.

She replied with all the snooty indignation she could muster, "That is called a HOMburger, monsieur."

Rising to the challenge, as I was already insufficiently impressed with the service and commensurate lack thereof, my prepared and immediate retort to her was, "Yes, but you do not have HOMburgers on your menu! You only have cheeseburgers," I replied back, perhaps not quite as gentlemanly as I should have.

I thought the couple next to us were going to fall out of their chairs laughing.

I did not leave an overly impressive tip, but it did reflect what I thought of the service. Fortunately for Andrea and me, that waitress must have just been having a bad day, because, during our entire week in Paris, she was the only person we encountered who was cranky. One hears about the haughty attitude the French have, especially toward Americans. However, I have no idea where that baseless rumor started. Except for the one waitress who may have just had a long day, we never encountered even a hint of unpleasantness. Just the opposite. We would go back in a heartbeat.

By the way, the real estate now called Vietnam used to be called French Indochina. Ah, the ties that bind.

- 61 -

PREFLIGHT AT DA NANG

AC-119 parked within protective revetment walls at Da Nang

AC-119G (no jets) Ditto the above

We had no revetments to provide at least some protection from rockets at NKP nor at Bien Hoa. There is a reasonable argument for this apparently questionable situation. There were no incoming rocket attacks at those two bases. Mystery solved. Da Nang was a horse of a different flavor. (I like to mix or modify metaphors; that way the Reader does not get bored to sleep, perchance to dream. The latter was me borrowing a couple or so words from Shakespeare again. It is difficult to write anything original anymore, what with all of the great mass of literature that precedeth. Shakespeare or Chaucer or Leon Redbone probably wrote that one, too. I don't think Shakespeare would mind; after all, he has spent his time on Earth and moved on.)

The typical rockets the North Vietnamese graced upon us were about six-feet long and very portable. Some could be aimed and fired from a supported shoulder-mount position (first photo below). Others could be set up with timers and abandoned to launch long after the NVA had left the area (second photo below). These timers were, as often as not, simply wrist watches, some with the hour hand broken off. If the rocket emplacement was later discovered by the Army of the Republic of Vietnam (ARVN, i.e, the good guys), they would not know if the rockets were set to launch in a few minutes or in a few hours.

(Above) NVA ready to launch rocket propelled grenades (RPGs)

Rockets being prepared for launch

Airborne-launched flares

In the aftermath of a rocket attack, it would ruin your whole ~~day~~ night

Another tactic employed by the NVA to try to destroy the operations at Da Nang was by using sappers. These were native Vietnamese people who would blend in with their fellow countrymen/women/children of the South and smuggle, steal, or use other methods to get explosive material, which they would clandestinely place at locations designated by their superiors. Often they would merely get as close as they could to a perimeter fence —which was close enough to an area where damage would be done—if they were not caught. The perimeter fence was patrolled by soldiers on foot, but it was not rocket surgery (sorry, couldn't resist) to time the patrols, get to a designated target area, arm the explosives, and then get back out quickly.

After getting our aircraft assignment, intel, weather, enemy activity, and other briefings, the ten of us Stinger aircrew men with our carry-on equipment and manuals would get into the back end of a crew transport truck to be taken to the aircraft. The crew transport truck was much like any of the ones you see in movies with a wooden or metal bench seat on each side in the back of the truck. Our carry-on went in the middle. The sides of the truck were thin aluminum, tin, or other metal, which could keep any rain out but were definitely insufficient to stop or even slow down the penetration by any supersonic-speed shrapnel from a rocket explosion.

If we were lucky—and by "we" I'm referring to everyone on base in harm's way—the control tower siren and others would begin their wailing, warning of an imminent attack. All a person could do then would be to get prone on the ground. This would create a low profile, minimizing the possibility of getting injured, or worse, by invisible, speeding, hot jagged pieces of shrapnel that might be headed one's way. Unless you unfortunately happened to be in too close of a proximity to the rocket impact site, or you happened to be in the less likely line of a piece shrapnel flying at ground level, lying prone could save you from having your body begin leaking red fluid. Any other color of fluid would certainly be understandable and not be a cause for shame.

As you can surmise from the photos above, the rocket and sapper attacks were taken very seriously. Unless a rocket hit in the revetment itself or in front of it where there was no protective wall, minimal damage would be done to an aircraft and any personnel within its boundaries. However, aircraft wings and fuel systems were full of thousands of pounds of JP-4 or other highly volatile aviation fuel. Any shrapnel finding its way to these targets could set off secondary explosions dwarfing the detonation of the rocket itself.

Once the crew truck dropped us off at our aircraft du ~~jour~~ nuit, we all began our respective preflight checklists. Before we began the Engine Start checklist, whoever felt the need or precaution deboarded the plane for the ritual emptying of the bladder up against the revetment walls. When everyone was back in place aboard the aircraft, the copilot—me, in my case—radioed the ground controller in the tower for clearance to start engines. Any time after the beginning of engine start, if the incoming rocket attack sirens began their aural warning and the tower announced the attack over the military guard channel, which is always monitored by US military aircraft, it became time for immediate aircraft evacuation. This managed to happen one night as I was part of a crew preparing for a mission. We two pilots and the FE shut down the engines and feathered the props immediately, not bothering to wait for engine oil scavenging, while the captain simultaneously shouted over the intercom, "INCOMING! GET OFF THE PLANE NOW!" And everyone did. The primary importance of getting the reciprocating engines shut down and the props feathered quickly was for safety. When under a rocket attack, the adrenalin instantly gets the body mobilized. Get off the plane NOW! Don't think about it—just do it.

No one needed to potentially make a bad night infinitely worse by running face-first into a spinning propeller blade. In any metal-to-flesh contest, the metal always wins. So it would be with propeller blades, especially spinning ones; the prop blade was guaranteed to win in every case. That is why the flight engineer feathered the props to stop them from spinning. Running into a spinning propeller blade was usually fatal; running into a stopped blade would hurt and require a few stitches. One can live with a zipper-like scar; not so with a missing head.

There was not time to do anything but get off the plane and take cover. And wouldn't you know it, the best immediate cover was a prone position up against the nearest revetment wall—those same walls that we had just recently visited, in a standing position—and listen for the *WHOOMPS*.

No big deal. Bodies and flight suits could be cleaned after we got back to the Qs. In the meantime, when the sirens abated into silence once more, we got up and walked just outside the revetment walls to determine if we could see any damage around our area. Then the captain, table nav, and I re-boarded the plane to get on the radios. We contacted the tower, and the nav also contacted our command post. When the supervisor of flying, or whatever the Da Nang equivalent was titled, drove the taxiways and runway and radioed that none were damaged and all were cleared of any potential damaging debris, a.k.a. FOD (foreign object damage), we got the rest of the crew back on board and carried on with our mission. We may have done some shooting that night, I don't remember for sure, but I am almost certain that we "let off some steam" within authorized limits. Too little, too late for that night, however.

- 62 -

TARGETS OF OPPORTUNITY

The Stingers at Da Nang Air Base were primarily tasked with flying perimeter defense missions. With the Da Nang Bay (or the
Gulf of Tonkin, depending on who is reporting) to the north and
the South China Sea (or the East Vietnam Sea, again, whoever
the mapmaker happens to be) to the east, both of which are mi-
crocosms of the South China Sea (you may mentally insert the
Shakespeare rose quote again here if you so desire) and mountains
not far to the west, this meant we were to fly around at about
3,500 to 4,500 feet AGL southwest and south of the base within
about seven nautical miles. (A nautical mile is 1.15078 statute
miles; I always round off the factor to 1.15, which is close enough
for practical purposes and allows you to mentally figure conver-
sions to statute miles easily.) We looked for North Vietnamese
military or any other militants setting up positions from which
to launch rocket attacks onto the base. These rockets were about
six or seven feet long and very portable. They could be set up

anywhere that was convenient for the NVA. The rockets could be set to launch by using a simple timer, giving the perpetrators time to leave the area before the Stingers flew overhead. By the time the rockets were launched, the perpetrators could be long gone.

While flying night perimeter defense missions just south of Da Nang, we were searching for guys on the ground who looked to be engaged in nefarious activities. Whenever we saw any such suspicious targets of opportunity, we would fly a firing circle above them while getting both night sensors tracking the targets, getting the guns ready, and getting into a good altitude and airspeed. One might reasonably think that we could then just start shooting and save the day—er, night. But, there was a war going on, so we were told, and there are rules of engagement in warfare. Really. Okay, no problem. We knew what the mission was that we were tasked to do. One might reasonably think that also.

And One would be wrong on both counts.

Even though we had identified potentially viable targets, there were certain Rules of Engagement (ROE). ("Rules, Butch? In a knife fight?") There were procedures to be followed:

The sensor operators would track the target.

The table nav would plot the latitude and longitude coordinates and relay this information to the USAF command post at Da Nang . . .

who would relay the information to their VNAF (Vietnamese Armed Forces) command post equivalents . . .

who would relay the information to their army units in the field . . .

who would plot the coordinates and check with other scouting units in the area to determine whether the target was any of their troops or "the other guys" . . .

then they would relay the information back to their command post . . .

who would relay the information to our command post . . .

who would relay the information to us.

If the target was the good guys, we would move on and look for targets elsewhere.

If the target was the bad guys, or at least confirmed to not be good guys, we were given clearance to fire upon the target.

This target confirmation process took about 45 minutes, give or take a few minutes. Finally we could start shooting. Lucky for us that we had six radios plus intercom to listen to.

One slight problem which the analytical Reader may have determined by now:

The target of opportunity had become a target of opportunity lost; the enemy on the ground were no longer around. (That sounds rather Dr. Suess-ish, although completely unintentially. Honest.)

After several years of conducting these little exercises, the North Vietnamese knew the sound of Stinger engines and could make themselves scarce. The rockets themselves did not give off a heat signature until their engines ignited. Of course, by then it was too late for us to do anything to prevent it. We would press on looking for other targets. After all, we had to justify the cost of all those radios and intercom.

The Reader may wonder how we managed to be effective at all, but the process I just outlined above was for targets of opportunity.

At our pre-flight intel briefings, we were given specific areas where we were already cleared to shoot. The table nav would have those areas plotted, and we would search there. Sometimes we lit the target areas by having the illuminator operator launch flares and/or use our "big flash-light."

As I recall, the flares only lasted a few minutes before another one might need to have been launched. No problem there; the flare launcher carried twenty-four flares, and I do not remember ever running out of them on a mission. Naturally we didn't use the big light if known or suspected enemy AAA fire was close enough to be a hazard for us. No sense in showing them exactly where to shoot. "Hey you guys down there, we're over here; see the light?" I would think that situation would be similar to a downed crewmember shooting his six 38 caliber tracer rounds during a gunfire fight with guys on the ground who were looking for him and armed with AK-47s, the difference being a matter of scale.

And so it went.

- 63 -

BRASS—NOT THE KIND THAT SAT AROUND TABLES SMOKING CIGARS AND PLANNING STRATEGY

The Vietnamese were very resourceful people. Entrepreneurs abounded.

While the South Vietnamese Army (SVA) were firing artillery rounds of various sizes all over the country, not to mention beau-coup 7.62, the NVA were firing right back in kind. The business end of these types of ammunition, a.k.a. the projectiles, or "bul-lets," if you prefer, were made of lead alloyed with hard metals, lead filled with explosive and/or incendiary material, et cetera. These projectiles were a bit harder to "entrepreneurial-ize" since they were located in territory infested with surviving enemy; or were embedded in the ground, trees, bodies, buildings, and trucks; or were blown to small bits and scattered if they were of the explosive variety; or were just plain hard to find.

On the other end of the artillery rounds, as with most any am-munition, were the brass cartridges. One nice thing about these cartridges was that after the 105 mm Howitzer cannons, 40 mm cannons, 37 mm cannons, 23 mm cannons, 20 mm cannons, and 7.62 mm AK-47 rounds were fired, the cartridges were ejected somewhere close by and were easily findable. In the case of the Howitzer rounds, they probably managed to get in the way at times. After all, those cartridges were over four inches in diameter and over fourteen inches long. With a bunch of them lying around it would not be hard to trip over one. Hundreds and thousands and millions of rounds of ammunition were fired during the decades of strife from imperialism and civil war, especially after President Lyndon Johnson drastically escalated US involvement across the "pond." All of this brass provided a vast supply of raw material to clever Vietnamese craftsmen and women. I imagine that most of the brass was lying around waiting to be found, or in piles, or in ammo cans waiting to be discarded. I would not doubt it at all if some of the ARVN types thought to make a buck or few—or Dong or few—by selling the expended brass shell casings to the locals.

 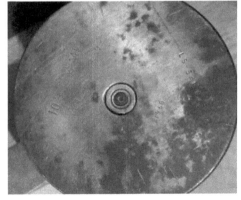

A 105 mm shell casing made into a "mug." This shell is dated 1968, which you can see (maybe) at about the 3:30 position near the center of the right-hand photo. (Personal photos)

These crafts-persons (once in a great while I succumb to political correctness; rest assured that it will not happen often) worked their magic and transformed these materials of war and destruction into decorative household items and useful hand tools. Mugs, ash trays, crucifixes (rather diabolical, don't you think? A crucifix made from 7.62 mm shell casings) and such. I have three 105 mm expended cartridges cut shorter and made into mugs; not particularly useful as mugs, unless you are drinking buddies with Hulk Hogan or Arnold Schwarzenegger. They weigh about 4.2 pounds empty and can easily be used as a paperweight for a whole ream of paper. Mine are engraved with the Stinger logo and some data about who (me), what, where, and when. (Notice the conspicuous absence of "why.") I had one made to give to my grandfather and one for Charlie as well (more about him back in chapters 50 and 51). Of course, I also had one made for myself. I wish I had bought a nicely fluted flower vase made from a 40 mm cartridge. On the other hand, they *are* brass and someone (me again) would have become the official polisher of everything made out of brass back at home, wherever that turned out to be.

- 64 -

WATCH OUT BELOW!

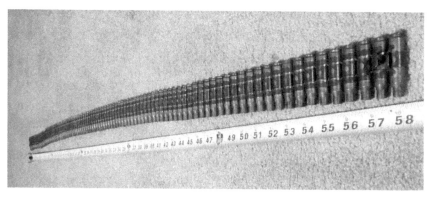

One hundred linked 7.62 mm cartridges—ONE second's worth of ammunition from one mini-gun, two inches shy of being five feet long. (Personal photo)

Many Readers may have never seen a visual of the concept of what those belt-fed 100 rounds per *second* fired from a mini-gun look like. A little arithmetic reveals that 58 inches per second is 3,480 feet per minute. That comes to just a shade under two-thirds of a mile per minute or just over 39 ½ miles per hour. Not very fast if you are slugging along the interstate in rush hour, but 100 rounds per second is 360,000 rounds per hour. That is a nice gee whiz number but relatively (EIR) worthless as far as any practicality is concerned, as the Reader has most likely concluded.

When our mission was finished for the night, which meant that our replacement was airborne (unless we happened to be the last sortie of the predawn morning), we returned to base. We rarely even got out of visual range of Da Nang. The procedure was to fly out just past the coast over the South China Sea and dump brass. That means that all the spent 7.62 mm and 20 mm brass cartridges on board were to be dumped overboard. The low-light scope and the infrared scope searched for signs of life below. Many Vietnamese people lived in their sampans and were anchored for the night. Many knew to keep a light or other heat source visible to the sky so that we could detect them and avoid "bombing" them with all that brass.

Even though empty, thousands of brass cartridges falling from 1,000 feet would reach a terminal velocity of 242 feet per second, which is about 165 miles per hour, after 7 ½ seconds— enough to smash clean through a wooden sampan and seriously injure or kill any humans on board. We made every effort to avoid collateral damage of both humans and their boats. I never heard any feedback about injuries and/or damage being done, but that does not mean that it did not inadvertently occur on occasion.

As we entered the flight pattern and were on short final to land from the north over Da Nang city, we were occasionally shot at by small arms fire from within the city. Da Nang, being a hundred miles south of the Demilitarized Zone (DMZ), was a refugee center, but not all of the refugees were friendly. The small arms fire, meaning hand-held rifles or pistols, never did any serious damage, and I never heard of any crewmembers being injured from it. The only evidence we had was when a maintenance crew discovered a small bullet hole somewhere in the aircraft underside. Naturally we could not retaliate by firing into a crowded populous. Besides, our guns were stowed in place, the sensors were off, and we were too low.

After debriefing the maintenance and intel types, we headed back to our Q rooms to unwind. I usually went to see if there was an opening in the bridge game that I had left about four and a half hours earlier.

Such was life in a war zone.

PART 4

- 65 -

ANDREA ARRIVES IN BANGKOK

Most countries have customs and courtesies that are common throughout the world, and most countries have other customs and courtesies that are peculiar to that country. There are also cultural differences within countries. This is no news to anyone.

These are neither profound nor even original statements, as they are fairly common knowledge, especially among those people who have travelled to distant lands—distant from their perspective—or who live near international borders. They have experienced these cultural differences firsthand. Others have read or studied about them, or seen movies depicting realism, or at least the Hollywood version of sorts. And, of course, with the advent of the internet and its world-wide coverage over our planet, the world has indeed become smaller, though it certainly may not seem that way to anyone flying from New York City to Australia or hiking the 2,160 miles of the Appalachian Trail. (For anyone considering hiking that journey or who have already walked part or all of the Trail, I recommend for your reading pleasure Bill Bryson's *A Walk in the Woods*, his detailed and laugh-out-loud account of his own particular trek.)

Most of us living in occidental cultures naturally expect to encounter considerably different cultures when visiting the countries of the Orient. My first venture to the Far East, as considered on a planetary scale, was my trip to Southeast Asia, complements of the US Air Force. My first stop was Clark Air Base in the Philippines. Well, technically, that was my second stop, but I can hardly give any consideration to the one-hour layover at Yokota AB outside Tokyo enroute to Clark AB. And though Hawaii might possibly be considered by some to be quasi-oriental, it is totally east of the 180th meridian, making it very west. My ten days in the Philippines were spent entirely on the base or just on the periphery outside the gate; I really did not need to acclimate to any culture shock.

Thailand, however, was a different story. Part of the in-country orientation briefing when I arrived at Nakhon Phanom addressed the cultural differences we were strongly advised to recognize and adhere to. Some of the Thai traditions are different even among the other countries in that region of the world. (If perchance the Reader has forgotten, a quick review can be found back in chapter 38.) Thai customs can explain some of the initial uncertainties we experienced when I met Andrea when she arrived at the Don Muang International Airport in Bangkok.

Among the more unusual Thai customs—unusual to me anyway—involved the body. As I discussed in an earlier chapter, to the Thais, the human body has a hierarchy—the top of the head being held in the highest esteem, for lack of a better term, and the lower the body part, the lower its esteem.

A Thai custom that took getting used to after Andrea arrived in Bangkok was remembering that displays of affection in public between members of the opposite sex were frowned upon. Admittedly, in the more internationally sophisticated capital city of Bangkok, the influence of western cultural habits made it perhaps more acceptable, or at least less frowned upon.

So imagine, if you will, a young couple having been married for only a smidgeon over three years (for those of you from the regions unaccustomed to that phraseology, "smidgeon" means "just a little bit") and who are still newlyweds, except by Hollywood standards. You have most likely already applied your best Holmesian deductive reasoning and properly concluded that the said aforementioned young couple was my wife, Andrea, and me. Add to the scenario the fact that we had parted when I had boarded the Southeast Asia-bound C-141 on April Fool's Day over three months earlier.

I had been given three days leave to meet Andrea at the airport in Bangkok. She was flying from Cleveland, Ohio. The one-way trip cost $300. She had probably flown via LAX or Hawaii, then to Tokyo, then to Bangkok. After such a trip anyone would be glad the journey was over, but no one more than a bride anxious to see her husband.

I had taken the C-130 "Klong" shuttle from NKP to Bangkok. The trip only took a couple of hours or so. Since I was traveling on a military aircraft, I was wearing my flight suit. I had packed my A-3 bag—an olive drab green canvas bag that can hold a lot of stuff when necessary—and left it with other travelers' belongings to be loaded by the C-130 loadmaster. I only needed perhaps half of its potential volume for some civilian clothing, ditty bag, shoes, et cetera. The C-130 landed at Don Muang because, at the time, the airport was shared by the military and commercial aviation. So far so good. I had arrived a bit before Andrea's scheduled arrival time. *I* had arrived, yes. But not my A-3 bag. The military agent on the civilian side made a call back to NKP for me, and my bag was found—still sitting on the tarmac at NKP. Grrrr. Now I had no change of clothes, no toothbrush, and no shaver (I was still using an electric shaver back then). All I had was the lovely olive drab flight suit I was wearing and whatever may have been in the various pockets, of which there were several.

Well, my bag would be on the Klong shuttle the next morning. With nothing further to be done about the situation at that point, I got a taxi to take me into Bangkok to the Chaophya Hotel (Chaophya is also found to be spelled as two words: Chao Phya), the hotel used almost exclusively by the US military or contract civilians. Did I have a reservation? No, and of course there was no room in the Inn. Not until the next night. Grrrr. What else could go wrong? Fortunately the Florida Hotel—go figure—was just across the street, and I was able to secure a room there for the night. I remember nothing particularly bad or good with the hotel. It would be for just the one night. It was not until some months later that a friend told me something about The Florida that I had not known at my check-in time: The rooms came "with" or "without." I do not remember being offered a selection; maybe it was just my naïveté. As luck would have it, though, my room came "without," which was a good thing—a very good thing. Rooms "with" included a girl. By a "girl" I mean—well, you know what I mean; no need for further elaboration. Andrea and I might not have been married much longer if, when I took her up to our room, I had had to say, "Andi (I call her Andi), I'd like you to meet Chulorn. (I just made up that name; it sounds Thai-ish to me.) She will be spending the night with us."

Like that would have happened.

Remember a few moments ago when you read the part about not showing displays of affection between the sexes in public? After I got checked into the "without" room in the Florida Hotel, I got a taxi back to the airport to meet Andrea's flight. The Don Muang Airport did not have jetways. It was a nice sunny afternoon when she arrived. Bangkok in July was pretty much like Savannah, Georgia: 98° temperature and 90 percent humidity. When she de-planed she was met by what must have seemed like a blast furnace. She got through customs and to the area where we could finally meet after being apart for over three long months. I had briefed her in a letter about Thai customs. We saw each other, and I am sure my smile was as big as hers—or it would have been if my smile were physically bigger than it is, which it isn't. We walked toward each other, got as close together as we could without actually touching, or even giving the appearance of doing so, inhaled and exhaled, and said "Hi" to each other.

Then she told me she was sick from the flight, so we found what served as the infirmary in the US military area of the airport. It turned out she had gotten a mild case of food poisoning on the last flight over. She was given something for it, and she rested there for a while. Amazingly I do not remember any details of that episode. She had reminded me of it when I was discussing with her what I had written so far in this part of the story.

In the meantime I had retrieved her luggage. As she planned to stay for an indefinite period, she had brought along an enormous gold-colored, soft-sided Amelia Earhart bag, probably large enough to hold our 1970 Pontiac LeMans that she had left at her parents' house in Euclid, Ohio. When she was feeling better, we got a taxi back to the hotel. On the way we let our hands secretly touch where the taxi driver could not see. It was never explained to us the particular definition of the boundaries that constituted what was and was not permissible in public, and the particular definition of the boundaries that constituted what was and was not public. However, there was no sense in taking a chance on offending anyone our first time together. The ride from the airport to the hotel was about forty-five minutes, but time was no longer an issue for us. We paid no attention to the taxi driver negotiating the Bangkok traffic, and there were no mishaps to be concerned about.

The taxi driver spoke some English—certainly much more than we spoke Thai, so once we arrived at the hotel he asked if we would need a taxi the next day. I said sure, then asked how much we owed for the ride. He said not to worry, we could pay at the end. I told him a time to meet us at the hotel the next morning and our general plans for the next couple of days. He seemed happy to have a fare and to be our chauffeur for our duration. We never talked price beforehand.

He met us on time the next morning; in fact, he had probably been waiting for us for a while just to ensure that another taxi driver did not claim us. At a minimum we had to go back to Don Muang to get my A-3 bag, then get back to the hotel where I could change into my civilian clothes and shave; I didn't want to leave telltale beard burns ('nuff said about that). We wanted to do some sightseeing, and our driver offered to be our extemporaneous guide.

But before the sightseeing, we needed to check out of the Florida Hotel. We left our baggage with the registration desk in the Chaophya Hotel across the street, since our room there would not be ready until later that afternoon.

Andrea and I would visit places of interest, then in between we would find an air-conditioned shop to duck into to cool off and get a respite from the heat and humidity, especially since she was not completely over the food poisoning episode yet, nor had she had time to acclimatize to the Bangkok climate. About the only air-conditioned taxis in Bangkok were the Mercedes and limousines. There was an obvious dichotomy of affluence levels in the city. There were the Mercedes-Benzes—I believe there was a manufacturing plant not far away. At the other end of the spectrum were the samlars, which were, and may still be, motorized, three-wheeled open-air two-passenger vehicles. The non-motorized versions were akin to the one man-powered rickshaws found in Hong Kong.

There was very little in between. In a current (1972) Bangkok newspaper I saw an advertisement for a Ford Fairlane. In the States one would have cost about $2,500 more or less. In Bangkok it was going for about 200,000 baht, or about $10,000. At that rate, imagine what a Mercedes would go for. I did not notice any BMWs over there, which I am now partial to, but back then I was not looking for any. I only had a vague idea how to spell them.

The afternoon of the third day when we would no longer need our driver, I asked him how much we owed him. He asked if I could get him a carton of US Marlboro cigarettes. I have never been a smoker, but he knew where the BX was and took me there. Thinking nothing of it, I went in and bought a carton for about two dollars or thereabouts. The driver seemed quite happy, as if I had just paid him a month's wages. For the amount he was probably able to sell them individually on the black market, it may well have been close to that. He was happy, and I was happy. A driver and tour guide for three days for two bucks. "How 'bout them apples!" as the saying goes.

We got Andrea an apartment, then I had to return to NKP to resume fighting the war. After all, somebody had to. The Adventures of Andrea in Bangkok will be covered in the next chapters. You will have time to refill your wine glass before we begin.

- 66 -

ANDREA'S ADVENTURES IN BANGKOK—THE APARTMENT

A fellow Stinger had told me of an apartment building in Bangkok where a number of the guys' wives (as far as I knew, that was a one to one ratio) were staying. Andrea and I checked it out, and it seemed quite acceptable. There was a two-bedroom unit available, and it was quite reasonably priced, especially if she got a room-mate. Shortly after moving in she did in fact get a roommate—Debbie Barbee, the wife of Larry, one our Stinger navigators.

One officer's wife, who had three young children, was in another apartment in the building. She had her fourth baby while a resident there; a US Army hospital was available in Bangkok. Talk about adventuresome. . . .

All the US wives in the apartment building had maids. The usual rate was 600 baht, or $30 per *month*. Andrea paid Somroum, the maid she hired, $35; the extra five dollars was because Som-roum was competent in English and therefore could take tele-phone messages. Somroum came in six days a week. She would make beds, dust, mop; wash, dry, and iron the laundry; do the grocery shopping (being a local, she could get far better prices in the markets than an American could); prepare meals; wash, dry, and put away dirty dishes, pots and pans, et cetera. When Andrea and/or Debbie entertained, Somroum prepared snacks and beverages, served, and cleaned up after guests left. When dinner guests were expected, Somroum would stay late to clean up afterwards.

She did all that for $35 a month. Today we have a maid service that comes every two weeks to vacuum, clean, dust, change the sheets, and make the beds; it takes them about one hour to do everything, a little longer if we need the top floor attended to. Seventy dollars, plus the ten-dollar tip we always choose to give each of the two girls.

Often, whenever I got down to Bangkok, Andrea and I would go to the restaurant in the Chaophya Hotel for a cool and refreshing dinner: Baked Alaska. It was about the size of a National Football League football and served quite well by itself for our evening meal. We also noticed what was to us an amazing feat: other couples would also get the baked Alaska—for dessert—*after* they had eaten dinner. After dinner is, of course, when one usually has dessert. That was not what we found incredulous. What we found incredulous was the fact that they even had any room remaining in their upper gastronomical tracts after dinner to consume this dessert. Maybe they had a freezer somewhere that they could keep any leftovers in.

Andrea was in Bangkok for about a month—long enough for her to get bored (not really)—when she heard about the International School Bangkok (ISB). Her being a teacher came in quite handy throughout our military and subsequent civilian

lives. Andrea managed to get a teaching job everywhere we have been for any extended period of time, including Thailand.

Being a teacher certified in Ohio, Texas, and Florida, she applied for a substitute position at the school. Her timing was serendipitously impeccable. One teacher was late getting back after her summer in the United States, so Andrea was hired to substitute and started from the first day of classes. After one week, the former teacher notified ISB that she would not be returning, and Andrea was employed full time as an English teacher. She was paid about 13,700 baht per month, which was the equivalent of just under $700 USD. No Medicare, no Social Security, nor income taxes were taken out of her pay. The $700 was more than enough to pay her half of the apartment rent and Somroum's services, other living expenses, and to have enough left over for her to shop to her heart's content and otherwise live comfortably. She was earning more than enough to support herself, so I did not need to send her money to live on. Things worked out just Jim Dandy. (Who was Jim Dandy anyway? Or Pete as in "For Pete's sake?")

- 67 -

A SHORT SOJOURN TO CAMBODIA

Speaking of shopping, she had what was then a rare opportunity to do a little shopping in Cambodia, of all places. As I mentioned much earlier in this magnum opus, apropos Cambodia during the United States military intervention in Southeast Asia at the time, "The Secretary *still* disavows any knowledge of. . . . " He was probably getting tired of disavowing by now, and I am not even finished yet. Regardless of the position of the POTUS and the Secretaries of State, of Defense, of Agriculture, of Much Ado About Nothing (for a long-dead guy he seems to pop up a bit in my writing), et cetera, concerning our military dissemination throughout the world, Andrea was, and still is, a civilian. Any Executive Orders forbidding *overt* military involvement in "certain places" were not binding on regular, everyday citizens.

Her entry visa to Thailand was only good for thirty days, at which time she had to leave the country and re-enter to get her thirty-day visa renewed. As it just so happened, there was a company in Bangkok that had a bus and scheduled day trips to Poipet, Cambodia to accommodate—for a small fee, of course—specifically such purposes as visa renewal. Poipet is on the Thai/Cambodian border. Although not shown on the above map, it is just across the border from Aranyaprathet, about an hour or so bus ride east from Bangkok, as best as Andrea can recall. When she and the other travelers arrived, their passports were stamped, and they were then free to dispose of some negotiated portions of their income in exchange for various and sundry locally crafted whatnots; i.e., they went shopping.

Small Cambodian silver which, with thin copper wire,
I converted into Christmas tree ornaments

Andrea bought several small items, most of which we still have. She got a decorative woven silver bowl. I do not believe that a bowl made of a woven metal would be particularly useful as, say, a soup bowl. However, it does serve well for holding bread to pass around at dinner, or just as a decoration. Rather than let otherwise decorative things just sit around looking pretty, she often uses them. She also bought several small engraved, or whatever the process is called, silver animals and two small silver bells. By small, I mean two or three can easily be held in one hand. After we returned to the States I attached some copper wire to each one, and they have been decorations for our Christmas tree ever since. These are not Cartier by a long shot, but that is of little concern to us.

As it turned out, it was just as well that Andrea did not spend much money on the Cambodian items. On the way back to Bangkok, the bus was stopped at the border again, naturally. This time armed Cambodian "border guards" boarded bus and confiscated most of their purchases on some pretext. They were armed, and the passengers were still in Cambodia; options were limited: 1) Comply. 2) See number 1. That was it. No other options. There may have been some complaining afterwards among themselves for what it was worth, which was nothing. However (this is a good however), Andrea and her seatmate had been at the rear of the bus and the Cambodian border ~~crooks~~ er, guards must have serendipitously ~~stolen~~ uh, gotten enough stuff before they (the guards) reached them (Andrea and her seat mate; I didn't want to leave confusion with indefinite antecedents). They confiscated nothing from Andrea or the other lady. The "guards" did not do this on the bus's way *into* the country; such antagonism would have disrupted the local economy and made the small merchants very unhappy.

I can't help but wonder if the bus driver got some payola for each trip; I would not be surprised. The Thai border people stamped the passports again and issued new thirty-day visas. They did not try to confiscate anything. They probably knew that the Cambodian guys just over the border had already routinely taken everything. Or maybe they had more scruples than their Cambodian counterparts, who had none. The Cambodian guards probably had a nice racket going for themselves and the local merchants. The merchants made money selling their craft ware, the guards made money selling their confiscated goods back to the merchants at an arranged price, the merchants re-sold the stuff to the next group to arrive, and the daily micro-economy flourished. Keep in mind that I *did* say probably.

Fortunately for Andrea, ISB took care of her visa after that time since she was a full-time employee and therefore did not have to make that trip again. However, she has actually been in Cambodia; I have never even as much as flown over the country.

For decades now Andrea and I have had a tradition of buying trinkets or other small gift-shop-type items from wherever we visit to hang on our Christmas tree. It always brings back happy memories when we decorate with them.

About every six weeks I enjoyed three days of Crew Time Off (CTO), meaning that I was free for three days to venture wherever my heart's desire led me, except for Cambodia probably. I was not the only person afforded such privileges, of course; everyone on a crew in our unit, and possibly everyone on crews in other units, were granted days off. It is entirely conceivable that other non-crew types on base had days off also. Their days off might have been called ATO (AdminTO), BXWTO (Base Exchange WorkerTO), ONCOAEPDOTNCRTO (Officers, Non-Commissioned Officers, And Enlisted Personnel Doing Other Things Not Crew Related TO). Or not. I am just guessing.

Of course, my heart's desire led me to Bangkok to be with Andrea, and a couple of times she was able to fly Thai Airways to NKP whenever we could arrange coinciding days off. Her bedroom in her Bangkok apartment was comfortably larger than my entire room at NKP. Plus, she had a private bathroom, a living room/dining room area, a kitchen, and a patio balcony. All the comforts of home.

Including geckos.

- 68 -

CRITTERS

While on one trip visiting Andrea in Bangkok, I was suddenly awakened early one morning to find Andrea sitting on the side of the bed rapidly brushing the sheet with her hand. Concerned, I asked her what the matter was. She said, "Tennis bugs! Tennis bugs!" as she continued sweeping at the sheet. I didn't see anything from my perspective, so I got up and went around to her side of the bed to take a closer look. From there all I could see was her still sweeping the bed, though not quite so vigorously now, and still saying, "Tennis bugs," though now not quite so exclamatorily. I bent over for a closer look, never having personally seen a tennis bug before, but I still didn't see any crawly creatures or whatever they were (oh, yes—tennis bugs). I ventured a tentative brush with my hand—still nothing.

Just about then she began to wake up; she made another brush stroke or two, saw me, and asked what was happening. I told her she was brushing away tennis bugs. By now she was alert enough to ask me what tennis bugs were. I said, "I don't know; I never saw any. I don't even know what they look like."

We had a good laugh about that little episode—and the story has continued ever since. For those of you curious Readers who have lived sheltered lives and have never seen or heard of a tennis bug, consider yourselves enlightened:

The following year we related this story to creative and imaginative friends around the dinner table at our home in Fairborn, Ohio. The next time we were together they presented us with this little fellow. We are forever grateful. It goes on our Christmas tree every year. (Thanks, Larry and Kathy.)

Four years later we were stationed in California at Beale AFB, about forty miles north of Sacramento. Larry and Kathy Tom were stationed at Fairchild AFB outside Spokane, Washington. Yes, they are the same two mentioned just above. In fact, Larry does not have a mere two mortal first names, he has three: Lawrence Craig Tom. But he does not have a last name unless you consider

Tom, which his family does. The Reader may recall that I had spent a couple of weeks at Fairchild going through the Basic Survival School. Andrea and I drove up to Fairchild that August so I could attend a two-week Life Support Officer training class at the base. She was seven months pregnant at the time; I did most of the driving. Naturally, we spent most of our (my) free time (all of hers was free time) with the Toms, who had in the interim become very good friends. Andrea and I stayed in the VOQ on base, and since the Toms were living in on-base housing, we would often go over for dinner and to play bridge. Their daughter Nikki was fourteen months old and learning to talk. She heard a word often used in bidding while we were playing bridge. She would stand by the table and say in a clear voice, "Pass!" That was the only bid she knew, but it was cute when she said it.

Lo and behold, after our daughter, Allison Marie, was born that October, we received another creation from the Toms:

A baby girl tennis bug

Since we are talking, so to speak, about small critters, I would be remiss if I did not include geckos; i.e., lizards, some of which look surprisingly like the one in the Geico Insurance commercial that talks with a slight English accent, except none of the ones I saw while in Southeast Asia ever so much as even greeted me with, "A jolly good day to you, kind sir," or whatever such English greetings were in vogue at the time. Like most earthly creatures, they come in a variety of sizes, shapes, colors, and other ornamentation. They range in size from about a half inch to two feet long. The ones I am familiar with were about four or five inches long, plus or minus. They were friendly, from a human perspective; not so, perhaps, to a little bug that appeared tasty to them. Their feet can form suction cups for climbing on the ceiling above your bed at night. Occasionally a curious gecko, while exploring whatever things geckos explore (or one that is a bit klutzy), might happen to find itself on a very large, warm, mobile creature which could even be a non-alert human. It can be quite startling to the person who happens to be the gecko's landing zone.

However, it is supposed to portend good fortune for you if one should jump or fall on you. Don't ask me how that is supposed to work. If I knew the answer, I would be keeping a whole flock of them around the house.

One variety of Gecko

Another real gecko

The Geico gecko

- 69 -

INCIDENT AT THE LIBRARY

Not all of Andrea's Bangkok adventures involved small creatures. In fact, many of her ventures were associated with human creatures of the high school student size.

There was one experience involving three or four of the aforementioned culprits, plus Andrea, their English teacher (for seniors), American Literature teacher (for juniors), teacher at ISB, and myself. For some reason – most likely a topic of the academic persuasion – except for me – we all made a visit to a Bangkok public library. I was a tag-a-long just because I was coincidentally in Bangkok on CTO visiting Andrea. Again, I have no memory of what "our" research was about, and it has no relevance whatsoever to the story, but a librarian came over and happened to mention that our conversational noise level was perhaps a decibel or two in excess of that normally tolerated in such an august (or whatever month it was) and serene setting. As the adult in charge, Andrea apologized for all of us and promised we would lower the decibels. Remember, this may not be (meaning definitely is not) a literal and exact transcription of this and subsequent conversations in the library. We may have possibly been looking through books and magazines for photos of late eighteenth century American dress codes attributable to the First Continental Congress in Philadelphia—the one in Pennsylvania, America. Let us make that assumption and continue from there.

One might reasonably inquire as to the purpose of such an exercise in 1972 Bangkok, and one would be totally justified in making such an inquisition. And, as incredulous as it may at first appear, there actually was a quasi-logical explanation. The drama department at ISB was going to produce the musical *1776*, which contains a cast of two females in semi-minor roles and a couple of dozen, more or less, actors of the masculine gender. I say "quasi-logical" because one (the collective "one") may well wonder, and I include myself and Andrea in that number, why, of all the musicals and plays in the world composed and written to date, was this particular one chosen for a high school production 8,709.53 miles from the site of the actual historical setting? And why was our little research group looking at photos in the library? And what instigated our commotional disturbances? (And why are there so many questions?)

The basic underlying answer was that Andrea had volunteered to assist the drama department, as she had enjoyed being in student productions in high school and in college. It seems (or seams (that will be evident very shortly)) that she was assigned to be in charge of having the costumes made. Thai seamstresses were plentifully available. However, it is indeed dubious at best that any of them had any clue what constituted the attire of an eighteenth-century

Continental Congressman. And imagine how silly they must have thought all that frilliousness was, what purpose it served, and why anyone would dress that way—on purpose. Alas, we—i.e., Andrea—had no answers for them; the best she could do was show them photos.

Considering the nature of our expedition and resulting mirth while observing photos and wondering how to convey any seriousness to potential seamstresses, our possibly nearly boisterousness may have on occasion caught the attention of any librarian within ten nautical miles. More than once, I might add. Incredulous as it may seem, it is entirely possible that I might have contributed to our apparently (to others more studiously indelved (EIR) than we) slight raucousness by recounting, in an entertaining fashion as I am wont to do from time to time, to an eager young audience—one of whom was applying to the US Air Force Academy—my version of "war (and other) stories."

Since we are discussing musicals in a round-about way, Marion the librarian had nothing on the librarians distracted by the commotion from our table. Eventually we were all asked, politely but unequivocally, to relocate ourselves to any premises which did not include the library and within a half mile surrounding radius. Yes, incredible as it may seem, especially to those who know me for the sedate, mature adult that I am (ahem—fingers crossed)—I, being an Air Force officer, and Andrea, being a high school teacher, were unceremoniously ejected from the library, along with Andrea's retinue.

At least two of those rapscallions still stay in contact with Andrea and come by to visit us in Atlanta from time to time. Both are grandparents now. One is a retired USAF pilot (he made it into the Air Force Academy with ease in spite of my influence), and the other is a Merchant Marine Academy graduate.

Oh, and although I did not see the ISB production, the play apparently went very well; probably none of the Thai viewers had any frames of reference for how the costumes should have looked anyway.

- 70 -

A COMMAND PERFORMANCE IN LAOS

Among her other volunteer activities at ISB, Andrea was an assistant to the director of the ISB Young Internationals (YIs) performing arts group. Young Internationals groups are in many schools around the world. While she was associated with the YIs, they were invited to perform before King Sisavang Vatthana and Queen Khamphoui in Vientiane, the capital of the country then known as the Kingdom of Laos. The King's full title was twenty-three words long; if you are curious, Google it. Andrea was among the adult chaperones attending with the high school student performers.

The students were mostly Americans attending school in Thailand and performing before high royalty in Laos. Talk about a life-broadening experience! What an adventure for those ~~kids~~ young adults. So what did you do in high school? Me neither.

I thought attending my very first integrated school at age sixteen was an experience, but it was nothing compared to these world travelers. For my high school graduation present, my dad shelled out

431

$250 and bought me a 1956 purple and white Chevy Bel Air, which was nine years old at the time. One of Andrea's ISB students—who over the years must have run up a record for long distance telephone calls (this was before cell phones) while keeping up with his classmates and teachers—was given (not taken—given) a trip to Singapore and a new camera for his high school graduation.

Getting back to Vientiane: since it is a dominate gene in most female-type persons, Andrea's shopping gene was not neglected; rather, it was exercised with gusto. Not inordinately, but certainly in keeping with the opportunity. She still has the gold Four Seasons bracelet and matching ring that she bought, plus a pair of gold earrings and probably some other stuff I don't remember. But I am sure that she does. She no habla Lao, and the Laotian shopkeepers no sprechen sie Anglais. However, Andrea's four years of high school French were useful in bargaining in a country with a history of French influence.

A jewelry store in Talat Sao Shopping Mall in Vientiane
(Photo: Trover)

Under President Nixon, the United States had gone off of the gold standard just over a year prior. As a frame of reference, at the time of the YI's Laotian trip, gold was valued at $38 per troy ounce. I was told that Four Seasons bracelets were selling in the States for $2,000. Without adding up prices, which I could not possibly do today anyway, I don't think we paid that much money for all the stuff we brought home in total. Today the bracelets can be purchased for somewhere in the neighborhood of $10,000. I am glad Andrea still has hers.

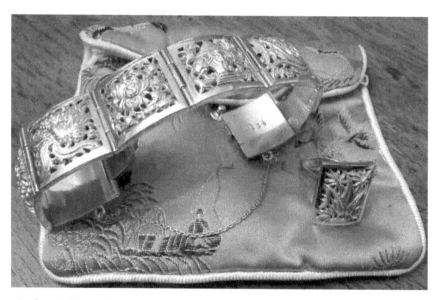

Andrea's Four Seasons bracelet and matching ring with silk pouch

There was a civil war going on in Laos in those days, but apparently at the time its effect on Vientiane was minimal. Still, there was a very strict curfew in place from 2100 hours to 0600 hours (translation to civilian-ese: 9:00 P.M. until 6:00 A.M.). Naturally, the YI chaperones were obliged to ensure that all their students were back inside the hotel before the evening curfew. From what Andrea tells me, it was a scramble getting everyone out of the vehicles expeditiously, but fortunately there were neither casualties nor international incidents requiring diplomatic intervention.

Andrea's school time was spent with the ISB students in the formal classroom structure as well as in the various less formal after-school activities. She was young-ish (EIR), lovely, and an affably personable teacher, which ordinarily one would think would be an asset. However, eventually propinquity became a factor, and some of her male students started getting a bit too flirtatious. She explained to them that they needed to tune it down. When they replied something to the effect of, "Aw, come on, Ms. Freund, you aren't that much older than us," she was ready with a quip for them:

"Keep in mind: When I was your age, you were in the *fourth grade*." That prime little example of EIR-ness put things into a perspective they could not help but understand.

- 71 -

THAI AIRWAYS OR THE KLONG SHUTTLE?

Whenever I had my CTO, I would catch a flight to Bangkok or Andrea would fly to NKP. I generally had two choices: Thai Airways or the Air Force's C-130 Klong shuttle. Andrea could not simply go out to the Don Muang Airport/military installation and catch a hop on a C-130 unaccompanied (i.e., without me along). Decisions, decisions.

The C-130 was free. Well, free in that I did not have to pay to ride in it to and from Bangkok wherever and whenever there was space availability. Not free considering that my salary was from the US Treasury; I received most of it, or at least a majority of it. However, *all* of it was taxed, such tax being paid to—right, the US Treasury, which collects revenue via the IRS. Then Congress allocates some of it to the military, some of which is then allocated to the USAF, some of that which is allocated to weapon systems acquisition, some of which is directed to the Research and Development (R&D) of, the construction of, and the operation of aircraft systems, some of which is allocated to the C-130 program. In that sense, my flights on C-130s were hardly free, considering that I was, in fact—and still am with my military retirement pay— financing the entire United States government. Admittedly, I was/am not personally providing *all* of this multi-trillion-dollar financing alone. I am getting some help from a few other folks. Like it or not, you, the Reader, are very likely one of them.

Bottom line, since the C-130 acquisition was a sunk cost (if you do not have a business degree, ask a friend who does what that means) and funds were already being allocated to operations, I did not have to contribute any further out-of-pocket. I didn't even have to tip the flight crew.

So, I assume we can all agree that "free" is not an inconvenience. However, there was a non-monetary cost to be endured. The C-130 cockpit—or flight deck, if you prefer the modern, politically correct euphemism—was the loudest in the Air Force inventory, according to a study that was done about such things. Riding in the back of the plane—i.e., in the cargo bay—was even louder. (What's that you say? Speak up. My ears are still ringing, and my hearing aid batteries just died.) Those four large turboprop engines made/make quite a piercing racket. C-130 passengers (pax) were issued and instructed in how to insert the soft, pliable yellow or orange (depending on the color du jour) ear plugs, described in an earlier chapter. They helped somewhat, but only a little somewhat.

Pax seating was not too horrible, if one was not overly particular about life's small creature comforts, and especially if the flight was not going to be of an overly long duration—say, like that of a trip across the Pacific Ocean, a.k.a. the Big Pond. Even a relatively short leg (EIR) while island-hopping across the Big Pond is one of several hours duration, even in turbojet—powered aircraft. You may remember that the C-130 is a turbo*prop*, meaning that the four sets of large, four-bladed propellers are driven by jet engines instead of reciprocating engines like on "normal" propeller airplanes. If you need further disambiguation on aeronautics, I suggest you pursue other disquisitions on the subject; right now I need to get back to C-130 pax seating.

As I was saying before I distracted myself onto another topic (very unlike me to do so, of course), the seating on the Klong shuttles was referred to as troop seats. You have no doubt seen them in movies, but you would be a rare individual if you even noticed or paid any attention to them. Usually the "infiltration team" of Navy Seals or Green Berets or James Bond had been sitting on them before jumping out the rear cargo door, usually wearing parachutes—except for James Bond, who would have to wrestle some other guy for his parachute on the way down.

C-130 troop seats

As you can see from the photo, they were/are not exactly first-class commercial airline seats, but the price was right, except that most of the time, the Klong shuttle was crowded with either all pax or pax and cargo, more like the photo below. Notice that the seats face sideways and are in double rows: outboard seats faced the center, and center seats faced outboard, so the pax were pretty much sitting knee to knee. Any non-human cargo would be loaded in the center in place of some or all of the center seats. The C-130 was versatile in that the cargo bay could be configured in whatever way was necessary for the particular flight or mission. For example, if dignitaries—meaning officers or civilians way above my pay grade—were aboard, airline seats could be installed facing forward in lieu of some of the troop seats. As a pilot, I was occasionally able to ride a jump seat in the cockpit if one was available.

Typical of the crowded C-130 Klong shuttle in Thailand

On the Klong shuttle between Nakhon Phanom and Bangkok, the flight usually made two or three stops to other bases enroute to drop off and pick up pax and/or cargo, so there was rarely an empty seat. These interim stops made the total travel time longer, trip time about four or five hours, but at least they provided a few minutes to stretch one's legs.

Many of us would carry our own lunches or snacks on board. For others who chose not to do so, inflight box lunches could be purchased at nominal cost before boarding the plane. If you have ever had an Air Force in-flight box lunch, you will understand why I took my own lunch with me. The only thing I found edible in the in-flight lunches was the fruit—typically an apple, orange, or banana—and Hershey bar. That was several decades ago, of course. Perhaps the meals have improved since then. I would certainly hope so. But if not, would anyone know the difference? More recently, MREs (Meals Ready to Eat) are being used by the military—at least they were twenty years ago when I last had occasion to consume one. They were at least better than the box lunches; some could be heated to provide a warm meal. Since cooking time would be involved, I suppose one could call them MNREs—Meals Nearly Ready to Eat.

Did I mention that while waiting on the ground before engine start, the C-130 was not air conditioned? Did I mention the tropically warm temperatures and humidity? Did I mention that there were only about five or six windows on each side?

I'm pretty certain I did mention that the flight was, in a sense, free.

By now you may be wondering about my Thai Airways option. Less description is needed here since most Readers are familiar with flying via commercial airlines.

The only detrimental feature to Thai Airways was that it was not free, and even that objection was minimized by the fairly low fares—no pun intended; okay, maybe it was. I do not recall the cost, but it seems to me that a round trip ticket was less than $30. I once accidentally broke a nice (EIR) glass of a nice (EIR) vintage of a nice (EIR) cabernet sauvignon; the glass and the wine in it each cost about that much. It was enough to make one cry; no crying over spilt milk, but over an '06 BV Georges de Latour Private Reserve in a Riedlel cabernet glass, I sure felt like crying. I couldn't even find consolation in blaming anybody else; the accident was mine, alone and unassisted.

Naturally, as would be expected, the Thai Airways ride was more comfortable from just about any perspective compared to the crowded Klong shuttle. The planes were air conditioned and had regular forward-facing pax seats with windows for each row, much quieter Rolls-Royce engines, and did not stop at each base along the way, making the trip time enroute considerably shorter.

And let us not forget cabin service. Back then the pleasant people in pleasant uniforms—not the military "green bag" flight suit—were referred to as stewardesses. Male flight attendants, to use the more current nomenclature, were a rarity then, as were male nurses. But in this age of quasi-enlightenment, there are female doctors and even female commercial and military pilots. When I left active duty in 1980, the Air Force was just beginning to train female pilots. Occasionally we would hear rumors of a fellow pilot claiming to have actually having seen one (a female pilot). But we all know about rumors.

After all the passengers were seated on the Thai Airways plane, the stewardesses would offer us a lightly-scented moist cloth rolled into a cigar shape. Sooo refreshing. Such things were, and may still be, typical on East Asian airlines. Some European airlines offer them also. On a trip to Europe several years ago, Andrea and I booked our flights with Delta Airlines. Our flight to Europe was aboard an Air France plane. Air France and Delta had formed a partnership agreement, as some airlines do these days. On the Air France flight the flight attendants distributed the moist towels. I do not recall such a pleasure on our return trip on a Delta plane.

During flights on Thai Airways, the in-flight meal was something with a local flair. I remember fruit such as pomelo, papaya, lychee, mango, and/or jackfruit. I don't recall the rest of the meals, but they generally were light, not heavy like perhaps a water buffalo double cheeseburger.

The choice between modes of transportation—military vs. civilian—appears to be a no- brainer. However, I usually based my decision on which organization had a flight in the direction I was going on the day I wanted to go and at the most convenient time for me.

To summarize, below is a list of the attributes I have mentioned, and which choice was more favorable—the Klong shuttle or Thai Airways:

Price: Klong
Noise: Thai
Seating: Thai
Price: Klong
Comfort: Thai
In-flight meal: Thai
Trip time: Thai

Price: Klong

A critical cost/benefit analysis reveals that on an unweighted basis, Thai Airways would be the hands down choice. On the other hand, if the factors are compared on an unbiased weighted basis, Thai Airways would still be the choice. Naturally I usually chose the Klong shuttle.

- 72 -

AWOL—OOPS...

At the end of one of my trips to Bangkok, I had some difficulty getting back to NKP. I called the in-flight services number and was told that the C-130 flight was booked but that I could come in anyway in case a seat opened up from a cancellation or no-show. Since I was riding stand-by, I caught a taxi from Andrea's apartment for the 45-minute taxi ride to the airport to hopefully be able to get on the morning Klong flight. As it happened that morning, and many mornings, the flight was full and none of the scheduled pax had the courtesy to cancel or not show up. The in-flight services guy told me I could try again the next morning, which I did. I called before leaving Andrea's place and was told, almost as if it were a recording, that no seats were available but I could come in . . . and I was unable to get on that second day either.

Ditto the third day except for one fortuitous event: As I was sitting around waiting, the flight crew for the Klong shuttle happened to pass by in front of me. Lo and behold—no, there were

no strippers around—the copilot on the crew was "Gualt" Gualtieri, a fellow classmate from my Undergraduate Pilot Training
class, the very same guy from the very same incident I wrote
about a hundred pages or so ago. After expressing mutual surprise
at seeing each other eight thousand miles from Del Rio, Texas,
he asked me what I was doing there. I explained my situation to
him, and he said, "Come on and take the jump seat," which I was
quite ready to do. Thus I was able to get back to my squadron.

Three days late.

Having been young and not too bright, it had not occurred
to me to try to call my squadron the first day when I could not
get back and advise them of my predicament, one reason being
that I did not consider myself to be in a predicament. Don't ask
why I did not try Thai Airways; that thought did not occur to me
for reasons stated above—young and not too bright.

As it turned out, as soon as I got on base I was told to report to
my squadron commander, a lieutenant colonel. The shininess of my
fairly new first lieutenant bars had not yet lost their luster. When I
got to the colonel's office, the normally affable and easy-going commander was all business. Apparently the three extra days I had in
Bangkok were unauthorized; i.e., technically I had been, inadvertently and unwittingly, AWOL (Absent WithOut Leave). Okay, so
Iwasveryquicklyapologeticandwouldneverletithappenagain. Sir.

After a sufficient chastising, which was not nearly as bad as it
could have been, I left his office humbled and a little wiser. Had
he chosen to do so, the commander could justifiably have taken
a serious career-ending action against me. Instead, he had had the
admin sergeant amend my leave orders to include the extra days
I had been gone. Whew! Thank you, Colonel.

- 73 -

THANKSGIVING IN HONG KONG

When military types are on extended unaccompanied assignments—meaning no spouses or families can accompany them—such as in, oh, say, war zones, for example, there is usually a provision for the military person to have a week or two of what is called R&R: rest and recuperation, or rest and relaxation, or rest and recreation. Choose whichever moniker suits your fancy; although the word choices suggest slight nuances of difference, they are all called R&R.

I coordinated with Andrea so I could take my R&R with her in late-ish November 1972. Most people in the environs of Southeast Asia chose to meet spouses and/or families in Hawaii. However, many families opted for Australia also. Those two destinations were the usual choices du jour, although there were many other places to visit, such as Bangkok, the Philippines, Okinawa, or Tokyo, to name just a few. That being said, we decided to go to Hong Kong, which was still a British protectorate at the time, whatever a protectorate was, not that that was any concern of ours or that we were even aware of it.

I should amend that last phrase in that it was not much of a concern, although it did occur to us that neither of us spoke or read Chinese. On the other hand, we did not speak any Thai or Vietnamese (or Cambodian or Philippine) before we left the US of A, and yet we were managing. One can find English spoken among a surprisingly large portion of the world's disseminated population. Neither of us had been to Hong Kong before, and we were excited about the trip.

I flew down to Bangkok the day before our scheduled departure flight for our three-day Hong Kong visit. The flight time was about two and a half hours non-stop. I do not recall which airline we used, but the service was pleasant and much as I described Thai Airways earlier.

I had the window seat as we were on our approach descent into the Hong Kong airport. Being a pilot, I preferred looking ahead out the cockpit windows in the direction we were flying. Much better views, of course. However, as a passenger looking out a cabin window, all I could see was the up and down sideways view. I could hear the flap drive screws operating as the flaps were lowered and could feel the slight aircraft pitch attitude change when airspeed was decreased as the wings generated more lift. We needed to be going down, but we needed to lower airspeed so that we would not be like a rocket when we landed.

As I looked out the window on short final—meaning almost to the runway—I noticed water below us and skyscrapers perhaps a half mile or a mile away to the right. When I heard and felt the landing gear lowered into place, I was looking up—yes, up—at the buildings; the water below was getting pretty close. Then it started getting really close. Then it got uncomfortably close. I knew what was going on; after all, I was an experienced pilot having logged nearly 650 hours of pilot time. Just as a frame of reference for you, the cockpit crew probably had, between the two of them, well over thirty or forty *thousand* flight hours. So much for my "experience." EIR. As it has been said, a little knowledge can be dangerous.

However, I still got momentarily concerned when I heard the engines pulled back to idle for the landing flare, and the water was still getting closer. Really uncomfortably closer. I knew that the plane was not going to make a scheduled water landing; I had seen the landing gear when we were waiting at the gate before boarding. But before I could get all worked up about it, we touched down on a hard surface. The runway was built out into the water. Imagine that.

Hong Kong Airport Runway (tough crosswind landing)

It was a gray, overcast day when we arrived, but it did not put a damper, per se, on our excitement in being in another "new" country. As far as we were concerned, it was a country; we did not bother a whit about the technicalities that it was a protectorate territory under the British Empire at the time, not to mention that it was a city and not a whole country. The combined populations of the *countries* of Monaco, Liechtenstein, and San Marino in 1972 were just over 66,000 people; the population of the *city* of Hong Kong was over four million more than the total of those three countries combined. Though geographically Hong Kong was a city, politically it was a country and a protectorate. Hong Kong even had its own currency, the HKD (Hong Kong Dollar).

From the airport we caught a taxi to our hotel. It was not one of the US international chain hotels like Hyatt, Hilton, or Marriott, but it was comfortable, even if not luxurious. If you will remember, I was merely a low-paid first lieutenant. As a frame of reference, the annual base pay of a four-star general, eight pay grades above me, responsible for billions of dollars of assets and thousands of personnel, was $36,000. A full-time McDonald's employee in California where the minimum wage now is fifteen dollars per hour makes, or could make, around $30,000 a year. Again, EIR.

After we checked into the hotel and rested a short while, we planned our upcoming excursions around Hong Kong using the various pamphlets, maps, and brochures we collected at the airport and the hotel lobby. Sufficiently rested, we caught a taxi and then one of the ferries to the Star Ferry Pier, a vast two-story enclosed structure extending a considerable distance out over Kowloon Bay. I do not remember the statistics for how long it was or how many shops, restaurants, tailors, boutiques, and other mall-esque purveyors to humanity there were in it, but it was at least a couple of hundred yards or maybe a half-mile long—to the half-way point. There were four central walkways running the length of the pier: two sets of upper and lower walkways, with stores, et al., along both sides of all four. Fortunately for us, there was a sidewalk café in the middle that served the most marvelous whipping cream cake—seven thin(ish) layers of alternating whipping cream and cake. It was nearly as light as cotton candy and utterly and delightedly pleasing to the palate. "Should we have seconds?" "Sure, why not!" It was such a wonderful discovery that we made it a point to stop for another expression of heaven each time we passed the middle of the pier.

We found a restaurant on the top deck with a menu that looked appealing for dinner. I do not remember what I ordered, being a much less adventurous gastronome than Andrea. However, she ordered shark's fin soup, bean curd, fried rice, prawns, and some other local dishes. As we were enjoying the ambiance while waiting for dinner to arrive, it occurred to us just then that that day was Thanksgiving, although it is not a holiday much celebrated in Hong Kong, or in the rest of East Asia, or in most of the world, I suppose. No turkey, pumpkin, corn stalks, or horn-of-plenty decorations to be found anywhere. Our dinner was certainly a departure from turkey and dressing, gravy, mashed potatoes, gravy, and the other usual feastial delights of Thanks-giving dinners we remembered from back home. (Pass the gravy again, please.)

I do not know why we were surprised, but there were no knives or forks. Just chop-sticks. Go figure. Somehow our waiter surmised that we were "not from around these here parts" and was kind enough to teach us how to hold and use chop sticks. Our initial endeavors were done without any alacrity whatsoever, and I thought I was going to get very hungry before the evening was over. But good fortune smiled down upon us as we managed to convey our edibles from plate or bowl to our mouths. Luckily, Andrea was given a spoon for her shark's fin soup. We would still be there if she had had to use the chop sticks for soup.

The local diners around us managed a few not unkind smiles at our efforts as displayed by our lack of adroitness at the table as we ate. As we successfully negotiated the learning curve, I noticed at least a nod or two around us of what could be interpreted as "Congratulations." The Chinese are a polite people.

For dessert we went to the café where we had another serving of the whipped cream cake.

Among other things, Hong Kong is noted for its quality tailoring, the oriental version of Savile Row, where today one can buy on-line a "Black Slim-Fit Peak Lapel Wool Suit" for $4,000. Might as well get two suits while you are at it should you happen to spill some gravy on one.

On our first day at Star Ferry Pier, Andrea and I wandered into a leather shop and had custom-tailored leather sports coats made. I thought I also needed a Marlboro Man fleece-lined leather jacket. After some due consideration, I decided to have one made that was a knee-length coat rather than just a waist-length jacket. Besides, I wasn't a smoker. Still aren't. Or amn't (a smoker). We went back the second day for a second fitting and another piece of whipping cream cake—at the café, not in the tailor shop. My

Marlboro coat weighed about ten pounds. Incredibly, although the three coats would not be ready for us before we left Hong Kong, we paid for them with the assurances that they would be shipped to us wherever we liked. I am fuzzy on the details, but after some back and forth correspondence with the tailor shop as to where we would be and when, our coats finally arrived as promised, although it was a while later—we were already back in the States. It was indeed a shop run by honorable people.

Shortly after our final arrival at my post-Vietnam assignment at Wright-Patterson AFB in Dayton, Ohio, we bought a blue 1972 MGB. For those not familiar with British-Leyland products, it was a two-seat sports car convertible. That was in the early summer of 1973. About six months later I really got to put my Marlboro-style coat to the test with the top down in an Ohio winter. The coat was heavy, thick, and stiff, making it a tight fit for me squeezing into the driver seat of the MGB. However, the cold did not penetrate through the coat. My face was another matter, though; the ice in my frosted moustache inconveniently melted whenever I went indoors into heated air space.

In Hong Kong we had also bought a pale green jade bird which stood in a custom-crafted and lacquered rosewood stand. It was also shipped to us, but sadly, the tips of the crest feathers and wingtips were broken. It still looks nice today, but it does not look quite as delicate as it once did. Carved ivory was expensive and may have already been made illegal to bring into the United States, but we did bring a small, delicate, oriental scene intricately-carved from cork (I believe) and enclosed in a small lacquered display case. The carving made it home without damage.

Lombard Street, San Francisco

San Francisco has its famous floral-lined Lombard Street, which is one block long as the crow flies. Whoever thought up that expression? It is a complete misnomer, like "straight as a clam" (a phrase my friend Bennett devised while watching one of my rare straight tee shots). But Lombard Street is at least twice that long as the car drives downhill. After all, it is a one-way street. Hong Kong has its equivalent with Ladder Street, which is a short pedestrian street made entirely of laterally wide stone steps. It has appeared in James Bond movies and other films where the motor scooter or car chase scenes show these motor-ized, wheeled vehicles hurdling their way down all those steps. I have never seen a scene with the chase going *up* Ladder Street. Andrea and I walked up the crowded street. It is respectably steep, and those of us unaccustomed to it stopped part up way to rest. It goes without saying that walking back down was much easier, although I just said it anyway.

Ladder Street, Hong Kong

For our third and last night in Hong Kong we decided to be nice to ourselves and splurge a little. We checked out of the hotel and checked into the Hong Kong Hilton. Although it was a bit more expensive (EIR)—over a hundred dollars a night—it was only for one night, and the room was worth it. We were pleased with the decision to switch hotels.

We noticed one thing in particular about the people in Hong Kong. After having spent some time in Thailand, Vietnam, and the Philippines for me, and Thailand, Laos, and Cambodia (briefly) for Andrea, not only were they polite, but we felt that as a people they were generally more physically attractive. I cannot offer any details to justify this observation; it was just something we both noticed and agreed upon.

- 74 -

PATTAYA BEACH

At this juncture I chose not to spend a lot of time doing a lot of work searching through a lot of boxes and drawers and albums of photographs just to determine the date of this next Vietnam "War" anecdote. My rationale is that, after all was said and done, the specific dates really do not affect the flow of the general storyline in any way. However, it was sometime in January 1973 during my leave enroute in Bangkok on my way to my next assignment.

Pattaya Beach, Thailand (Photo: FritzDaCat (really))

Andrea and I took another mini-vacation to Pattaya Beach, about 62 miles southeast of Bangkok. Sixty-two miles along a rural stretch of the Interstate system in the US would take about 44 minutes (with me driving), or about nine minutes longer if one plods along at an average speed limit of 70 miles per hour.

In 1972 there were no interstates connecting Bangkok with Pattaya Beach; as far as I know, there were no interstate-esque highways in Thailand connecting anywhere with anywhere else. However, since Andrea and I were in no particular hurry, the four-hour bus trip was tolerable, although air conditioning would have been nice. Just a ride through the pleasant countryside.

Pattaya Beach is approximately 892 statute miles north of the equator, give or take a couple of feet, and so has a tropical climate year round. The average diurnal temperatures for January are 87° for the high and 73° for the low. Even the record high of 99° and record low 58° are endurable with only a bathing suit and a light-weight jacket. For comparison, Key West, Florida, is 1,679 miles north of that very same equator, nearly twice as far north as Pat-taya Beach. However, these little details matter naught; a tropical sandy beach is a tropical sandy beach. Some are definitely nicer than others, of course, but we were not especially particular then. The beaches we have seen and been on in the Mediterranean were all rocky or pebbly, even along the Spanish, French, and Italian Rivieras, although surely there must be some nice sandy beaches somewhere along the Mediterranean coast. We have just not come across any ourselves. On the other hand, the beaches along the San Destin area of Florida are spectacular, or were in 1972. The white sand around three quarters of the lake at Calla-way Gardens near Warm Springs, Georgia, was all imported from

Puerto Rico, or so I was told circa 1955 or so. On reflection, perhaps I oversimplified with my comment about a beach being a beach.

We went down to Pattaya for two or three days of fun in the sun and stayed in one of the hotels along the beach. The tropics are definitely the place to have tropical drinks. The orange slices, melon slices, and other frills are fresh as well as picturesque and inviting. Nothing quite like a Mai Tai (Thai?) on a beach in Thailand.

I remember seeing people parasailing over the water. It reminded me of the two times I had been parasailing. Even though they occurred in survival training situations, they still had an element of fun, like a ride in an amusement park. At the time my only experiences parasailing had been free; I had never thought about people actually having to pay for the pleasure, but it made sense. I checked on the price; it was $5 per person, and I do not remember seeing any tandems back then. When I asked Andrea if she wanted to go for a parasailing ride, she politely declined.

Although I do not remember too many details of our stay, there is one thing I definitely remember. Just before checking out of the hotel, I made sure I emptied my bladder before boarding the bus for the four-hour return trip. Then we had our baggage loaded on the bus and found some seats. For some unknown biological reason, within minutes after the bus started on its way north back to Bangkok, I needed to "go" again. Not urgently—yet. However, I was concerned about the four-hour *non-stop* ride on a hot—as in no air conditioning—and sometimes bumpy, trip. Only three hours and fifty-six minutes to go . . . it shouldn't be a problem though, I thought. I had not had that much to drink, and I had gone to the potty, to use correct Air Force nomenclature. (I am trying to keep the verbiage discreet; my grandkidlets may want to read this story someday. Actually, they are both old enough to read it now.)

I was beginning to feel a little bit uncomfortable, but since there was nothing to do about it—there was no toilet on the bus—I had to grin and bear it. Only three and a half hours to go. I could make it.

Okay, I was definitely beginning to get uncomfortable. Still two and a half hours to go.

At around the halfway point I was wondering how offended the driver and especially the Thai passengers would be if I got up close to an open window and . . . no, I thought that probably would not be a good idea.

Still an hour to go; sixty minutes, plus or minus. I was hoping for the minus.

Misery. . . . I did not think I could physically and physiologically hold it in any longer. A big wet spot would be very embarrassing.

The miles and time could not have crept by any more slowly. I had to try to take my mind off of it. Yeah, right.

Finally in the city. By this time I was way past urgency. Getting close. The end is in sight, metaphorically speaking, as I could neither see nor even know where our drop off building was.

Aha! The bus was stopping to drop some passengers off at their hotel. I indicated my necessity to the driver and asked if he could wait a couple of minutes while I found a toilet. It did not really matter to me, because I was getting off the bus regardless. I could get a taxi the rest of the way if I needed to.

I found the men's room off the hotel lobby. I almost ran the short distance to it. If all the toilets had been occupied, I would have gone into the Ladies' room. I could deal later with any consequences such an action may have precipitated.

Any urologists reading here may be able to explain the frustrating situation I had faced, but without going into personal details, suffice it to say that I had, much to my consternation, considerable difficulty emptying my bladder. What should have taken seconds could have been better measured in minutes. However, this little episode ended well, and I was feeling much better when I finally made it back to the bus.

I had relatively (EIR) few *un*pleasant memories from my life's detour to Southeast Asia, but you have just read about one of them. If the Reader at some future time decides to read my Vietnam-era story again, no one would blame you for skipping this chapter.

- 75 -

BEFORE LEAVING BIEN HOA AIR BASE

Bien Hoa Air Base was in the Republic of Vietnam, a.k.a. South Vietnam, a.k.a. the land of the Good Guys, as opposed to the Democratic Republic of Vietnam—a.k.a. North Vietnam, a.k.a. the land of the Bad Guys (EIR). The term "Republic" was in both names. One would have thought a democratic republic would have been more in favor with the US government—with the Democrats, at least. After all, the United States form of government is—contrary to the common misperception that it is a democracy—is in reality itself a democratic republic. Just like the "Bad Guys." As preposterous as that may seem, it is nonetheless the truth. However, Shakespeare's line about "A rose by any other name . . ." is incongruous in this instance.

I was TDY at Bien Hoa for the two weeks wrapped around Christmas 1972. The very final Bob Hope USO Show in Vietnam was going to be at Tan Son Nhut (*tahn son noot*) AB in Saigon on Christmas Eve. The military had made arrangements for busloads of us at Bien Hoa to travel the twelve miles to attend the show. That is, for those of us who were not flying, guarding stuff, peeling potatoes ala Beetle Baily, or otherwise on duty. Technically, while on active duty one is always "on duty, 24/7/365," though not always actively.

Andrea had wanted to meet me in Saigon, but I had to remind her that there was a war going on in Vietnam. I did not want her in harm's way; she got enough of that in the crazy Bangkok traffic. I really believe that the painted lines on the streets and roads there were used as general guidelines only and otherwise considered as nothing more than street decorations. Two lanes of traffic in one direction stopped at a red light would usually be occupied by at least five vehicles of varying sorts: Mercedes, beat-up Fiats, mopeds, bicycles, samlars, and here and there an oxcart drawn by a water buffalo.

She was not happy about my not wanting—insisting, if you will, and as I did—her to come to Vietnam and meet me for the show. In retrospect (everything is disambiguated in retrospect, is it not?), had I let her come to Saigon, she could have added another country to her countries visited list; she did not actually have a list back then. That came years later. However, the one hand greatly outweighed the other as far as I was concerned: Stay safe (EIR) or take a chance on getting shot at. For me that was a non-decision. I was being paid to venture into harm's way. She was not.

- 76 -

THE LAST BOB HOPE VIETNAM USO SHOW

Who does not remember Bob Hope? Perhaps only the youngest (EIR) of my Readers may not be familiar with the ski-nosed man of many talents and ventures. However, I dare say that it would be a rare military serviceman or woman from the twentieth century who does not appreciate his service to us. He lived for nearly all of that century and indeed attained centenarian status, having been born in May 1903 and having died in July 2003. Among his many tributes were the 57 United Service Organizations (USO) tours he made from 1941 to 1991 to entertain active duty troops all over the world, especially in war zones. In 1997 Bob Hope was declared an honorary veteran of the United States Armed Forces by an act of Congress. The Spirit of Hope Award was created in his honor and is presented annually by the Department of Defense. It is appropriate that he was the first recipient of the award.

*The **Spirit of Hope Award***

On 24 December, Christmas Eve, 1972 I was among the fortunate military personnel to get to see a Bob Hope show during his last Vietnam USO tour. At the time I was on temporary duty for two or three weeks at Bien Hoa Air Base in southern South Vietnam, near the capital of Saigon. The Bob Hope tour was not scheduled to appear at Bien Hoa, possibly because of all the associated war-like activity going on there. Much of the Bien Hoa claim to fame of having been the busiest airport in the world could have been attributable to the nighttime activity. The airfield was operational and busy 24/7. None of this "we attack at first light" business.

Possibly another reason for the show to be held at Tan Son Nhut AB in Saigon and bypass Bien Hoa was the convenience and the fact that it was a venue better suited for handling the large number of military personnel expected to attend the show. I do not have accurate attendance numbers for you, but I was one of the guys in the crowd.

A number of us at Bien Hoa that were not scheduled to be working the day his show was scheduled to be in Saigon were fortunate enough to be provided transportation gratis from the USAF motor pool. Any Readers of sufficient vintage to remember *The Phil Silvers Show* on television way back in the—well, you remember the decade and the age of black and white TV— might also happen to remember that Sergeant Bilko's outfit was the Army motor pool. An Army or Air Force public relations officer—I am not sure why Bien Hoa would have even needed a public relations office, and perhaps the operation was handled by some other office anyway, not that it really matters at this point— coordinated the travel for us and managed to acquire twelve Air Force buses and drivers for our use. These were not the relatively (EIR) comfortable long-haul Greyhound-type buses. They had basic seats and interior, but the windows opened. They had to; the buses were not air conditioned. No big deal, one might think. But consider that Bien Hoa is about eleven degrees north latitude, which may mean nothing to you if you are not geographically enhanced. But if you have ever been to Miami, Florida in the summer, or Key West, which is about 75 miles farther south, you were still at 24½ degrees north of the Equator. If by some outside chance all these latitude and degree terms have no meaning in your personal frame of reference, Bien Hoa is still over eight hundred miles farther south than Miami, or about six hundred sixty miles from the Equator. You may have never been to equatorial latitudes, but you have certainly heard that it is always hot.

So were those twelve buses as we boarded them and remained sitting, going nowhere, for about an hour.

At some point a couple of guys on each bus were asked to get off and accompany another uniformed person. As we sweltered, anxious to be on our way, they returned after another long while, accompanied by an official looking officer with a clipboard. The latter had boarded the bus to give us passengers an intel(ligence) briefing. An intel briefing for a twelve-mile bus trip to see Bob Hope? That seemed rather odd. However, what the intel officer had to say was less than encouraging. The two guys who had returned with him had already been briefed and were armed with M-16 rifles. They were not to keep us on the bus. As we were briefed, there was a 100% chance that we would be shot at either on the way to Tan Son Nhut or on the way back. Armed with this new information, we all wanted to get off the bus and get weapons so we could be really armed, but that did not happen.

We were told to keep arms and all other body parts inside the bus at all times. It was common in Saigon for Vietnamese on mopeds or small motorbikes to zip along past a bus or taxi and slip a watch or bracelet off of a wrist in a flash. Depending on the item being worn, it could be an uncomfortable experience, not only to the wrist and the arm to which the wrist was attached, but to the psyche as well. "I just paid eight dollars for that brand-new Seiko!"

Eventually the bus convoy was on its way. Nice hot breezes from the open windows provided a little comfort, more from the cooling effect of drying our sweaty uniforms than from actual cooling. Although the scenery on the ride was pleasant, the half of us on the window side of the seat were getting the benefit of the open window while the other half had a human body between themselves and any bullets that were as much as guaranteed to come from outside. However, the trip to the show was otherwise uneventful, although upon reaching the city of Saigon we were reminded once again to keep our arms inside the bus. Suggestions were made to close the windows, but that did not happen.

Once we arrived at Tan Son Nhut, we disembarked the buses and were led to the actual show venue. As one might expect, it was just a wee bit crowded, since all of Mr. Hope's shows packed in as many troops as could attend that were not otherwise out in the jungles shooting at things.

The last Bob Hope Vietnam USO Christmas show;
at Tan Son Nhut AB, Saigon 1972

Not all of us had front row seats. In fact, most of us did not have seats anywhere near the temporary stage constructed especially for the show. Many did even not have seats at all. As you can see from the photo taken from where I was standing, I really could not see much at all of the show and especially the girls; he always brought the girls. I think Ann Margaret might have been accompanying him on this tour, but I am not sure. It was not so much a matter of actually having good seats, or any seats, or being able to see the show very well. The memorable and important thing was that we were there. I was there. And The Man Himself was there.

For anyone who might be interested, I found this link to a short video of his last show:

https://www.youtube.com/watch?v=kODDgJRYF5I

Contrary to the intelligence information we had been given, not only were we not shot at on the bus trip to Saigon, but we received no incoming fire on the way back. (Incoming fire usually refers to artillery, but in this instance I am referring to not being shot at by anything at all). The day after the visit to the Bob Hope Show was Christmas which, in Bien Hoa, South Vietnam, was pretty much like any other day. My mother had sent me a table-top artificial Christmas tree, about thirty inches high, complete with decorations and colored lights. I still have that tree and its accoutrements; we get it out every year and it decorates our — actually, my—pool room.

I flew another combat mission Christmas night; like I said— just another day at the office.

- 77 -

ON MY WAY HOME VIA BANGKOK

In his last show in Saigon, Bob Hope mentioned Henry Kissinger and the Paris Peace Accord as not yet having reached—well, an accord (as in an agreement, not as in a Honda). However, shortly afterward an accord was indeed agreed upon, such as it was, by all parties concerned, and a "cessation of hostilities" was declared. That meant, theoretically, no more shooting, bombing, strafing, napalming, and other associated war-esque activities. Since I was in a gunship outfit whose primary purpose was to carry on a bit of shooting, one of the categories of activities just mentioned, our services were no longer needed. The 18th Special Operations Squadron, among others, was given orders to cease operations and disband.

Those of us not necessary to overseeing the unit's closure details were issued orders to new units, nearly all of which were stateside. The Cold War was still in existence and, although this bit of trivia was not known at that time, it would continue nearly twenty more years. Strategic Air Command (SAC) and Military Airlift Command (MAC) readily absorbed most of us. The popular phraseology of the day was that SAC sucked, a less deferential and alliterative wording than SAC "absorbed."

The Air Force had a Form 9, with which one could request desired future assignments. I am sure the other services had equivalent forms. Ours was called a dream sheet, mainly because the infinitesimal chance of actually getting one of those cozy assignments near the Italian Riviera was only in your dreams. I had lived in Ohio for the seven years leading up to my first active duty assignment to pilot training in Texas. Following that fourteen-month tour, I was assigned to Ohio for three months for the first half of winter. Shortly after arriving at my unit in Thailand, I updated my dream sheet to include any number of assignment locations, none of which were even in the United States. Europe, sure, in a heartbeat. South America, definitely. East Asia also worked for me.

Since Andrea was enjoying herself and her teaching job in Bangkok, we decided that I would request to extend my gunship assignment until her school year ended in June, after which we would take a month to visit Singapore and Europe before going to wherever my next assignment would be. We even planned to buy an MG Midget in England and have it shipped to our new home. (That was before I became more intimately familiar with British Leyland electrical systems than I ever cared to be when I bought an MGB while at my next assignment. The perspicacious Reader may have guessed by now that that assignment was back to Ohio.) All of this planning was done, of course, prior to unimagined events like, oh, say, the end of the so-called war that had been going on since before I could remember, thwarted our adventure.

The shooting part of the war was halted, however, and I was issued orders to report to Wright-Patterson AFB (WPAFB) to continue my Air Force career as a KC-135A tanker copilot. WPAFB is in Dayton—the one in Ohio. Back to Ohio again. Join the Air Force and see the world. At least we had seen more of the world than we would have if left to our own devices, although I have read that Vietnam is a desirable tourist destination these days.

Before leaving NKP I went to an on-base Thai tailor and had some shirts and slacks made. The procedure began with the tailor taking my measurements. For the shirts these measurements were quite encompassing: neck, chest, waist, shoulder to wrist, armpit to wrist, biceps, forearms, and wrist. He was equally diligent in taking measurements for the slacks. I could choose fabrics for the shirts and slacks from the rolls of cloth that he had, and he would magically convert the necessary material into clothing custom tailored to my then relatively thin (EIR) body. The clothes were ready for me to pick up within a week. They fit just fine, of course. However, the Thai tailor had apparently used the absolute minimum amount of fabric necessary in making the garments. Never having had custom-tailored clothing made for me before, except for the leather jacket and Marlboro Man-style coat done in Hong Kong and which I had not yet received, I had no circumspection concerning this little detail, and I was ignorant of the need to be concerned. I don't remember the cost of the two pairs of slacks, but the seven tailor-made shirts cost me twenty dollars. Not each—total for all seven shirts, including the material and labor, tax, tags, title, dealer prepping charges, shop costs, shipping preparation fees, yada-yada-yada. Actually, disregard all after labor.

I was at my pre-marriage "fighting weight" at the time the clothes were made. When life resumed and I was able to eat Andrea's cooking on a regular basis, those custom-tailored shirts and slacks naturally tightened. The material I had selected must have been adversely affected when it crossed the International Date Line on the way back to the USA. No problem: among her many talents, Andrea was proficient with a sewing machine. I figured she could let the clothes out a little to accommodate the increase in my body mass. Problem: the frugal Thai tailor had left no extra material to afford any enlargement adjustments. The Thai people were/are generally a little smaller than we Western folks and most were not overweight. I have never heard of a Thai sumo wrestler. Eventually I reluctantly had to agree with my wife that the clothes were best donated to Goodwill.

On her last visit to NKP, Andrea and I had a "party suit" made for each of us. A party suit was basically a flight-suit-designed one-piece outfit with appropriate names and unit patches, and such embroidered on them. They were tailored much like everything else over there, meaning it did not take long for both of us to outgrow them.

I requested and received a couple of week's leave enroute to Ohio. The Air Force shipped most of whichever of my "stuff" I did not anticipate needing until I relocated. The rest—some clothing, uniforms, toiletries, et cetera I took with me to my wife's apartment in Bangkok. She continued in her teaching position until the end of the semester later in January. We managed to do a variety of last-minute shopping before leaving Southeast Asia.

I was allowed six hundred pounds of hold baggage, which included my shipment from NKP when I made my final departure from the base. That shipment was just over two hundred pounds. I had the nearly four-hundred-pound balance at my disposal, which was a good thing, since we needed to add Andrea's things in our shipment from Bangkok. And the roomful of rattan furniture that we had bought: a couch, two end tables, a coffee table, two swivel chairs, two bookshelves, a rocking chair, and a foot stool. Of course, no such furniture assemblage would be complete without a large papa-san chair. Plus all the associated cushions. We, meaning my wife, picked out the material for the various cushions, and the Thai furniture dealer made the covers for them. Two sets.

We were cognizant of the weight restriction for our Bangkok shipment, so we had weighed the furniture beforehand. Andrea bought herself bunches of Thai silk scarves and other things of negligible weight while she was there. We bought one temple rubbing we liked for ten baht (fifty cents) and had it framed. I do not know what the process was called, but the Thai frame maker three-dimensionalized it, matted it in white and hunter green mattes, and framed it, all for ten dollars. It also occurred to her to have one of her silk scarves framed; I think she may have gotten the idea from seeing something like that during her stay.

I found a bootery shop (for lack of a better term; cobbler, perhaps?) where I thumbed through some old US magazines for pictures of some boots that I wanted made. The Thai craftsman suggested some materials. One pair of boots would be made from elephant hide and the other pair from kangaroo. People were not as concerned back then about conservation of the various species.

After I decided on boot styles and materials, the Thai guy asked me to remove my shoes and socks, or sandals, if that is what I was wearing (with no socks, of course), and he put a spiral notebook on the floor. He turned to a blank page, made some notations, traced an outline of my right foot, and took what seemed like copious measurements. I wonder if he was the shirt-maker's brother. . . .

Then he turned to another page and repeated everything for my left foot. A couple of days later I tried on my new custom-made boots. They fit like gloves, except they were gloves for the feet. One pair was brown leather cowboy-ish style but with squared toes rather than pointy toes. The other pair was smooth plain black leather, which happened to conform to suitability for wearing with my military uniforms—except with flight suits, naturally. They cost me twenty dollars total for both pair. Years later it cost me more than that just to have the black pair resoled. Both pairs seem to have shrunk after about forty years of use. I didn't know that when one gains a little weight—Andrea snickered at the reference to "little" (EIR)—some of it settles in one's feet.

Somewhere along the way I managed to buy several Thai silk ties to go with the early 1970s-style polyester suits I had. This may be a bit hard—ne'er I suggest painful—to imagine, but one particular tie was a free flow design of shiny, silky lavender on a shiny, silky chartreuse background. And it went very well (1973 remember) with one suit I had when I wore a pale green dress shirt with it. Talk about Mr. GQ!

Well, perhaps not. I still have the ties, though, but not the polyester suits.

While wandering around Bangkok we came across an Oriental rug dealer. I immediately became fascinated with these wonderful carpets favored by Sinbad and genies. The dealer explained some pertinent details one should know before buying a Persian rug. The names Persian and Oriental seem to be used interchangeably in the industry. One important thing to check is the knot density, or knots-per-square-inch (kpsi).

(The white area inside the above square is one square inch.)

The more knots, the more expensive the carpet. It is hard to imagine the patience required to tie two thousand hand-tied kpsi. At this density, an eight foot by ten foot carpet would equal eighty square feet, which would equal 11,520 square inches, which would equal 23,040,000 knots. No wonder they are so costly, even at Middle East manual labor wage rates. Material (usually wool or silk or a mixture thereof), design, size, country of origin, age, and even color are other factors contributing to the cost, disregarding profit margins added between the place of manufacturing and your home or office.

Andrea and I had decided to buy a couple of four-by-six-foot wool Bokhara rugs, which the dealer arranged to have shipped to her Bangkok apartment. At the time they cost us about $200 - $300 each, which is not expensive in the overall scheme of things. However, to this day I regret not having also purchased a beautiful four-by-six-foot green silk carpet of a design I no longer remember.

Naturally, it had more knots (tighter weave) and was a bit more expensive, but one of the reasons for its cost was the color. Apparently green is a sacred color in some eastern cultures. Think about that next time you are shopping for Oriental (not just Oriental-style) carpets. You are not likely to find many predominantly green ones. For us it would have been a hang-on-the-wall fixture rather than a walk-on-it carpet, although the dealer assured us that it could indeed be walked upon. When asked about cleaning the carpets, he said we could put them out in the snow—we were being stationed in Ohio (again)—and wash them off.

Um, I don't think so.

To this day, the first thing I do when I see a carpet I like is to look under a corner of it and notice the knot density and regularity. Machine-made carpets have tell-tale, very even and regular lines of large (EIR) knots.

There are any number of things that are common just about anywhere in the world. In Thailand, for example, the items we bought were common in the orient, but not so much in Cleveland, Ohio. It seemed that nearly everyone wore a gold baht chain or chains made of small solid rectangular links. Even the GIs wore them. The Thai used to wear them as money; the links had been able to be broken off individually. The US had gone off of the gold standard in 1971, so the price of gold was set at $38 per troy ounce. A typical one-baht baht chain cost twenty dollars, easily affordable by most people. Therefore, they were ubiquitous. Although Andrea had bought herself some jewelry while living in Bangkok, she never bought herself a baht chain. Too common for her, I suppose. Everybody had them.

It was not until three or four years later after, we had returned to the States, that she decided she would like one. We were stationed at Beale AFB in Northern California by then. I was flying KC-135Q air refueling tankers, and we made frequent trips to Kadena AB on Okinawa. Guys brought "stuff" home that was much cheaper to acquire when overseas. From my first TDY over there, I brought Andrea her first baht chain. We were definitely off the gold standard by then, and that first one cost $110 for a one-baht chain. On subsequent trips I bought her six more gold chains of different sizes and one silver baht chain.

Wooden elephants of every size and brass candlesticks were other very common items bought in Southeast Asia by GIs. I was given specific instructions to *not* buy any of either one. I'm not sure why, meaning I haven't a clue; she does not dislike elephants, and we had a variety of candlesticks in storage with our hold goods somewhere in the US. When the moving company had packed and loaded our household stuff into a moving van in Del Rio, Texas, I had no idea where it had been taken to be stored.

Andrea found a bamboo pattern of flatware—what I know as knives, forks, spoons, and serving pieces—in bronzeware that she liked. She bought place-settings for eight, or maybe twelve. Although, I think it is actually brass; bronze has a more reddish tint. They have a nice, heavy feel to them. She also bought some decorative bronzeware bowls which complement the dining utensils or look nice just sitting out. The set of monkey pod serving plates and trays were very lightweight.

Before leaving NKP, I had assembled a belt of 100 expended 7.62 mm cartridges from the vast supply available and had taken it with me to Bangkok (See photo in Chapter 64). Before having it shipped with our hold baggage, I had to take it to the Joint United States Military Advisory Group, commonly known as JUSMAG. I did not know what it was or did, just that I was told I would have to have someone there authorize the belt to be included with my shipment. The person I saw looked the belt and cartridges over, verified that all cartridges were expended, and gave me a written authorization of approval for shipment.

All of these things were accumulated in Andrea's apartment. We weighed everything on a bathroom scale to see if we were under, or at least not over, my remaining hold baggage weight allowance.

Surprisingly, everything, including all of the rattan furniture, the two Bokhara rugs, and the bronzeware, weighed in with a handful of pounds to spare. That was a relief.

Over four decades later, most of the rattan furniture had seen better days and is gone; only the three tables, the two bookshelves, and the rocking chair remain with us. The temple rubbing hangs in our foyer; the framed silk scarf hangs in our bedroom. The shirts and other clothes that we had made, and the polyester suits, are long gone, except my Thai silk ties; I only have occasion to get them out at Halloween or such events. The boots lasted until just a few years ago. The Oriental rugs are still in use and have been added to. Andrea still has her baht chains. I still have the 7.62 cartridge belt; it provides a very visual appreciation for people when I am asked about Vietnam. Hearing about six thousand rounds per minute is usually impressive, but actually seeing what one *second*—one hundred rounds—looks like gets a visible reaction of incredulity every time.

Oh, one more thing. Before leaving Bangkok, I surreptitiously bought the smallest wooden elephant I could find—one about two inches long. I presented it to Andrea after we got back to the States; she managed a smile. I put some copper wire around it and it adorns our Christmas tree every year.

- 78 -

SAWADEE

While diligently doing my duties during my days and nights as a Stinger copilot for nine months, I managed to engender the "cessation of hostilities" in Vietnam. I might mention that I had a modicum of assistance in this effort from Dr. Henry Kissinger's negotiations at the bargaining table in some lush hotel in Paris, but between the two of us, and perhaps a couple or three million or so other US military types over the previous ten years, we "got 'er done."

However, I, for one, was not ready to go home yet. Andrea and I had other plans, which were interrupted by the timing of the announcement of no more war. So much for our spending Easter in Singapore, our trip through Europe on the way home, and our buying an MG Midget in England and having it shipped to wherever in the world we would be assigned next. Technically, Andrea was not "assigned," since she was a nonparticipant in the military, but since we were still newlyweds, having been married fewer than four years at the time, and planned on living together for a few more decades, the mundane details apropos the definition of "assigned" were moot at best.

Flexibility is, or should be, an important facet to just about any plans, with the possible exception of a NASA mission to the Moon or Pluto, and even under such circumstances as space travel, unexpected bugaboos occur despite "the best laid schemes o' mice an' men." (Thank you Robert Burns.) Ergo, having gotten my notification of impending travel orders to somewhere dictated by "the needs of the Air Force," I requested and received two or three weeks of leave enroute to wherever we might next find ourselves living. (As "impending" indicated, I had not yet actually received assignment and travel orders to WPAFB.) After having some shirts made and buying an indispensable item or two, the likes of which could not have been too important as I have no clue now what they would have been, I spent my last couple of weeks in Southeast Asia in Bangkok with Andrea.

She was also disappointed to have to be leaving so soon. How many Vietnam veterans and spouses do you know that could honestly say that? However, as I already described earlier, we did a little shopping and enjoyed our last days there. On one occasion I accompanied Andrea when she went to a Thai bank where she had established an account to cash her final paycheck from International School Bangkok and close her account. The check was for about 13,700 baht, or just under $700. I do not remember how much she had on her remaining account balance, but it was fascinating to watch as the Thai teller totaled the transaction. He had a little machine into which he placed a wad of 100 baht ($5) banknotes. The machine flipped through them like flipping the edges of a tablet on which some stick persons or animals or—depending on the creative aptitude of the artist, things a bit more interesting—are drawn to appear in motion as the pages are rapidly, well, flipped (I couldn't think of a different word). Voilà! In the time it takes to say antidisestablishmentarianism the machine had counted out over two hundred banknotes. Of course, it took me a wee bit longer to confirm the amount by manually counting them. The machine was indeed accurate.

We paid cash—i.e., baht—for many of the things we bought before leaving Thailand. The intent was to incur only a minimal transaction fee to pay, if any, if we had any currency remaining to exchange before leaving the country. US Customs always wants to know how much foreign currency one has upon entry. I suppose if one had a large (EIR) amount, by whatever definition Customs applies to "large" —a suitcase full, or a zillion Vietnamese Dong (about three US dollars)—questions might be asked. However, the amount we had with us was negligible. I had been used to carrying small amounts of US dollars, MPC, Thai baht, and South Vietnamese Dong in my wallet, but apparently not enough to raise the Customs agent's eyebrows or curiosity.

- 79 -

SAWADEE LUNCHEON

Andrea had made friends of her fellow teachers and staff at ISB, and when they learned of her impending early departure in the midst of the school year, they gave her a sawadee luncheon. Sawadee is the English translation for the Thai word *sawadti*, which is used as a greeting or farewell, much as aloha is used in Hawaii. (One may find different spellings of the word, depending on the source.) Nothing spectacular; they were mostly teachers which were/are hardly over-paid, but there were over a dozen of us who went to a Thai restaurant for a sawadee lunch for her. I do not recall the particular restaurant. I do recall the little Thai waiter passing out the menu booklets. I say booklets because the menu items were numbered in Arabic numerals. For the uninitiated, those are the numbers we use, which in no way resemble Thai numerals. There were well over four hundred items for all of us to peruse. Notwithstanding, as soon as the waiter had finished handing out menus to everyone, he stood there, pad and pencil in hand, waiting to take our orders.

Some of the teachers who were already familiar with some of the menu items or who already had in mind what they wanted to eat may possibly have been ready. Even if so, they still needed to find the correct menu item number for the waiter. The rest of us had a lot of scanning to do and questions to ask. "Is number 373 fried eel with hot dipping sauce or a water buffalo burger?" My reaction was something like, "Holy moley (or words to that effect), I'm only up to number seventeen!" Fortunately, one of the people at the end of the table nearest the waiting waiter advised him that we might need a little more time to decide. I do not remember anything else about the luncheon except that it was a sunny day and the company was pleasant, but I will always remember the little waiter, whoever he was . . . waiting.

PART 5

- 80 -

RETURNING TO THE STATES

We, meaning Andrea, made sure that any accounts, outstanding bills, and the like were taken care of. I had already taken care of things on my end before leaving NKP. With everything packed up and, I would guess, shipped to a temporary storage facility at Wright-Patterson AFB, we were ready to leave tropical Bangkok and be on our way to Ohio. In January.

Leaving her apartment was a bit sad for both of us. My assignment to the "War in Vietnam" some sixteen months prior, and all the perils that such an assignment one could envision, had not turned out at all as we had anticipated. The memories of our experiences in those totally foreign settings in Southeast Asia—Bangkok, NKP, Cambodia, Laos, Hong Kong, the Philippines, and oh yes, South Vietnam—were, and are still to this day, memories of pleasant times. Not everything was peaches and cream every day, but even our recollection of perhaps less pleasant experiences forty-five years ago are nonetheless, for the most part, remembered fondly and with a smile. We were young, happy, and had grown accustomed to a lifestyle totally different from anything we would have imagined in our typical suburban American upbringings. If I may borrow and paraphrase from Charles Dickens, Andrea and I enjoyed the best of times during what many would consider the worst of times. Life is mostly what you make it.

Andrea flew via a commercial air carrier from the Don Muang Airport to LAX. In case there are any Readers immersed in this "travelogue" unfamiliar with international airport identifiers, LAX is the three-letter designator for the Los Angeles Airport. Since there were still five and a half years until the fall of 1978 when OPEC (Organization of the Petroleum Exporting Countries) raised the price of oil on world markets from about eight dollars a barrel to thirty-two dollars a barrel, her air fare eastbound across the Pacific was much the same as it had been when she had come westbound six months earlier—about $300. No, there are no zeros missing.

Since I had been on an unaccompanied tour, there were no provisions for her to fly back with me on a military-chartered airline which, as you might well imagine, was at least two or three orders of magnitude more comfortable than the back end of a C-141. (Ironically, after Andrea retired from teaching in 2007, she got a job as a flight attendant with Omni Air International, a charter airline that catered mostly to DOD (Department of Defense) needs. My commercial flight left Don Muang also, not too long before, or after (?), hers. Our flights were scheduled to arrive at LAX within about two hours of each other. I do not recall which of us arrived first, but whoever did arrive first met the other at the other's arrival gate for yet another happy reunion.

- 81 -

ARRIVING "IN-COUNTRY" (THE USA)

There were no cheers for "soldiers" arriving home. No patriotic red, white, and blue signs. No welcoming crowds. No bands playing. No flags waving. Nothing like what you find in the airports these days, at least like at the Atlanta Hartsfield airport. Those were different times. We were not the returning victors, the conquering heroes with reason to celebrate. On the other hand, I suppose I should be grateful there were no jeering crowds and other outward signs of animosity and negativism.

Photo I took in the Atlanta Hartsfield Airport 11 Jan 2018

On a brighter side, these days whenever I make a purchase and show my military ID for what is usually good for at least a ten percent discount, or show it when asked for an ID when buying wine at a beverage store, most of the time I am thanked for my service to my country. Although it has been quite a few years since I have worn the uniform, I sincerely appreciate the acknowledgement. The Home Depot stores in my area always give a 10% military discount; Lowes stores finally followed suit a few years ago, whereas previously they only offered military discounts on such holidays as Memorial Day, the Fourth of July, and Veterans Day.

Many businesses now offer military discounts; it would be unnecessarily difficult to memorize them all or carry around a list. It is easier for me to just ask for it wherever I go. You would be surprised at some of the places that honor the military this way. You would also be surprised at some of the places that don't. In my case, if the business does not give military discounts, I ask for an "old people" discount. Usually I can get one or the other. Usually the discount is the same percent for either. Fuddruckers Restaurants gives 30%, or did last time I ate at one. Every now and then a company will give both. The owner of the barber shop (or hair salon, or hair styling joint) I use, until recently gave four discounts: old people discount on Wednesdays, military discount; good customer free haircut discount after twelve visits, and another two dollars off for registering a visit online and getting a code number. When I went to get a haircut on a Wednesday as a good old customer—as in good, old customer (enough to qualify for an old people discount), not good old—and with a code number, plus military, my haircut was $4.99. I tipped my barber/hair stylist—no, barber, by golly; I don't need to get my hair styled—more than that. It's kind of like the snake thing with me: All snakes are poisonous. All barbers are men. Hair stylists do ladies' hair. That being said, my barber is a female lady-type person. Like the sage advice my dad always used to give me: "Do as I say, not as I do."

The owner of the aforementioned tonsorial foreshortening emporium decided he was losing too much money giving all these multiple discounts (duh), so now I pay just under ten dollars on Wednesdays. Still a bargain.

Once again I digressed (quelle surprise). Returning to the story-line, we were last at the LAX terminal.

Andrea and I then boarded together a commercial flight to Cleveland Hopkins Airport, where we were met by her parents.

Welcome back to reality—the "real" world. January 1973. Cleveland, Ohio. Dirty snow banks and ice. People in winter coats. Cars rusted out along the bottom sides from road salt. We didn't care; we were at long last back home—Andrea's home anyway.

Surprisingly, for Andrea and me both it was like arriving in another foreign country. Reverse culture shock. Prices for every-thing were so much higher than in the third world countries we had recently left behind. A hefty five-dollar tip to a waiter at a restaurant across the Pacific would elicit whole-face smiles (one hundred baht in Thailand; 113,500 South Vietnamese Dong). It would bring a look of dismay or disgust from waiters and wai-tresses in the good ole' US of A. This was in 1973, many years before the currently politically correct term of server. We had ap-parently gotten quite spoiled. Being your basic poor lieutenant tightwad, I wondered how anybody could afford to live in my country of origin. Obviously my unexciting Air Force salary—even including the little extra I got for flight pay—was not going to stretch nearly as far as it had while we were overseas. I have always thought of "overseas" as referring to Europe and its envi-rons: "We were stationed overseas" (read: Germany) or "My dad was stationed overseas in WWII" (read: France) or "When we were overseas . . ." (read: Italy).

I suppose compared to the Pacific Ocean, the Atlantic Ocean might be thought of as a large "sea" to be over. EIR.

When we flew to Hong Kong from Bangkok, the flight took about two and a half hours. That is about half the time it takes to fly from New York City to LAX, where upon landing you will find yourself still in the same country as the one you departed. Well, technically it would be the same country, although there is a world of difference, so to speak, between New York City and Los Angeles. Just ask anyone from The Bronx or Rodeo Drive.

That trip is generally about a half hour shorter when flying eastward from LAX to NYC due to the generally eastward direction of the jet stream in the northern hemisphere; flying west, headwind; flying east, tailwind. The United States is the third largest country in the world based on area. (I just looked that up I had always thought China (the People's Republic of China, not Nationalist China) was third. I wonder when it shrunk. . . .)

Driving across the USA along interstates at a reasonable (EIR) speed (about 85+ mph in my professional opinion) for eight hours a day will take four to five days to accomplish. Driving 2,600 miles in 1972 Southeast Asia would have to have been measured in weeks—assuming you even arrived alive. Everything "back home" took getting re-used to. Americans talked funny—meaning they spoke in English, for the most part, although I am sure any urbanized college-educated Englishman, from England, would adamantly disagree about exactly what language we really do speak on this side of the Atlantic. Just listen for what Professor Henry Higgins has to say on the topic next time you are watching *My Fair Lady*.

I admit it was fun getting to drive my (our) own car again. Not so much fun in Ohio, though, as I do not think any roads in that state, including interstates, have been resurfaced in over half a century. We went to Ohio earlier this year (2018) to see friends. As soon as we crossed the state line over the Ohio River—which, for some odd reason, is in Kentucky, at least around the Cincinnati area—the road quality seriously deteriorated.

- 82 -

AFTER-THOUGHTS

This is the imaginary place where I write about what I would do or would have done differently if I had it to do over again. Not so much in the way of regrets, but more of "I wish I had done that."

As you have already read, unless you skipped from the Preface to here to get to the exciting conclusion, my memories of Southeast Asia and the Vietnam conflict are overwhelmingly of the pleasant and happy variety. As I reviewed what would hopefully be my final draft before sending the manuscript (typing with two fingers should qualify as manual scripting) to the publishing system, I noted that in just about every case but one—our arrival in Hong Kong—started on "pleasant, sunny days."

I suppose I am and always have been a little on the naïve side when it comes to experiences outside my life's frame of reference. I tend to be not as adventuresome as the Reader might expect nor as I would like to be. Perhaps now that I am in my early seventies it might be too late to change. On the other hand, perhaps not, at least about many things. Forget seafood (that refers to any food coming from water (sea), not to South East Asia food). As long as there is still pot roast and gravy, I do not see a need to change. I accept that I am a minority in that regard, but do not confuse me with someone who cares. Ditto with cheese, although not quite as blatantly and inviolably as with seafood.

Thousands of khom fai in Mae Jo during Loi Kratong

Starting with the "I wish I hadda's," I wish I had visited Chiang Mai, considered the cultural heritage center of Thailand. That was a trip Andrea and I could have made together during one of my three-day leaves for Crew Time Off. Chiang Mai is 435 miles north of Bangkok, a flight of about an hour.

There was no Internet or Wikipedia in 1972, at least none for public use, so I could not do a little online research for sights to see. Ergo, one sunny—see, even without premeditation it was sunny—afternoon I went with a fellow Stinger who had made a number of trips to the town of Nakhon Phanom. We stayed a couple of hours walking along a main street looking around at shops, markets, and people. For no particular reason, I felt I had seen enough and never ventured back. Some guys went into town frequently; they had found "girlfriends" there. Some of those girl-friends eventually became wives.

While I was stationed at Da Nang, I never ventured off base, and I missed lounging on a beach on the South China Sea. Part of the in-country briefings at both NKP and Da Nang contained warnings from several sources of inherent dangers for careless visitors, so I just avoided the temptations. Thailand, Vietnam, and most of the rest of Southeast Asia are now popular vacation loca-tions. Andrea and I might perhaps go back on a vacation one of these days, but there is a lot of world out there that we have not been to yet. Of course, it is expensive to travel anywhere; often the airfare costs as much or more than half of the trip. Most of my visit to the Far East in the 1970s was free.

I am occasionally asked about my "feelings" considering the type of missions we flew. Nothing specific is mentioned, but I gather they are asking about if I have personal regret, remorse, flashbacks, PTSD-type effects, et cetera.

No, no, no, no, and no (to the et cetera).

Unlike the up-close and personal combat contact that Army, Marine, and other forces on the ground that slogged through rice paddies and whacked their way through jungles faced when con-fronted by enemies—people that they could see—I flew in mis-sions about 4,000 +/- feet above the ground. I had no view through the low light NOS scope nor the forward looking in-frared scope. Sitting on the right side of the cockpit, I had no view of the ground except possibly out to the horizon, since we flew in left-hand firing circles. Besides, my job was to maintain aircraft airspeed and altitude, so during the firing circles I had to maintain a strict vigilance on the airspeed and altimeter instruments.

And I am pretty certain I mentioned several times in preceding chapters that we flew at night. Even with 20/12 vision and a full moon on a cloudless night, I never actually saw any enemy. I did not even get to see the supply truck explosions when our 20 mm rounds made contact. In other words, I had no "up close and personal" experience with NVA, nor Viet Cong, nor other North Vietnamese sympathizers.

The guys directly involved in face-to-face fire fights with the enemy only feet away—where they could see the faces, look into the eyes, and hear the screams as the enemy died . . . and hear the screams as their fellows-in-arms right next to them died the same way—that is what I mean by those who were up close and personal. Like Donnie Johnson, when he and his platoon were ambushed. There is no way to know for sure now, but I think I would not have done well in those situations.

With modern technology today, technicians somewhere in Nevada sitting in the safety of comfortable chairs with high tech video screens, cameras, and a variety of weapons at their disposal, and about 7,500 miles separating them from the site of conflict, have a couple of orders of magnitude more of "personal" exposure than I ever did from only 4,000 feet above the Ho Chi Minh Trail. One can access actual videos on YouTube showing high resolution combat situations from the air of ground targets. You plainly see the tracer rounds fired and hitting trucks, which burst into explosions. Even more personally, you can see people abandoning their vehicles and hurriedly scattering, unsuccessfully, as the mini-gun tracer rounds strafe over them, their bodies no longer moving targets.

Anyone interested may get more emotionally-inspired responses from the military persons controlling these far away high-tech machines. Then again, maybe not. Combat is personal for everyone involved. Some can just walk away, putting it all behind. Some can never recover. The dead have no opportunity.

I had different experiences.

I had survived a "war," with fond memories.

- APPENDIX 1 -

About ACRONYMS

ACRONYM—A Considerable Regimen Of Non-Yoga Manipulation

That is one possibility of what an acronym is. However, according to Merriam-Webster, an acronym is a word formed from the initial letter or letters of each of the successive parts or major parts of a compound term.

That is a definition worthy of a bureaucrat or an attorney.

The military thrives on acronyms, and as I am retired military, and as this a military-ish collection of anecdotes, you may (i.e., you definitely can) count on coming across one or a few of them from time to time here within. In fact, it is highly improbable to even imagine that you have managed to read this far without having encountered at least one acronym already. However, I have made a conscientious effort to disambiguate as we go along and define any acronyms at the time (as opposed to sometime after the fact) that, in my estimation, may not be otherwise intuitively obvious to any non-military types who may perchance be sufficiently curious to be reading these parcels of—let us just call them history.

(For any literary and grammar critics, yes, I am fully cognizant that the previous sentence does run on, but it runs on grammatically correctly.)

There are hundreds of acronyms—indeed, hundreds of hundreds of them, and that is just in the military. We will not even consider the (non-military) government, our education system, the computer and technology fields, the various other industries, and just about any other "field" you can think of. For example, let us start with a simple one: ARCP—Aerial Rendezvous Control Point. That is the latitude, longitude, and altitude where USAF (notice how I smoothly slipped that acronym right in) aircraft, or sometimes Navy or Marine aircraft, would meet a KC-135 Stratotanker to begin air refueling. Of course, there is a fourth dimension—an ARCT(ime)—associated with the three-dimensional ARCP. The aircraft obviously have to be in contact with ARTCC (Air Route Traffic Control Center). That is where the guys and gals on the ground keep track of all those green or yellow blips on large radar screens. They tend to get a little panicky if two blips merge and they do not know about it ahead of time. The flight plans filed with the FAA (Federal Aviation Administration) included the ARCP and the ARCT, as well as the subsequent refueling track (route) such as AR459NE, which is obviously—yeah, right, of course it is—Air Refueling (track) #459, heading Northeast. None of us wanted another flock of airplanes heading along AR459SW at the same time. This information is passed on to the appropriate ARTCC, or ARTCCs if the air refueling flight path crossed into a second

ARTCC geographical area. And that is just a sample from air refueling operations.

Only Rod Serling knows about flying in the fifth dimension—one not of sight and sound, but of mind. And only Stephen Hawking (R.I.P.) and a handful of specialized physicists and mathematicians in the world could/can comprehend 18 dimensions.

Then, selecting some examples at random, there is ABCCC, which is Airborne Battlefield Command and Control Center, which is an airborne aircraft close enough to an area of conflict, with lots of communications equipment on board and an officer with appropriate authority to make real-time, on-scene decisions. ACP is an acronym I looked up and have listed just for fun. It means either 1) Alternate Command Post; 2) Assault Command Post; 3) Allied Communications Publications; or 4) Airspace Control Plan. I guess you have to be there to know which one applies at any given time. Try putting this on one line on a business card: ACSI/HQUSAF (Assistant Chief of Staff Intelligence, Headquarters United States Air Force). That is a real one; I did not make it up.

How about an oxymoronic acronym? ACTEDS stands for Army Civilian Training, Education, and Development System. Army civilian? Does that refer to an Army person or a civilian person? An Army reservist or National Guard troop perhaps, but not at the same time. ADACP, Alcohol & Drug Abuse Control Program, probably evolved in California in an AVA (American Viticultural Area, a designated geographic wine-making area. Okay, so that one is not a military acronym, but it seemed to fit with the ADACP). On the military acronym website where I found ADACP, it was the 101st acronym on the list, and alphabetically speaking, it is barely into the "ADs". You probably already know that scuba, radar, and laser are examples of acronyms that have been absorbed into the English language as words unto themselves. You may remember scuba comes from Self-Contained Underwater Breathing Apparatus, or perhaps it was the other way around, as many acronyms have been created as stretches of the imagination. "Let's think of an acronym word and make up something to fit this breathing underwater thingy." Radar is another—RAdio Detecting And Ranging; and laser—Light Amplification by Stimulated Emission of Radiation. CINCSAC (Commander in Chief, Strategic Air Command) is no longer around since SAC itself no longer exists as such, or if it is, it refers to the commander of a different organization. POTUS—President Of The United States—is seen more and more often these days and, I suppose, could be considered a military acronym since the person holding the office is the CINC of the entire US military establishment.

One actual non-military term you will find scattered about is one I use frequently, although I will attempt to not overuse it within these pages: Everything Is Relative (EIR). Oops—probably too late. You may to want remember this one. It has a little history with me. I was an Aeronautics major in undergraduate school at Miami University (MU: the REAL Miami, in Oxford, Ohio, where the Little Miami River is and where the Miami Indians used to roam. I have no clue—nor do I care—where that "other" Miami got its name. Maybe it came from Native Americans who wintered in south Florida and decided to stay.). There were a gazillion, plus or minus seven, accounting majors and English majors, but the aeronautics (aero) department at MU was rather small. Most of our aero classes only had about twenty students, and we were mostly the same students in all of the classes. There was one instructor who taught all of our "in-house" classes, Mr. Cocanhaur. His favorite expression was, of course, Everything Is Relative. We heard it for four years in every class he taught, be it Introduction to Aero, Thermodynamics, Celestial Navigation, whatever.

"Sir, that is a complicated curve you are grading us on."

"Son, everything is relative." (For some reason we had no female-type persons in aero classes back then, but that was okay with me. I had found my Life's Love, Andrea, at the end of my freshman year. She was even with me somewhat in Southeast Asia, as you may have read by now.)

I have thought about that phrase over the years, and I have never been able to discover anything to dispute it. Everything really Is Relative to something else in one fashion or another, even in super-string theory or Einsteinian time-space universes. If you think of anything to dispute it, please let me know.

Over the years, many, if not most of us in the military, have speculated about the source of all the various and sundry acronyms that bombarded and governed our lives. Way back when computers occupied entire rooms—they were probably steam-powered monstrosities that Robert Fulton would have been proud of—acronym creation was most likely delegated to some poor lieutenant just out of post-graduate school with shiny new brown bars on his or her collar and a crisp doctorate degree under his or her belt. He or she was probably put into a windowless dimly lit closet in a remote corner in the basement of the Pentagon and given a stack of manuals, a few reams of paper, some boxes of pencils, and instructions to streamline the language. He or she must have had a sense of humor and a bent toward sadism.

Maybe he or she became friendly with the woman or man in the other dungeon room who invented the PCS without a PCA, as I described in one of the Da Nang chapters.

That is one theory anyway.

At some point I am sure that the task of acronym development was transferred to people operating computers small enough to only occupy part of a room, then to those using desktops, and now to a world full of teenagers who can text like wildfire. It is the natural evolution of things on Earth. We have all seen dorky acronyms that were obviously made up from phrases concocted just for the sake of said dorky acronym. A similar situation exists with 1-800 numbers. Supposedly they are marketing tools to help us remember the phone numbers, like 1-800-THE-DUDE (which would be Jeremy, my son-in-law's, if he had a need for a 1-800 number). That may be all well and good, and I may certainly be more likely to remember the words than the actual number, but just try dialing those letters. I can find an 8 reasonably easily on a phone dial—er, keypad, but I have to really have a dire need to make the call to warrant my spending twelve minutes looking up the numbers associated with each letter, then pressing that correct number, and repeating the operation for the next associated alpha-numeric grouping, then beginning the next one—oops, wrong one, delete previous number, try again two more times . . . oops again, my finger slipped on the tiny number keypad. By then I hear, "If you would like to make a call, please hang up and try again." Grrrr. This time I look up each alpha-numeric, write it down somewhere, and then make the call. Is it too much to ask for the actual properly-associated numbers to be included with the cutesy acronym listing? I don't think so. I really should be consulted about these matters.

Personally, when I am reading, I hate having to search back through material I have already read trying to find out what some abbreviation or acronym means that may have been explained once 347 pages back but which I have by now forgotten. Ergo, for your convenience, I have decided to put a bit of an appendix at the end. After all, who ever heard of putting an appendix at the beginning? The Reader may have noticed a heading in the Contents page that says Appendix. That means that as I was skipping around here and there writing this book which, at the time, I did not even know would be long enough to be considered a book, I decided to indeed include one and that I would most likely do so in a few months from next Thursday, depending on how long it takes me to finish expounding on the rest of what we could call the Appendix Support Source Verbiage, or ASSV. That is not particularly catchy, but I have never been a particularly creative-type person. It could turn out that writing an appendix of acronyms could be more drudgery than I am willing to subject myself to just for your benefit. After all, there is a good chance that I do not even know you. However, after all has been said and (not) done (yet), I think I have made a good argument for including an acronym appendix for your convenience.

As it turned out, I discovered that by scattering pictures about here and there within the volume between the Acknowledgements and Appendix, there might just be enough material to build a book.

Depending on your curiosity and memory, you can find the actual acronyms themselves used in the preceding verbiage in Appendix 1A. And as the Reader may have noticed, I actually have six Appendices, including this one, which does not really contribute to anyone's disambiguation of any preceding content.

While reviewing this book for the first time in its assembled format, I decided an appendix on another topic might be helpful. What would have been helpful indeed, to me at least, would have been if I had made myself a note on actual paper of just what the appendix topic was to be about. Alas, that particular topic has since escaped into the ethernet. Scientists used to have the populous convinced that there was an invisible ethernet all around us. As it turned out, they were not too far off—except that it is spelled Internet.

Appendix 1A: Acronyms used in this book, in alpha order, listed by the first page the acronym is encountered

(Technically, many of the following are not true acronyms according to some definitions; regardless, I have listed them below for the Reader's convenience. The source of the list in this appendix ends on page 501.)

AAA—Antiaircraft Artillery—Preface

AB—Air Base

AC—Attack Cargo or Aircraft Commander—Acknowledgements

AFA—Air Force Academy

AFB—Air Force Base

AFROTC—Air Force Reserve Officers' Training Corps—Acknowledgements

AFSC—Air Force Specialty Code

AGL—Above Ground Level

AH—Attack Helicopter (Also see Appendix 3)

AK-47—Avtomat Kalashnikova 1947

ARVN—Army of the Republic of Vietnam

ASE—Aerospace Engineering

ATC—Air Traffic Control

AWOL—Absent Without Leave

BDA—Battle Damage Assessment

BMW—Bayerische Motoren Werk; translation: Bavarian Motor Works

Bn—Battalion

BOTH—not an acronym here; capitalized for emphasis

BV—Beaulieu Vineyards

BX—Base Exchange

C&C—Command and Control

CBPO—Consolidated Base Personnel Office

CCR—Creedence Clearwater Revival

CD—Compact Disc

CMSgt—Chief Master Sergeant—Acknowledgements

CONUS—Continental United States

Co—Company

CTO—Crew Time Off

DMZ—Demilitarized Zone

DNIF—Duty Not Involving Flying

E&E—Escape and Evade

EC—Special Electronic Cargo (Also see Appendix 3)

EFIS—Electronic Flight Instrument System

EIR—Everything Is Relative

ER—Emergency Room

ESPN—Entertainment and Sports Programming Network

FAC—Forward Air Controller

FARs—Federal Aviation [Administration] Regulations

FCS—Fire Control System

FE—Flight Engineer

FL—Flight Level

FLIR—Forward-looking Infrared Radar; also, the operator of it

FM—Frequency Modulation

FMS—Flight Management System

FNGs—Friendly New Guys

FOL—Forward Operating Location

FRSoA—Future Rocket Surgeons of America (the Reader is not likely to find this acronym elsewhere else as it is one I concocted from a mixed metaphor)

FYI—For Your Information

GDI—Gamma Delta Iota

GI—Government Issue—Preface

GMT—Greenwich Mean Time

GQ—Gentlemen's Quarterly

HEI—High Explosive Incendiary

HH—Heavy Helicopter (Also see Appendix 3)

HHQ—Higher Headquarters

HKD—Hong Kong Dollar

HQ—Headquarters

HUD—Head Up Display

IFR—Instrument Flight Rules

IO—Illuminator Operator

ISB—International School Bangkok

JFK—John Fitzgerald Kennedy (airport identifier)

JROTC—Junior Reserve Officers' Training Corps

JUSTMAG—Joint United States Military Advisory Group

KC—Cargo Tanker (Also see Appendix 3)

KISS—Keep It Simple Stupid

KP—Kitchen Police

Kpsi—Knots per square inch

LAX—Los Angeles (airport identifier)

LED—Light-emitting Diode

M&Ms—M&Ms

MAC—Military Airlift Command

MARS—Military Affiliate Radio System

MBA—Master of Business Administration

MG—Morris Garages

MIA—Missing In Action

MPC—Military Payment Certificates

NATO—North Atlantic Treaty Organization

NBA—National Basketball Association

NCO—Non-Commissioned Officer

NKP—Nahkon Phanom

NOS—Night Observation Scope; also, the operator of the scope

NVA—North Vietnamese Army

NYC—New York City

OANG—Ohio Air National Guard

OCS—Officer Candidate School

OOPS—(not an acronym; just oops, as in oops-y daisy)

OPEC—Organization of the Petroleum Exporting Countries

OTS—Officer Training School

OV—Observation Vehicle (Also see Appendix 3)

P1D1—Fresh pineapple with vanilla ice cream

PACEX—Pacific Exchange

Pax—Passengers

PX—Post Exchange

QU—Unmanned Utility (Also see Appendix 3)

R & R—Rest and Recuperation/Relaxation/Recreation

R&D—Research and Development

R.I.P.—Rest In Peace

RB—Reconnaissance Bomber (Also see Appendix 3)

RC—Reconnaissance Cargo (Also see Appendix 3)

Regt—Regiment

RTAFB—Royal Thai Air Force Base

RTB—Return To Base

SEA—Southeast Asia—Preface

SA—Surface to Air

SAC—Strategic Air Command

SCO—Summary Courts Officer

SMV—Slow Moving Vehicle

SOF—Supervisor of Flying

SOS—does NOT stand for anything in this case

SOS—Special Operations Squadron

SVA—South Vietnamese Army

TACAN—Tactical Air Navigation

TDY—Temporary Duty

UPT—Undergraduate Pilot Training—Acknowledgements

USA or US of A—United States of America—Preface

USAF—United States Air Force—Acknowledgements

USD—United States Dollar

USMC—US Marine Corps

USO—United Service Organizations

UTC - Coordinated Universal Time (don't ask!)

VFR—Visual Flight Rules

VNAF—Vietnamese Armed Forces

VND—Vietnamese Dong

VOQ—Visiting Officers Quarters

VVI—Vertical Velocity Indicator

WAG—Wild * Guess

WSG—Writers Support Group—Acknowledgements

WWII—World War Two—Preface

YIs—Young Internationals

- APPENDIX 2 -

US MILITARY SERVICES RANK AND COMMENTARY ABOUT OFFICER RANK FROM HIGHEST RANK TO LOWEST RANK

(lowest to highest in photo below)

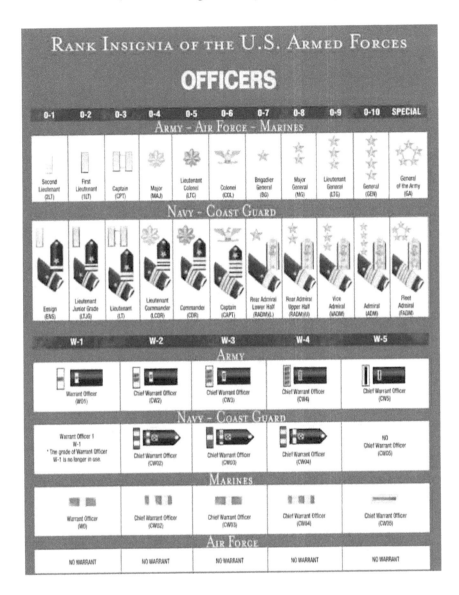

The following commentary on rank is about officer rank from highest rank to lowest rank:

Most of the information and my personal commentary to follow pertains to the US Air Force rank, abbreviations, insignia, and other tidbits of information. The Army and Marine officer ranks are basically equivalent to that of the Air Force, with some relatively minor differences here and there. Navy and Coast Guard officer and enlisted ranks differ considerably from the other services, so other than some interspersed commentary consisting of my sage considerations (he said modestly) about Navy rank, the focus is as it pertains to the Air Force.

In the charts above, the ranks of all services are grouped by ascending pay grades, meaning that a 2nd Lieutenant in the Army/Air Force/Marines is the same pay grade as an Ensign in the Navy/Coast Guard, whereas a Navy Captain is three pay grades higher than an Air Force Captain. Captain ranks and pay grades are different; only the rank titles are the same.

The rank of the Commander In Chief of the entire US military establishment is not shown in the photos above. That rank is held by a civilian, as established by the US Constitution, Article II, Section 2, Paragraph 1: The President of the United States (POTUS). Military personnel of even the highest ranks address the POTUS as Sir.

The format I have used below is: Rank—Rank abbreviation—Rank insignia—Pay Grade —commentary, if any. (Did you ever wonder why the word abbreviation is itself such a long word? It even has its own abbreviation: abbr.) I have also subdivided them into appropriate groups.

General Officer rank: All generals are addressed as general in informal conversation; the full titles are used formally. As a more junior officer addressing a general, one cannot go wrong with "General, Sir."

General of the Air Force (or Army, or Navy Fleet Admiral)—GAF—five stars in a circle. I do not know what a 5-star pay grade was, but one might logically deduce that it would be O-11. This designation was reserved for wartime only and was established during WWII to provide for overall theater of operations commanders. Only one person has ever held the rank and title of General of the Air Force: Henry H. "Hap" Arnold. He is also the only person to have held that rank in two services; he was an Army 5-star until the creation in 1947 of the USAF as a separate service from the US Army Air Corps. There have been only five men to wear the rank of five stars: George C. Marshall, Douglas MacArthur, Dwight D. Eisenhower, Henry H. Arnold, and Omar Bradley. There is an interesting and detailed biography by Stanley Weintraub entitled *15 Stars: Eisenhower, MacArthur, Marshall: Three Generals Who Saved the American Century*. There were also four Navy officers who attained the Navy's equivalent rank of Fleet Admiral: William D. Leahy, Ernest J. King, Chester W. Nimitz, and William F. Halsey, Jr. The 5-star rank was retired in 1981 on the death of General Bradley.

General—Gen—four stars—O-10.

Lieutenant General—Lt Gen or LGen—three stars—O-9.

Major General—Maj Gen or MGen—two stars—O-8.
(A major outranks a lieutenant, but a lieutenant general outranks a major general; I still have never figured that one out.)

Brigadier General—Brig Gen or BGen—one star—O-7.
The Navy rank (and pay) equivalents to one- and two-star general ranks are Rear Admiral (Lower Half) and Rear Admiral (Upper Half). Any military person who manages to attain general and general equivalent ranks is certainly among the very upper echelons of the command structure. Of all the millions of people who are in or have been in the military service of our country, only a relatively few have shined in their careers sufficiently to reach this rarefied coterie.

That being said, one would think the Navy could choose a less discriminating and, to me, less demeaning title that includes in its name Lower Half. It sounds like the kids that scored in the Lower Half of the Bell curve on standardized tests. (If you are a teacher, I did not mean to bring up that sore subject to irritate you (or my wife)). The English language is rich with over a million words, and it is growing daily, absorbing constantly from languages and cultures from other countries as well as various language, cultures, and technologies within our own society. If you used words like "google" or "text" as verbs in, say, 1980, you would have gotten some strange looks. Most of these admirals have no doubt distinguished themselves to have reached this significant level of command; there is a chasm between "Colonel" (Captain in the Navy) and the general (and admiral) ranks. Once there, one has "joined the club." One should have earned a title recognizing that fact, something like Rear Admiral (to maintain some semblance of Navy tradition) for the lower rank, then perhaps Senior Admiral, or Next Higher Up Admiral. None of this Lower Half and Upper Half business. There is undoubtedly some naval history and tradition behind the current titles to which every recruit or officer entering the Navy gets exposed early on, I would assume. It is hard to change tradition, but I think my titles are superior, in case anyone asks. One of these centuries we will have to consider rank titles for the Space Command.

Field Grade Officers:

Colonel (ker-nul, as in a kernel of corn)—Col—eagle with wings outspread—O-6.
This rank is often referred to as full colonel, as opposed to lieutenant colonel, one rank lower. It is also known as "bird colonel" for obvious reasons. This rank is at the pinnacle of those below general rank. Just as there is a chasm between colonel and brigadier general, there is also a nearly as significant chasm separating full colonel from lieutenant colonel and all those below.

Lieutenant Colonel—Lt Col or Ltc—silver oak leaf—O-5.
Usually addressed as colonel, or more formally as lieutenant colonel.

Major—Maj—gold oak leaf—O-4.
This is another one I have never figured out. Gold is deemed more precious than silver, but silver oak leaves (and silver bars; see Lieutenants below) outrank gold ones. Go figure. Obviously these selections were not chosen by a think tank of retired Wall Street precious metals commodities arbitrageurs.

Company Grade Officers:

Captain—Capt or Cpt—two connected parallel silver bars, sometimes called railroad tracks—O-3.

Times may have changed since, but during my era, promotions from 2nd lieutenant to 1st lieutenant (see below) and then to captain were pretty much automatic. After X amount of time in grade (rank), one pretty much expected to pin on the next rank in each case. After one made captain, he or she would have to "meet" promotion boards consisting of more senior officers. By "meet" it is meant that one's performance records were reviewed by the board, not person to person. In my career I only knew of one officer, whose name I will not mention—because I do not remember it, but I am sure my friend Dave Brown does. He was one of Dave's fellow navigators who got passed over for promotion to captain. If you anger a general officer, which this 1st Lt. did, by doing something really stupid, as well as against regulations, which he did, especially away from your assigned base, which he was, even if it is relatively trivial, which it probably was considering one's perspective and attitude about such things (EIR), but which definitely was NOT trivial to the general, you might have considered updating your curriculum vitae and getting it spread around the civilian world.

Which he did.

While we are at this level, I might as well insert more of my commentary about the Navy again. The Navy marches to its own drummer, to grossly mix a metaphor, and that is just fine. The Air Force is barely a few months younger than I am (just like the C-119); on the other hand, the US Navy is hundreds of years old.

Well, nearly a quarter of a millennia anyway. It was established on 13 October 1775. That makes it even older than the country that founded it. (Hmmm . . . that is something to think about.) The Navy is heavily steeped in tradition. The character Tevye sings a song about tradition in the play and subsequent movie *Fiddler on the Roof*. The song is, in fact, titled "Tradition." It has nothing whatsoever to do with the US Navy, however, but the song expresses the value and importance of tradition. So, granted the Navy has a long and admirable tradition, it is one to be proud of, even if their pilots do try to land their aircraft on moving, floating runways. (I just thought I would throw that in for the benefit of my retired Navy pilot friends.)

BUT, like their Lower Half admiralty, they once again degrade their officers. As you may note below, the USAF has second and first lieutenants. The Navy starts with Ensign (en-sin, not en-sine), but when an ensign gets promoted, the next rank up the ladder is Lieutenant Junior Grade (LTJG). My, now is that a title one dreams of aspiring to or what? I think—or what. Again, what is the Navy's preoccupation with using demeaning terms for its officers? Junior Grade—my granddaughter is in the fourth grade this year. (Well, she was when I started this appendix; she is in eighth grade now; I am not a very fast composer). That is certainly a junior grade, unless you happen to be her younger brother; he may have a different perspective on the issue. EIR. On a positive Navy note, the next promotion after Lieutenant JG is just plain old Lieutenant. No second or first lieutenants like the Air Force. In case you missed it, a Navy Lieutenant is the same grade as an Army/Marine/Air Force Captain. A Navy Captain is equivalent to a full Colonel in the other services. I have no idea how all this transpired—probably tradition. . . . However, as an Air Force captain, whenever I wanted to'stay at a VOQ on a Navy installation, I would call for reservations and announce, quite truthfully, that I was Captain Freund. To my way of thinking—which many of my friends often wonder about—it was incumbent upon the VOQ clerk to determine that my pay grade was only an O-3 captain and not an O-6 captain.

The Navy title disparagement gets even worse among the non-commissioned officer ranks, which we will come to below.

First Lieutenant—1st Lt or 1lt—silver bar—O-2.

Second Lieutenant—2nd Lt or 2lt—gold bar—O-1. (See note under Major, above.)
Far be it from me to bring this up (I erred. It is not far at all—it is right here, in writing), but it seems that when one has one's *first* officer bars pinned on, that person should be a *first* lieutenant. When that person is subsequently promoted to the second rank in the grade structure, that officer should logically then become a second lieutenant. I have never known, or known about, anyone who did not get promoted from second lieutenant. Or, rather than a second and first anything, how about a different word altogether for one of them. I will let you think up some fitting titles. Be nice, now; these young officers are serving their—and perhaps your—country.

Warrant Officers:

There is a class of five warrant officer ranks approved by Congress; they are rather a specialty category usually reserved for technicians or specialists and are basically a hybrid between senior non-commissioned officer (NCO) ranks and junior to mid-level officer ranks. They are senior to the highest NCOs (CMSgts) but junior to the lowest commissioned officers (second lieutenants or ensigns, depending on the branch of service). Whereas commissioned officers are designated as officers by a commission (duh), and non-commissioned officers are designated as such by virtue of seniority but without being commissioned, warrant officers are designated as such by a warrant. I had to do a little research (a little, not a lot) about "warrant" to determine the applicability of the term to satisfy my own curiosity and thereby possibly explain it for you. A definition of "warrant" as found in Merriam-Webster reads: "an official certificate of appointment issued to an officer of lower rank than a commissioned officer." That is the closest definition listed. The exclamation "duh" seems to be a particularly appropriate, if not elegant, comment now. So much for disambiguation.

The lowest warrant officer grade is (and at this point it may come as absolutely no surprise to you) Warrant Officer. (Surprised? I told you.) To complicate matters somewhat, the Warrant Officer, WO1, is *not* a commissioned officer. Of course not; he or she is issued a warrant. Contrariwise, Chief Warrant Officers CWO2—CWO5 *are* commissioned. If you are curious as to what distinguishes them from plain old commissioned officers, I do not know. You will have to climb the mountain and ask the Dali Lama; perhaps he has email these days (dalilamaonthemountaintop@himalaya,org)—but do not count on it.

(Oops! Was I ever wrong! I just made that ludicrous email address up in my very own little mind because it seemed so . . . ludicrous.

However, after I typed it out and it automatically turned itself blue and underlined itself, just like a real email address (or eddress, as I prefer to use now, to add a modern moniker to the language), I thought I would try to send something to it, just as an experiment and for its personal entertainment value. I fully expected to get a "Delivery to the following recipients failed" notice. Fortunately, it was a completely innocuous email. Subject line: "Really?" Message text: "I didn't think so." Boy, was I wrong. I am guessing that a college kid somewhere in Denver or Nepal got bored one evening. . . . Let this be a lesson to us all: Be careful when playing with frivolous email; you might irritate a crazed serial killer (not to be confused with an un-crazed serial killer). As yet I have not had a reply; I'll give it some more time, just in case.)

Getting back to officer ranks, we have non-commissioned officers, non-commissioned warrant officers, commissioned chief warrant officers, and commissioned officers. Do not concern yourself, however; there will be no test at the end. The Army, Navy, Marine Corps, and Coast Guard still have warrant officers. That is the term applied to the gamut of warrant officer grades, much as general refers to all general grades. Warrant Officer refers to the non-commissioned warrant officer grade. The Air Force stopped appointing warrant officers in 1959 and no longer uses warrant officer ranks. That may explain why I have never seen an Air Force warrant officer.

The following commentary on rank is about enlisted rank from highest rank to lowest rank (lowest to highest in photo below)

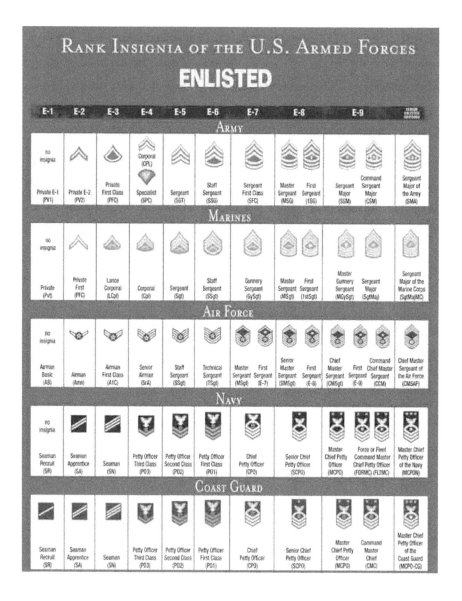

Non-commissioned Officers (NCOs):

Chief Master Sergeant (sar-jint)—CMSgt or CMS—three stripes up and five down—E-9.

The down stripes are sometimes referred to as rockers. In particularly formal situations, these senior NCOs are generally addressed as "Chief Master Sergeant," or in less formal circumstances as "Chief." However, I am not so sure that a Native American who happened to have earned this rank would be called that. In more formal circumstances, sergeants are addressed as "Sergeant." In less formal and more familiar situations, the term "Sarge" is often used, as in, "Hey, Sarge, the lieutenant is coming" (probably to ask how to get something done).

The top sergeant of a command, such as a Wing or numbered Air Force (e.g., 8th Air Force) has a designated insignia such as a diamond within upper and lower stripes. The Chief Master sergeant of the Air Force (CMSAF) is the top-ranking non-commissioned officer in the USAF and has certain special insignia designating this position. The CMSAF is entitled to billeting equivalent to a lieutenant general (three stars).

Senior Master Sergeant—SMSgt or SMS—two stripes up and five down—E-8.

Master Sergeant—MSgt or Msg—one stripe up and five down—E-7.

These three highest ranking sergeant positions are often referred to as "the top three." Clever deduction on someone's part. On some larger military installations there is even a Top Three Club for social functions, with an NCO Club for sergeant ranks below master sergeant and an Airman's Club for ranks below Sergeant.

Technical Sergeant (tech sergeant)—TSgt or Tsg—five stripes down—E6.

Staff Sergeant—SSgt or Ssg—four stripes—E-5.

Enlisted Personnel:

Senior Airman—SrA—three stripes down—E-4.

Airman First Class—A1C—two stripes down—E-3.

Airman—Amn—one stripe down—E-2.
Once upon a time there was the rank of Airman Second Class, but the Air Force decided that "second class" sounded too derogatory, like second-class citizen, so, in an inspirational moment (it no doubt took much longer than a moment) that designation was dropped in favor of just "Airman." I believe most of us would agree with that decision, although I, for one, was not consulted on the matter. The Navy, however, has third, second, and first class Petty officers—one-, two-, and three-stripers (not strippers) respectively.

Airman Basic - AB - no insignia designation—E-1.
Equivalent to an Army Private, which is two grades below a Private First Class (PFC). Perhaps the most famous private is Beetle Baily in the comic strip by that name, created by Mort Walker.

- APPENDIX 3 -

AIRCRAFT NOMENCLATURE

For those of you who may be curious about other military aircraft designations but who prefer not to tear themselves away from my intriguing (he said modestly) exposition to do their own research at this point, I will, as a favor, provide a brief description of the designation system. The rest of this paragraph will be mostly factual and relatively humorless, so you will not miss anything critical by skipping to the next paragraph. However, if you do, you will be depriving yourself of some nice trivia that you could use for bar-room betting. Since 1962 the US Department of Defense military designations have used a Mission-Design-Series format: (Status Prefix)(Modified Mission)(*Basic Mission*) (Vehicle Type)-(*Design Number*)(*Series Letter*). Alpha (meaning alphabet) combinations can get tricky or complicated, as they change from time to time and become non-standard. Aircraft design numbers also seem to have randomly illogical progression series with skipped numbers in the series or reversions to lower numbers. However, for simplification and disambiguation, below are some current and more common designations (some are not so common, yet); where more than one aircraft example is listed, the underlined one is the one in the photo:

A = Attack (e.g., A-10 Thunderbolt, a.k.a Warthog):

B = Bomber (e.g., <u>B-52 Stratofortress</u>, B-47, B-2, B-1 (a.k.a. BONE (B-ONE)):

C = Cargo (you know that already now) (e.g., C-47, C-141, C-5, C-17)

D = Drone director (not common yet, but are becoming more prevalent)

E = Special Electronic (e.g., EC-135, EB-57, <u>EB-66</u>):

F = Fighter (e.g., <u>F-22 Raptor</u>, F-4, F-15, F-16, F-35)

G = Glider

H = Helicopter (e.g., HH-3 Jolly Green Giant, shown with two Sandy A1-E's):

K = Tanker (KC-135 Stratotanker):

L = Cold weather operations (e.g., LC-130)

O = Observation (e.g., O-1A Bird Dog, OV-10 Bronco)

P = Maritime patrol (P-3 Orion); formerly Pursuit (e.g., P-40 Warhawk, P-41 Mustang)

Q = Unmanned drone (not common, but becoming more so) (e.g., QU-22B Pave Eagle, which was a manned USAF version of a Beechcraft Bonanza; QU is an odd nomenclature for a not-so-odd aircraft; the military version of the aircraft was initially planned to be unmanned)

R = Reconnaissance (e.g., SR-71 Blackbird, RB-66 Destroyer)

S = Strategic (e.g., SR-71 Blackbird)

T = Trainer (e.g., T-37B Tweet, T-38A Talon) A-37B Dragonfly

U = Utility (e.g., QU-22B Pave Eagle, which was a manned USAF version of a Beechcraft Bonanza)

V = Staff transport (e.g., VC-135; also for vertical/short takeoff and landing (V/SOL), e.g., Marine AV-8B Harrier)

W = Weather reconnaissance (e.g., WC-130 Hercules)

X = Experimental or special research (e.g., X-15, <u>XB-70 Valkyrie</u>)

Y = Prototype (e.g., YF-12 (a precursor to the SR-71))

Z = Lighter-than-air

Now you should be sufficiently equipped with a veritable plethora of almost useful information to have a little fun making up your own aircraft combinations, from the sublime to the ridiculous. How about an X-RAY (Experimental-Reconnaissance Attack Prototype)? I wonder what that one would look like. The possibilities are endless. Well, perhaps not endless, practically speaking. After all, there are definitely a finite number of permutations of the twenty-two letters currently used (I did not include I, J, M, and N above because they are special use designations) of the English alphabet. Even considering the exponentially increasing combinations possible by adding letters to the nomenclature string, at some point even the most maniacal enthusiast would eventually run out of coffee and tire of the game.

Wasn't that an exciting breath of fresh air? (Sarcastic? Who, me?)

Appendix 3A - Some Examples

SR-71

SR-71 Blackbird

Perhaps now the various letter combinations may make more — or at least some—sense. Usually. Some interesting examples: Had designation protocol been followed, the SR-71 should have been the RS-71, but Air Force Chief of Staff General Curtis LeMay preferred Strategic Reconnaissance, and four-star generals have a way of getting what they want. Funny how that works. Personally, I agree with the General, although he never asked for my approval; I was still in high school at the time. Reconnaissance Strategic sounds awkward; Strategic Reconnaissance simply sounds better and stealthier, but that might be because we are used to hearing SR-71 all these years. My choice of using this magnificent airplane as an example results from two reasons.

First, I was closely associated with the SR-71 program for the five years that I flew the KC-135Q, or Q model as it is called, as in, "I flew the Q." The Q model had modifications so that it could carry two different types of fuel. The JP-4 Jet fuel was used by nearly all of the US military aircraft until 1995, when it was replaced by JP-8; and JP-7, a special fuel developed specifically for the high temperatures and high supersonic speeds of the SR-71. The fuel modifications were mostly in fuel plumbing and tanker fuel management procedures, but they were critical procedures. There were some other modifications to facilitate SR-71 refueling operations, especially covert operations, but the fuel system was the major consideration. The KC-135 had ten fuel tanks with a capacity of nearly 200,000 pounds (nearly 30,000 US gallons) of fuel. I say "had" because there have been major design modifications and engine changes since I last flew a tanker in December 1979. We never referred to fuel in gallons; fuel was calibrated in pounds. The tanker had the capability to transfer fuel between tanks to maintain aircraft center of gravity and balance. Too much fuel forward or aft or left wing or right wing could cause some serious aircraft control problems, especially during landing. It was the copilot's job to monitor and manage the fuel control panel, which had ten fuel quantity gauges, a totalizer gauge, ten fuel transfer switches, associated fuel pump switches, two fuel pump offload switches, and an offload transfer rate gauge. The fuel offload rate was up to 6,500 pounds per minute, based on the rate the receiving aircraft could onload. Lots to keep track of.

Managing the fuel panel required planning the day before the flight, especially when carrying both types of fuel. Special procedures were designed to prevent contaminating the JP-7 fuel with the JP-4 Fuel. The SR-71 could burn JP-4 fuel, but its mission would be restricted or most likely aborted, as the plane could then not fly supersonic. If someone—specifically, the copilot, although the aircraft commander (pilot) is always ultimately responsible—made a mistake and inadvertently transferred some JP-4 into a JP-7 tank, the SR-71's mission would be curtailed and someone would have to answer to a higher authority. (No, not *that* high—just to a full colonel or general.) If it was an operational mission for the SR-71 (as opposed to a training or proficiency mission)—operational meaning a spy mission—oops, er, I mean, an intelligence gathering mission, heads would certainly roll, starting at the bottom and working up the chain of command, depending on the importance of the mission.

The second reason for my selection of the SR-71 is that it was simply unique in the annals of aviation. Its distinctive design is a work of art. Its performance has never been matched before or since, by any country on the planet. Kelly Johnson, the famous Lockheed engineer, designed the plane as well as a few others of note, like the U-2 spy plane that Gary Francis Powers was flying when he was shot down over the USSR in 1960. The time from concept to first flight of the prototype (A-71) was about a year and a half, which is nothing less than incredible. (Under the Obama administration the federal government could not even construct a working Obamacare website in that short of a time period. Furthermore, the government under the Trump administration is taking even longer to dismantle and replace the program.) There are numerous fascinating stories associated with the aircraft and the crews who flew them, many of whom I got to know during my tenure in the Q. Several of them have written books that I have read. One story not in any of the books was on a more personal level and not really directly related to the SR-71 program.

After the "cessation of hostilities" in Vietnam was reached, I was assigned to be a copilot on the KC-135A at Wright-Patterson AFB in Dayton, Ohio. At the same time, Captain Tom Keck was a B-52 Aircraft Commander in the same Bomb Wing, a unit designation which included both the bombers and tankers. When the powers on high in Strategic Air Command decided to close down the Bomb Wing at Wright-Patterson, I was transferred to Beale AFB in Northern California, about forty miles north of Sacramento, flying the KC-135Q. Tom apparently had applied for and been accepted into the SR-71 program, and he and his wife were transferred to Beale also, as that was the home base for SR-71 operations. Coincidentally he and his wife decided to start a family at about the same time that Andrea and I did. The four of us attended Lamaze classes together, Tom and I as coaches while our wives did their breathing exercises.

Tom Keck eventually went on to retire as a three-star general (Lieutenant General).

XB-70

Another aircraft with a different set of letter designations was the XB-70 Valkyrie, an Experimental Bomber. There is an XB-70 on display outside the Air Force Museum, now known as the National Museum of the United States Air Force, at Wright-Patterson AFB. I believe it has been moved indoors since. The supersonic bomber never made it into operational status in the Air Force inventory. If you are interested in aircraft and aviation history, the Air Force Museum at Wright-Patterson is the ultimate place to visit. There is a B-52 Stratofortress *inside* the main building; this bomber is 41 feet high and has a 185-foot wingspan. Next to it and extending under a wing is an SR-71, which is itself over 107 feet long. The Museum is quite impressive and educational.

Gunships

The AC-47 Gooney Bird—whoever thought of making a pokey old cargo plane into an *attack* aircraft? Talk about oxymorons. But the gunship concept worked rather well in Vietnam as Puff the Magic Dragon (call sign Spooky), as it did with the successors to the AC-47: the AC-119G Shadow, the AC-119K Stinger (my favorite, although I may be slightly biased), and the AC-130 Specter.

QU-22B

The QU-22B was a strange designation. One of the guys in my Undergraduate Pilot Training (UPT) class got assigned to one. No one in our class had ever heard of one. I don't think even our instructors—captains and majors—had heard of one either. Say it out loud: QU-22B. It even sounds strange. It does not exactly float off the tongue. But it must have been a real airplane of some sort; one of our newly-minted pilots was going to fly one.

As it turned out, the QU-22B was part of the Air Force Special Operations, as was my AC-119K and the OV-10 Bronco, which another UPT classmate got. All of these aircraft were part of the Special Operations Wing at Nakhon Phanom RTAFB. Nakhon Phanom was a small base, relatively speaking (EIR), and while I was stationed there, I had occasion to talk with some QU-22B drivers (as pilots are sometimes known). Their airplane was a Beechcraft Bonanza, known in the civilian world as the doctors' airplane, since it was just a bit on the pricey side. The Air Force modified its inventory of Bonanzas to be electronic monitoring signal relay aircraft. They were packed with black boxes. The trouble with the plane was that with all of the added weight of the equipment, the plane was underpowered, especially on take-off. There was a slight issue with the planes crashing on or shortly after takeoff. The pilots were not overly thrilled with this high-percentage potential for catastrophe and personal bodily harm. However, there was a bright side, as I was told. There were only twenty-one QU-22Bs in the Air Force inventory, so the theory was that when they all crashed and there were no more planes remaining to fly, they—pilots, maintenance and other support troops, commanders—the whole unit, in other words, could go home.

And thus it came to pass that when the QU-22B inventory dropped to ten aircraft, the unit was indeed closed, and the troops did get to go home. They all lived happily ever after, or whatever.

C-119

Flying the C-119G was a new and different flying concept for me on several levels. For the past year I had been accustomed to flying the trainer versions of small, zippy, two-engine, two-seat attack and fighter-type jets, either solo or accompanied by an instructor. Solo was the most fun, of course.

In no conceivable way did flying the C-119G resemble that experience. The C-119G did have two engines and the USAF star emblem painted on it, but there the resemblance ended. It had its own provocations for adrenalin rushes, however. Thoughts that occurred to us all as we rumbled down the runway were more in the nature of, "Is this thing ever going to get off the ground before we run out of concrete?"

When it was time for takeoff in the T-37, T-38, and other fighter-type aircraft, you pushed the throttles to 100% RPM, quickly scanned the engine instruments, released the brakes, and lit the afterburners, if the plane was so equipped. In the C-119, you carefully advanced the throttles and tried to set them at the calculated power settings before checking the rest of the engine gauges. The airplane would shake, rattle, and roll as it struggled with the stressful conflict of its need to begin movement for flight while being restrained by the brakes preventing it from doing so. In the meantime, the captain was anxious to get going down the runway, and the copilot—and the crusty old flight engineer— were trying to read the settings of all the engine performance instruments in the bouncy cockpit. Not quite the same as "kick the tires and light the fires."

For takeoff, even in jet cargo planes like the KC-135, the engines had to be set at the calculated power settings and not just shoved up to 100%. On the other hand, these planes were newer (EIR), generally larger, and more stable than the reciprocating engine planes, and it was easier to read the instruments because the airplane wasn't vibrating and wobbling all over the place.

Of course, on long flights (there *were* no long flights in a T-37 or T-38; a typical flight lasted about 1.3 hours) you were not necessarily confined to your seat the whole time.

- APPENDIX 4 -

MNEMONIC ALPHABET

Below is the ICAO (International Civil Aviation Organization) alphabet and numbers pronunciation used in aviation communications. The first word is the actual word used. The second word is my own selection; however, as yet the ICAO has not decided to change to my system. Go figure. The capital letters in the parentheses are the accented syllables.

A as in ALPHA (AL-fah) or Antidisestablishmentarianism
B as in BRAVO (BRA-vo) or ****
C as in CHARLIE (CHAR-lee) or Champagne or Czar (see T and Z)
D as in DELTA (DEL-ta) or Djibouti (see J)
E as in ECHO (EK-ko) or Euphemistic
F as in FOXTROT (FOX-trot) or Phenobarbital or Phlegm (see P)
G as in GOLF, or Gnome

H as in Hotel (Ho-Tel) or Herb (personally, I pronounce the H)

I as in INDIA (IN-dee-a) or Ichthyosaurus

J as in JULIET (JOO-lee-et) or Djibouti or Gist (the military uses GYST as an acronym (see Appendix 1) but I cannot translate it for you here)

K as in KILO (KEE-lo) or Knife or Knockwurst

L as in LIMA (LEE-ma) or Llama (double L pronounced as y in Spanish)

M as in MIKE, or Mnemonic (see N)

N as in NOVEMBER (no-VEM-ber) or Mnemonic (see M)

O as in OSCAR (OS-car) or Onomatopoeia

P as in PAPA (PA-pa) or Pseudonym or Psychiatrist or Psalter (see S), or Phonetic or Phlegm (see F)

Q as in QUEBEC (KAY-beck) or Qatar

R as in ROMEO (RO-mee-o) or Rheumatism

S as in SIERRA (See-ER-ra) or Psalter (see P)

T as in TANGO (TANG-go) or Thermostat or Tsar (see C and Z)

U as in UNIFORM (YOO-nee-form) or Ugly

V as in VICTOR (VIC-tor) or Ventriloquist

W as in WHISKEY (WHIS-kee) or Whence

X as in X-RAY (X-ray) or Xylophone (see Z)

Y as in YANKEE (YAN-kee) or Ytterbium

Z as in ZULU (ZOO-loo) or Xylophone (see C and T)

1 as in Wun

2 as in Too

3 as in Tree

4 as in Fow-er

5 as in Fife, as in Barney

6 as in Six (kind of far-fetched, but that's what it is)

7 as in SEV-en

8 as in ATE

9 as in NI-ner

0 as in ZEE-ro

And speaking of zero, that is how much is left of this book, a.k.a ...

The End.

CPSIA information can be obtained
at www.ICGtesting.com
Printed in the USA
JSHW021512030921
18373JS00001B/3